JAMESTOWN EDUCATION

D0474096

Five-Star Stories

Choices

17 Stories of Challenge and Choice
With UNITS for Mastering Language Arts Skills

by Burton Goodman

Titles in the Series

JAMESTOWN EDUCATION

Five-Star Stories

Choices

17 Stories of Challenge and Choice
With UNITS for Mastering Language Arts Skills

by Burton Goodman

Mc Graw Hill **Glencoe McGraw-Hill**

New York, New York   Columbus, Ohio   Chicago, Illinois   Peoria, Illinois   Woodland Hills, California

JAMESTOWN EDUCATION

Glencoe/McGraw-Hill

*A Division of The **McGraw·Hill** Companies*

Send all queries to:
Glencoe/McGraw-Hill
8787 Orion Place
Columbus, OH 43240-4027

ISBN 0-07-827354-4

1 2 3 4 5 6 7 8 9 10   116/055   09 08 07 06 05 04 03

Contents

To the Student

Choices contains 17 outstanding short stories of recognized literary merit. Within these pages, you will find stories by present-day writers as well as by time-honored authors. You will discover, too, that many countries and cultures are represented. The stories are varied, but they will capture your attention, and they will stimulate you to think. And, as you will see, the characters involved must make meaningful *choices*.

The stories have been arranged in five units, each with its own particular theme. Each unit is introduced by Previewing the Unit and concludes with a Review, which consists of questions for discussion and extended writing. These questions offer opportunities to compare and contrast information and ideas in the stories and to gain practice in writing the kinds of essays you are likely to encounter on standardized tests.

These stories will provide you with many hours of reading pleasure, and the exercises that follow each story have been designed with language arts mastery in mind. They employ an approach that utilizes **UNITS:**

UNDERSTAND KEY IDEAS AND DETAILS will help you improve your reading comprehension skills.

NOTE NEW VOCABULARY WORDS will help you strengthen your vocabulary skills. Often you will be able to figure out the meaning of an unfamiliar word by using *context clues*—the words and phrases around the word. All the vocabulary words in this section appear in the stories.

IDENTIFY STORY ELEMENTS will provide practice in recognizing and understanding the key elements of literature.

THINK CRITICALLY ABOUT THE STORY will help you sharpen your critical thinking skills. You will have opportunities to *reason* by drawing conclusions, making inferences, and using story clues.

STUDY THE WRITER'S CRAFT will give you opportunities to see how stories are crafted and to learn about authors' techniques, especially their use of language.

There are four questions in each exercise. Complete all of the exercises. Then check your answers with your teacher. Use the scoring chart following each exercise to calculate your score for that exercise. Give yourself 5 points for each correct answer. Since there are four questions, you can score up to 20 points for each exercise. Use the UNITS scoring chart at the end of the lesson to figure your total score. A perfect score for a lesson is 100 points. Keep track of how well you do by recording your score on the **Progress Chart** on page 198. Then plot your progress by recording your score on the **Progress Graph** on page 199.

The Questions for Writing and Discussion section offers further opportunities for thoughtful discussion and creative writing. Additional questions are provided in Questions for Discussion and Extended Writing in each Review.

On page 3, you will find **The Short Story—Literary Terms.** You may want to refer to these definitions when you answer the questions in the Identify Story Elements section. On pages 4 and 5 you will find **The Craft of Writing—Literary Terms.** You may want to refer to these pages when you answer the questions in the Study the Writer's Craft section.

I feel certain that you will enjoy reading the stories in this book. And the exercises that follow will help you master a number of important language arts skills.

Now . . . get ready for some *Choices!*

Burton Goodman

The Short Story— Literary Terms

Character Development: the growth and changes in a character revealed by a writer during the course of a story.

Characterization: the ways a writer shows what a character is like. The way a character acts, speaks, thinks, and looks *characterizes* that person.

Climax: the turning point of a story.

Conflict: a struggle or difference of opinion between characters. A character may also clash with a force of nature.

Dialogue: the exact words that a character says; usually, the conversation between characters.

Foreshadowing: clues that hint at what will happen later in the story.

Inner Conflict: a struggle that takes place in the mind of a character.

Main Character: the person the story is mostly about.

Mood: the feeling or atmosphere that the writer creates. For example, the *mood* of a story might be joyous or suspenseful.

Motive: the reason behind a character's actions.

Narrator: the person who tells the story. Usually, the *narrator* is the writer or a character in the story.

Plot: the series of incidents or happenings in a story. The *plot* is the arrangement of events.

Purpose: the reason the author wrote the story. For example, an author's *purpose* might be to entertain, to convince, or to inform.

Setting: the time and place of the action in a story; where and when the action takes place.

Style: the way in which a writer uses language. The choice and arrangement of words and sentences help to create the writer's unique *style*.

Theme: the main, or central, idea of a story.

The Craft of Writing— Literary Terms

Alliteration: the repetition of consonant sounds at the beginning of words. An example of *alliteration* is "Ten tame tigers sat sadly."

Allusion: a reference within a literary work to a famous person, place, work of literature, and so on.

Autobiography: the story of a real person's life, told by that person.

Biography: the story of a real person's life, told by another person.

Connotation: a meaning or emotion associated with a word. For example, the words *thrifty* and *cheap* have a similar **denotation** (dictionary meaning), but *thrifty* has a positive *connotation,* while *cheap* has a negative connotation.

Descriptive passage: writing that tells about people, places, and things in ways that help the reader picture what is being presented.

Dialect: a form of speech spoken in a particular country, region, or place.

Figurative language: language that creates vivid word pictures, especially through the use of figures of speech such as simile, metaphor, and personification.

Flashback: the interruption of the action in the plot to show an event or events that occurred at an earlier time.

Folktale: a traditional story that has been passed on from one generation to another, originally by word of mouth.

Imagery: language that uses words and phrases that appeal to one or more of the senses—sight, taste, touch, hearing, and smell. Often *imagery* helps create a picture in the mind of the reader.

Irony: a contrast, usually between what is expected and what actually occurs. There are many kinds of *irony.* Saying "Great work!" to a waiter who has dropped a tray is an *ironic* remark.

Metaphor: a figure of speech in which one thing is said to be something else. Unlike a simile, a metaphor does not use the word *like* or *as*. For example, "He is a bull" is a *metaphor,* but "He is as strong as a bull" is a simile.

Moral: a lesson, which is often the point of a story; what the story teaches the reader.

Onomatopoeia: the use of words whose sounds imitate their meaning. Some examples of *onomatopoeia* are *pop, hiss,* and *bang.*

Personification: a figure of speech in which an animal, object, or idea is given human feelings or qualities. An example of *personification* is "The sun crept slowly through the window and slipped quietly across the room."

Simile: a figure of speech in which two unlike things are compared through the use of the word *like* or *as.* An example of a *simile* is "She ran like a deer."

Story within a story: a story told by one character to other characters in a story.

Symbol: something that has its own meaning but also stands for, or represents, something else. For example, a red heart may be a *symbol* of love; a dove *symbolizes* peace.

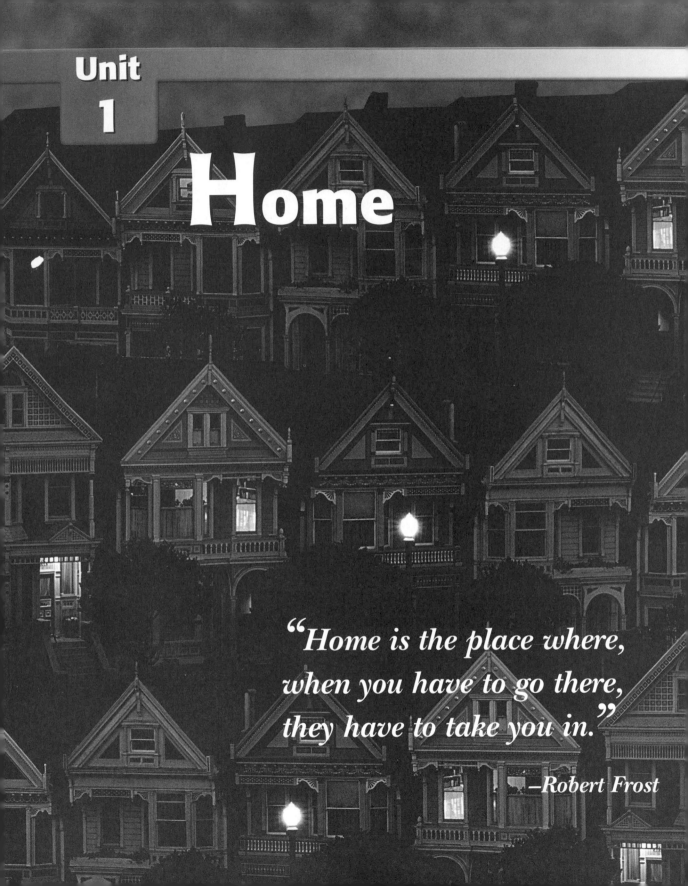

Home

"Home is the place where, when you have to go there, they have to take you in."

—Robert Frost

Previewing the Unit

In a famous poem, the great American poet Robert Frost stated that "Home is the place where, when you have to go there, they have to take you in." Frost is suggesting that, after all is said and done, home is a refuge, a safe harbor.

However, the word *home* cannot be limited to Frost's definition. The word has far too many meanings. We will explore some of them in the unit that follows.

AMERICAN SANDWICH Edite Cunhã was seven years old when she and her family emigrated from Portugal to the United States. Cunhã's story "American Sandwich" is highly autobiographical. It reflects the fierce yearning of a child to identify with her new country and her new home. The main character desperately desires to be an American. How she thinks that can be achieved is the basis for the story.

ANTAEUS In Borden Deal's "Antaeus," a group of boys attempts to convert a factory roof into a garden "with flowers and grass and trees and everything." To the boys, thrilled by what they create, the living roof becomes a kind of home. T. J., the leader of the boys, declares, "It's our earth. It's our land. Can't nobody touch a man's own land." What happens when the adult world intrudes is for the reader to discover.

THIS FARM FOR SALE To Jesse Stuart, home was the Kentucky hill country, the land he loved and the setting of many of his stories. In "This Farm for Sale," you will meet Dick and Emma Stone, who own an old farm in the hill country. Mr. Stone decides to sell the property. However, disposing of the farm may not prove easy, since it is situated in an isolated spot far from power lines, and it lacks the conveniences we associate with modern life. Stone calls in the shrewd Melvin Spencer to assist with the sale. Spencer makes his living selling real estate. He has a keen eye and, much like Stuart himself, is something of a poet of the land. What eventually happens may surprise you.

As you read, think about "Home"—what it means to you and what it means to the characters in these stories.

Edite desperately wanted to belong, but so much
depended upon an . . .

American Sandwich

by Edite Cunhã

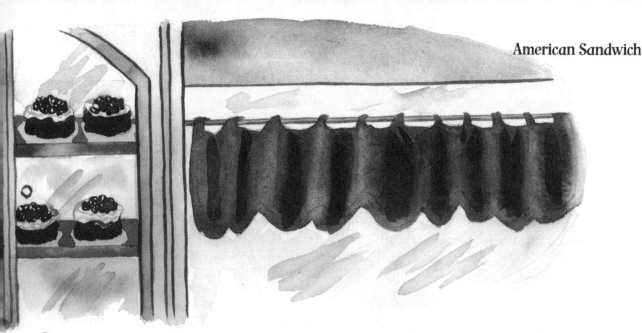

Carlos and I ran down the hill ahead of our mother, over dirty piles of snow, past the long wooden factory where our father worked, toward the rusty bridge and the river.

"Don't fall in," Ma called after us, as she always did when we walked downtown to the First National Store.

"We won't, Ma," we called back.

When we got to the bridge my little brother and I dropped down on our bellies on the rough wooden planks and stuck our heads under the railing. That day the river was bright green. We could see old tires and metal barrels in the shallow water under the bridge. I raised my head to look upriver. The tall tall smokestacks of the factories along the riverbank threw long shadows across the water and over the junkyard on the other side.

Once, when our washing machine broke down, I had gone to that junkyard with my father to buy a part. The man who ran it had a mean black dog who slept in an old refrigerator with no door. I didn't know how

to explain to the man what Pa wanted. The man was very patient, but Pa got frustrated and I got upset. Before we left the old man gave me a doll with matted hair.

Seeing that junkyard always gave me a headache. I lowered my head and watched a rusty bucket sail by on the green waves. Then I took two shiny pennies out of my pocket and gave one to Carlos. He knew what to do because before leaving the house I had taught him, just the way Yolanda and Raiza had taught me in school. We held the pennies tightly in our hands, closed our eyes and let the words appear on a blackboard inside our heads: "I wish, I wish, I wish, that Ma would buy some Sunbeam Bread." Then we blew a hot breath into the pennies in our fists before dropping them into the smelly green ripples. When she caught up with us on the bridge, Ma asked what we were doing.

"*Nada,*" we answered together, because Yolanda and Raiza had said it was important not to tell. And they had sworn that many of their wishes had actually come true.

American Sandwich

As soon as we stepped into the First National Store, Carlos and I broke from our mother and ran. Sunbeam Bread had a new display stand at the front of the store near the checkout counters: three neat wire shelves loaded down with loaves under the tipped blonde head that smiled forever.

The Sunbeam girl had a pretty blue dress and golden curls. Her ear lobes were smooth and unpierced. I always felt dark and bedraggled staring up at her. But she also made me feel hopeful.

"Will we get those little wells in our cheeks if we eat this bread?" Carlos wanted to know.

"Dimples," I corrected. "Maybe, but for sure we won't get them if we don't eat this." I handed him a loaf, grabbed one for myself and we walked off in search of Ma.

We found her in the produce section lifting a sack of potatoes into the metal shopping cart. The long floorboards creaked as we ran up and positioned ourselves in front of her with our loaves in our arms. When she looked at us I nudged Carlos to begin.

"Pleeeeeeze Ma," we begged, squeezing our eyes and tilting our faces up toward her. *"Por favor."*

She didn't say anything!

"What for?" she would usually say when we first approached her.

"For lunch, Ma, so we can have a real sandwich in our lunch."

"I could squirt some soap on it and use it to wash down the table." She always said this thoughtfully as she picked green beans or tomatoes into a bag. And Carlos and I would look at each other and nearly stop breathing as we waited.

"But I'd rather use a dishrag," she would finally add. And I would sigh loudly, disgusted.

That day, when we asked for Sunbeam Bread, Ma just looked at me as if she'd forgotten the joke. Then she moved off down the aisle. I took it as a hopeful sign.

Chasing our mother around the First National with loaves of Sunbeam Bread had become a ritual. It was my idea. There were twenty-six kids in my class. Most of them had beautiful lunches every day of the school week. Bologna and cheese with mustard on Sunbeam Bread. Peanut butter and jelly on Sunbeam Bread. Egg salad on Sunbeam Bread. More than anything I wanted to be like the others.

Once, only once, Ma tried one loaf. Our father took one bite and said with sarcasm, "This is bread?" in that tone that makes us want to be far away from him. Then he said that he didn't want his money spent on something that looked and tasted like sponges. Ma agreed that it wasn't as good as the crusty loaves she bought at the Portuguese bakery. They didn't understand that taste wasn't the point. I wouldn't let Carlos admit that he liked our regular bread better. I told him that if we didn't eat Sunbeam Bread we would never be American. In the end he ate it as if it were candy. Still, we never got another loaf. But I think Ma would have bought more if Pa had liked it. She always tried extra hard not to upset him.

My mother had no idea how I suffered over bread. She didn't know that lunch time was a time of mortification. At first I wouldn't bring out my lunch, telling Miss Leitenen that I wasn't hungry. But she always forced me to pull the brown bag out of my desk and spread the food out on my plastic place mat where everyone could see it. My sandwiches were always monstrous. Two fat uneven slices of bread that Ma cut every morning from the big crusty loaves *she* preferred, filled with scrambled egg and *linguiça,* or thick slices of brown marmalade, or the white cheese that she made herself because she was homesick. Sometimes she filled the bread with ham, or peanut butter and jelly. But even that was little consolation. Sometimes the slices of bread had huge air holes that allowed the filling to spill out when I tried to raise the sandwich to my lips. My grotesque sandwiches were so big that I could hardly open my mouth wide enough to take a bite.

Soon I began throwing my sandwich away before I got to school. At lunch I would eat my cookies and fruit and sip my milk. When Miss Leitenen asked how come I had no sandwich I would tell her that my mother had forgotten to make one; or that my mother had run out of bread; or that she had made it and forgotten to put it in my lunch bag. After a few days I began feeding my sandwich to Tony Mello's dog before I got to school because I felt guilty about throwing away good food. And it *was* good food. At home I gladly ate it and even asked for more. But in public my stomach got tight so that I couldn't eat.

On the day before this trip to the First National store, Miss Leitenen had called me to her desk as we were filing out to go home. She gave me a folded piece of paper and told me to give it to my parents.

"Edite, bring it back tomorrow with their signatures on it."

"My parents can't read English," I reminded her.

"I know that, I had Mrs. Donahue write it in Portuguese for them."

Out on the street I tried to read what Mrs. Donahue had written but I wasn't as good at reading Portuguese as I was at reading English. When Ma and Pa read the note they called me into the kitchen and asked me how come my sandwiches never made it to school.

"I feed them to Tony Mello's dog," I said because though I'd lied to Miss Leitenen about my lunch, I usually tried to tell the truth.

"YOU WHAT?" yelled Pa, standing up very fast.

"*Calma,*" Ma said, holding her hand up to Pa like a traffic cop.

"Why don't you eat your sandwich in school?" asked Ma.

"Because I can't open my mouth wide enough."

Pa stood up again. He was very angry.

"You can open your mouth up wide enough at home," Ma reminded me.

Pa started yelling about how much food cost. And how he wasn't getting up at dawn to work at that factory every day so that I could fatten up Tony Mello's dog. It was hard to tell the truth when he yelled like that.

"Why don't you want to eat your sandwich?" he yelled.

"Because the other kids make fun of me," I finally said, but by then I had started to cry and couldn't say anything else.

"It's because she wants Sunbeam Bread," said Carlos.

He thought he was being helpful, but what he said only made Pa madder. He yelled that he didn't come to America so that his children could eat fake food and

11

feed the good stuff to dogs. He didn't come to America to get letters from his daughter's teacher telling him how to feed his family. Ma put us to bed and he was still yelling.

In the bedroom Ma asked me what would make my sandwiches better.

"Sunbeam Bread," Carlos whispered so our father wouldn't hear. But I just turned and cried into the wall. Sometimes when I did that Ma would think about things and be a bit more benevolent.

In the morning Ma had written a letter to Mrs. Donahue and handed it to me before I left for school. She didn't need to tell me not to feed Tony Mello's dog anymore. At lunch time when I brought out my sandwich, I saw that she had tried to slice the bread very thin.

In the First National Store, Ma moved very slowly down the canned goods aisle scanning the shelves, though she never bought too much food in cans. As Carlos and I followed, I thought about that sandwich again. I was sure that the thin slices of bread Ma had cut were a sign that she finally understood. I was sure that on that day she would buy some Sunbeam bread. She might refuse each time we asked her, as she always did, but when we got to the checkout lane she would smile and put a loaf up on the counter. The wish would help it happen.

"Pleeeeze, Ma," we said again. But she just dropped two cans into the cart and ignored us. I looked at the cans.

"Beets? Why are you buying beets in a can, Ma?" I asked.

"If you're buying beets in a can how come you won't buy this sponge bread?" Carlos wanted to know.

"Beets?" she said. "This is that sweet sauce to eat with our turkey." She picked up a can and pointed at the picture of sliced red beets on the label.

"Ma, the picture looks like cranberry sauce, but the words say 'Sliced Beets.'"

"Well, find me some sweet sauce then, Edite," she said.

"Please, Ma," I said again as soon as I'd given her the cans of cranberry sauce. I thought she might buy the bread out of gratitude. But she just said "stop," and swept past, leaving Carlos and me standing in the aisle.

Carlos and I turned a corner and sighted Ma down another aisle in the meat department. She was picking up turkeys to see how much they weighed.

"That's a twenty-pounder," said the man behind the counter.

Ma smiled at him and said "ya" as if she understood what he said.

"Do you want a smaller one?" the man asked.

Ma said "ya" again and put the twenty-pounder in the cart. The man looked confused.

"She can't speak English," I said to him as I ran up.

"Speak English," Carlos said, running up behind me.

Ma gave me that look that meant "what did he say?"

"He wanted to know if that turkey was too big."

"Oh," she said. Then she turned to the man and said "good" as she pointed to the turkey in the cart.

"O.K., Lady," the man said without smiling. And he turned and disappeared through a door in the wall.

"Pleeeeze, Ma," Carlos and I said in unison. She was almost at the checkout counter.

"Get out of my way," Ma said.

And I could tell that she was trying not to shout. Carlos dropped his arms down by his side so that his loaf dragged on the floor. He took a deep breath and blew it out fast. He was giving up. I couldn't blame him. He wasn't as committed to the cause as I was. He didn't have to go to school every day with a monster sandwich in his lunch bag.

Ma was already at a checkout lane emptying the contents of her cart onto the counter. I went over and stood next to her.

"Please, Ma."

As I closed my eyes and hoped real hard, I thought about how even Raiza and Yolanda ate Sunbeam Bread.

My mother ignored me.

"PLEEASE, Ma!"

I think she thought I shouted it, but really, I didn't. It's just that my voice got desperate then.

Ma bent down and put her face very close to mine.

"If you say that to me one more time I will slap you right here in front of everyone." She kept her voice very calm but I knew she was serious from looking in her eyes and from what she said. Ma never threatened to hit us unless she was very mad. My eyes started crying even though I didn't want them to.

"Come on," I said to Carlos. As we headed back toward the Sunbeam girl, I decided that Ma did not really love us. She especially didn't love me. I felt sure then, that my hair would always be unruly, that my ear lobes would always have holes in them, that I

would always have to translate for Ma and Pa. I couldn't look up at the curly blonde girl.

Carlos wanted to know why this bread wasn't kept on the long aisle shelves with the other brands.

"Because the people at this store know that Sunbeam Bread is special," I told him.

On the way home I trudged along behind Ma as she pushed the rattling shopping cart up Main Street. My legs felt lazy and stunned. Carlos hopped along unaffected, being his usual self. Each time we walked by an alley he would stand back near the curb holding his hands up to his face like a camera. Then he would click a picture of the river and the factories which were visible at the end of each alley. We always played this game together. But that day my stomach was full of anger and misery all mixed up together. I used to get very upset at the thought that my mother might die, but that day I didn't care. I was so dejected I hoped that both Ma and Pa would die soon so that we could be adopted by an American family who bought Sunbeam Bread.

When we got to the bakery Ma left the shopping cart by the door and went in to get bread. Carlos and I followed her in and sat on the big window sill while she went up to the big glass counter.

Another customer moved along slowly in front of the counter looking at the fancy pastries. She held a little girl by the hand. The girl pointed to a giant brown cake and said something I couldn't hear.

"No you can't have a chocolate cake, Dear," her mother said. And the little girl began to cry. Carlos got very still and watched carefully as he always did when other children cried. He said he was trying to hear if they cried in English or Portuguese.

I was surprised when Ma called me up to the counter. She never needed my help in the bakery because the people who ran it were Portuguese.

"What kind of bread do you want for your lunch?"

She always bought the big crusty loaves without asking my opinion at all. Maybe she did love me a little. I looked at the different loaves that the bakery lady had put on the counter.

"French stick, Italian Vienna, Polish Scalli, Jewish Rye." She called out their names as she pointed to each one. I looked them over. They were all different sizes and shapes. The French one looked like the softball bat we played with at recess. I could see why they called it a stick. Each loaf had hard golden crusts, some with little seeds baked into them.

"Do you have any that are sliced?" I asked.

"I can slice any of these, except for the French. It's too long to fit in the machine."

I looked at each one of them again trying to imagine which one would make the neatest slices. I felt confused by this sudden gift of choice which seemed to be no choice at all. Why couldn't my mother love me better? Why couldn't she understand that my need for bread was different from hers? The girl at the end of the counter was crying louder. I wanted to tell Ma that the girl was crying because she couldn't have a giant chocolate cake. I wanted to say: "All I want is a proper loaf of bread for my lunch."

"Don't you like any of these?" the bakery lady asked with her hand on her hip.

I shook my head.

"Do you have any other kind?" I was about to ask this myself, but Ma surprised me by asking it first.

"Well, we have one more kind in the back, but it's not as good as these." She went through a swinging door and came back with a rectangular loaf. The crust wasn't as golden as the others and it didn't look as hard. There were no seeds on it at all. I could see that it would make nice square slices.

"I want that one," I said, pointing to the new loaf.

The bakery lady looked at Ma. For a second I was afraid that she would say no, but she nodded her head in agreement.

The lady went through the swinging door again to slice my loaf and brought it back in a clear plastic bag. I felt better when I saw it all sliced up. She put the sliced loaf into a paper bag with two of the crusty ones.

"What do you call that one?" I asked the woman while Ma was looking in her purse for money.

"American Sandwich," she said. And I felt something warm growing in my belly. That sounded even better than Sunbeam Bread. I imagined what my sandwich would look like on my place mat the next day. I imagined myself eating it slowly so that my classmates would have a chance to see it.

"I think it's like Sunbeam Bread, only without the fancy bag," I told Carlos as we followed Ma down the street toward the river.

"It's called American Sandwich," I said.

"American Sandwich, American Sandwich," Carlos yelled as we ran past Ma toward the bridge.

When we got to the river we lay down on the bridge and stuck our heads under the railing again.

"American Sandwich," we yelled together, projecting our voices into the green sluggish water. "AMERICAN SANDWICH!" I liked the way the name of our new bread echoed under the old bridge.

Across the river Pa's factory rose up four stories high and lined the street all the way to the top of the hill. Its roof slumped in the middle like the back of an old work horse. I wondered where, within that factory, our father worked. The windows at the bottom near the river were at street level and were covered with a thick wire mesh. When we walked past one that was partly open, I pressed my face against the mesh to look in.

Far across the room two men in leather aprons pulled a heavy metal cart through a wide doorway. The sounds of the squeaking cart echoed throughout the room, and I imagined them reverberating through the rest of the huge factory and reaching my father's ear. And without even knowing that I would do it, I suddenly closed my eyes tight and yelled as loudly as I could into the room.

"AMERICAN SANDWICH."

But I didn't wait to hear the echoes. I turned, fast, and ran after Carlos and my mother, up the hill, toward the rows of houses where the laundry flapped from the porches like banners.

About the Author

Edite Cunhã (1953–) has written several award-winning stories and an autobiographical novel, from which "American Sandwich" is taken. Cunhã was born in Portugal and came to the United States with her family when she was seven years old. Cunhã lives in Massachusetts, where she has held a variety of jobs, but she considers herself primarily an educator and a writer. She taught creative writing in private schools for many years and also teaches reading skills to adults. According to Cunhã, "'American Sandwich' came from the emotional truth of my experience. That is why the story is especially meaningful to me."

UNDERSTAND KEY IDEAS AND DETAILS. The following questions help you check your reading comprehension. Put an *x* in the box next to the correct answer.

1. "American Sandwich" is mainly about a
   ☐ a. mother who refuses to listen to her children.
   ☐ b. typical day in a school in the United States.
   ☐ c. child's efforts to convince her mother to buy a particular brand of bread.

2. Why did Edite throw her sandwiches away before she arrived at school?
   ☐ a. She did not like the taste of the sandwiches.
   ☐ b. She was embarrassed to eat the sandwiches that her mother made.
   ☐ c. She never got hungry at school.

3. When Pa learned that Edite had been discarding her sandwiches, he
   ☐ a. became angry.
   ☐ b. wrote a note to Edite's teacher.
   ☐ c. went to the school to speak to Miss Leitenen.

4. Edite's father worked in a
   ☐ a. factory.
   ☐ b. bakery.
   ☐ c. junkyard.

NOTE NEW VOCABULARY WORDS. The following questions check your vocabulary skills. Put an *x* in the box next to the correct answer. Each vocabulary word appears in the story.

1. Chasing their mother around the store became a ritual for the children. As used here, the word *ritual* means a
   ☐ a. routine that is followed on a regular basis.
   ☐ b. terrible hardship.
   ☐ c. difficult task.

2. For Edite, lunchtime at school was "a time of mortification." The word *mortification* means
   ☐ a. pleasure or pride.
   ☐ b. shame.
   ☐ c. astonishment or surprise.

3. Edite's father said with sarcasm, "This is bread?" When you speak with *sarcasm,* you
   ☐ a. express pleasure.
   ☐ b. make fun of something or someone.
   ☐ c. ask for assistance.

4. Her grotesque sandwich was so large that she could hardly open her mouth "wide enough to take a bite." What is the meaning of the word *grotesque*?
   ☐ a. monstrous
   ☐ b. expensive
   ☐ c. delicious

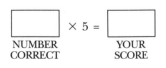

☐ × 5 = ☐
NUMBER   YOUR
CORRECT   SCORE

☐ × 5 = ☐
NUMBER   YOUR
CORRECT   SCORE

IDENTIFY STORY ELEMENTS. The following questions check your knowledge of story elements. Put an *x* in the box next to each correct answer.

1. Who is the *main character* in "American Sandwich"?
   ☐ a. Carlos
   ☐ b. Edite
   ☐ c. Edite's father

2. Of the following events, which happened last in the *plot* of the story?
   ☐ a. Ma purchased a loaf of American Sandwich.
   ☐ b. Miss Leitenen gave Edite a note for her parents.
   ☐ c. Edite made a wish and dropped a penny into the river.

3. The *conflict* in "American Sandwich" is best described as a struggle between a
   ☐ a. brother and a sister.
   ☐ b. girl and her mother.
   ☐ c. girl and her classmates.

4. Which statement best expresses the *theme* of the story?
   ☐ a. Most parents want their children to have a good education.
   ☐ b. What other people think about you is not important.
   ☐ c. Fitting in and belonging are important.

THINK CRITICALLY ABOUT THE STORY. The following questions check your critical thinking skills. Put an *x* in the box next to each correct answer.

1. We may infer that Edite's parents thought that the bread they ate at home was
   ☐ a. not as good as American Sandwich.
   ☐ b. better than American Sandwich.
   ☐ c. about the same as American Sandwich.

2. Ma probably bought a loaf of American Sandwich because
   ☐ a. it cost much less than the other breads.
   ☐ b. she was bored with eating the same bread all the time.
   ☐ c. she realized how much that bread meant to Edite.

3. Which statement is true?
   ☐ a. To Edite, eating sandwiches made with Sunbeam Bread symbolized being an American.
   ☐ b. Edite's teachers were often unkind.
   ☐ c. Edite and her brother, Carlos, were born in the United States.

4. Clues in the story suggest that Edite's parents
   ☐ a. did not care about their children.
   ☐ b. cared a great deal about their children.
   ☐ c. could speak and write English very well, though they chose to give a different impression.

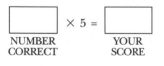

NUMBER CORRECT × 5 = YOUR SCORE

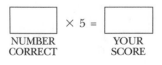

NUMBER CORRECT × 5 = YOUR SCORE

STUDY THE WRITER'S CRAFT. The following questions check your knowledge of skills related to the craft of writing. Put an *x* in the box next to each correct answer. You may refer to pages 4 and 5.

1. "American Sandwich" is based on events in the author's life. Therefore, it is
   ☐ a. an autobiographical story.
   ☐ b. a poetic story.
   ☐ c. a myth.

2. The French bread was "like the softball bat we played with at recess." This sentence
   ☐ a. is an example of foreshadowing.
   ☐ b. illustrates the author's purpose in writing the story.
   ☐ c. contains a simile.

3. "The river was bright green. . . . The tall tall smokestacks of the factories along the riverbank threw long shadows across the water." This is an example of
   ☐ a. the author's ability to create character.
   ☐ b. a descriptive passage.
   ☐ c. a legend.

4. The American Sandwich referred to in the story is best described as
   ☐ a. poetry.
   ☐ b. alliteration.
   ☐ c. a symbol.

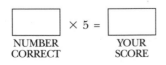

NUMBER CORRECT × 5 = YOUR SCORE

Questions for Writing and Discussion

- To Edite, having sandwiches made with Sunbeam Bread was important. Explain why. Give two reasons.
- In referring to her mother, Edite asked, "Why couldn't she understand that my need for bread was different from hers?" What did Edite mean?
- Do you think that Edite should have revealed to her parents *and* her teacher that children were making fun of her at lunch? Explain.
- At the conclusion of the story why were Carlos and Edite so delighted? Describe how they expressed their joy.

See additional questions for extended writing on pages 40 and 41.

Use the boxes below to total your scores for the exercises. Then record your scores on pages 198 and 199.

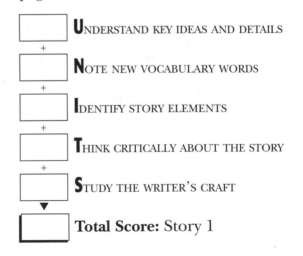

UNDERSTAND KEY IDEAS AND DETAILS
+
NOTE NEW VOCABULARY WORDS
+
IDENTIFY STORY ELEMENTS
+
THINK CRITICALLY ABOUT THE STORY
+
STUDY THE WRITER'S CRAFT
▼
Total Score: Story 1

In Greek mythology, Antaeus was a giant, unable to be conquered while touching the earth. Lifted off the ground by Hercules, the mighty Antaeus was crushed to death. In this story, you will meet a new . . .

Antaeus

by Borden Deal

This was during the wartime, when lots of people were coming North for jobs in factories and war industries, when people moved around a lot more than they do now and sometimes kids were thrown into new groups and new lives that were completely different from anything they had ever known before. I remember this one kid; T. J. his name was, from somewhere down South, whose family moved into our building during that time. They'd come North with everything they owned piled into the back seat of an old-model sedan that you wouldn't expect could make the trip, with T. J. and his three younger sisters riding shakily atop the load of junk.

19

Our building was just like all the others there, with families crowded into a few rooms, and I guess there were twenty-five or thirty kids about my age in that one building. Of course, there were a few of us who formed a gang and ran together all the time after school, and I was the one who brought T. J. in and started the whole thing.

The building right next door to us was a factory where they made walking dolls. It was a low building with a flat, tarred roof that had a parapet[1] all around it about head-high and we'd found out a long time before that no one, not even the watchman, paid any attention to the roof because it was higher than any of the other buildings around. So my gang used the roof as a headquarters. We could get up there by crossing over to the fire escape from our own roof on a plank and then going on up. It was a secret place for us, where nobody else could go without our permission.

I remember the day I first took T. J. up there to meet the gang. He was a stocky, robust kid with a shock of white hair, nothing sissy about him except his voice—he talked different from any of us and you noticed it right away. But I liked him anyway, so I told him to come on up.

We climbed up over the parapet and dropped down on the roof. The rest of the gang were already there.

"Hi," I said. I jerked my thumb at T. J. "He just moved into the building yesterday."

He just stood there, not scared or anything, just looking, like the first time you see somebody you're not sure you're going to like.

---

1. **parapet:** a low wall

"Hi," Blackie said. "Where you from?"

"Marion County," T. J. said.

We laughed. "Marion County?" I said. "Where's that?"

He looked at me like I was a stranger, too. "It's in Alabama," he said, like I ought to know where it was.

"What's your name?" Charley said.

"T. J.," he said, looking back at him. He had pale blue eyes that looked washed-out but he looked directly at Charley, waiting for his reaction. He'll be all right, I thought . . . except that voice. Who ever talked like that?

"T. J.," Blackie said. "That's just initials. What's your real name? Nobody in the world has just initials."

"I do," he said. "And they're T. J. That's all the name I got."

His voice was resolute with the knowledge of his rightness and for a moment no one had anything to say. T. J. looked around at the rooftop and down at the black tar under his feet. "Down yonder where I come from," he said, "we played out in the woods. Don't you-all have no woods around here?"

"Naw," Blackie said. "There's the park a few blocks over, but it's full of kids and cops and old women. You can't do a thing."

T. J. kept looking at the tar under his feet. "You mean you ain't got no fields to raise nothing in? No watermelons or nothing?"

"Naw," I said scornfully. "What do you want to grow something for? The folks can buy everything they need at the store."

He looked at me again with that strange, unknowing look. "In Marion County," he said, "I had my own acre of cotton and my own acre of corn. It was mine to plant ever' year."

He sounded like it was something to be proud of, and in some obscure way it made the rest of us angry. Blackie said, "Who'd want to have their own acre of cotton and corn? That's just work. What can you do with an acre of cotton and corn?"

T. J. looked at him. "Well, you get part of the bale offen your acre," he said seriously. "And I fed my acre of corn to my calf."

We didn't really know what he was talking about, so we were more puzzled than angry; otherwise, I guess, we'd have chased him off the roof and wouldn't let him be part of our gang. But he was strange and different and we were all attracted by his stolid sense of rightness and belonging, maybe by the strange softness of his voice contrasting our own tones of speech into harshness.

He moved his foot against the black tar. "We could make our own field right here," he said softly, thoughtfully. "Come spring we could raise us what we want to . . . watermelons . . . and no telling what all."

"You'd have to be a good farmer to make these tar roofs grow any watermelons," I said. We all laughed.

But T. J. looked serious. "We could haul us some dirt up here," he said. "And spread it out even and water it and before you know it we'd have us a crop in here." He looked at us intently. "Wouldn't that be fun?"

"They wouldn't let us," Blackie said quickly.

"I thought you said this was you-all's roof," T. J. said to me. "That you-all could do anything you wanted up here."

"They've never bothered us," I said. I felt the idea beginning to catch fire in me. It was a big idea and it took a while for it to sink in, but the more I thought about it the better I liked it. "Say," I said to the gang, "he might

have something there. Just make us a regular roof garden, with flowers and grass and trees and everything. And all ours, too," I said. "We wouldn't let anybody up here except the ones we wanted to."

"It'd take a while to grow trees," T. J. said quickly, but we weren't paying any attention to him. They were all talking about it suddenly, all excited with the idea after I'd put it in a way they could catch hold of it. Only rich people had roof gardens, we knew, and the idea of our own private domain excited them.

"We could bring it up in sacks and boxes," Blackie said. "We'd have to do it while the folks weren't paying any attention to us. We'd have to come up to the roof of our building and then cross over with it."

"Where could we get the dirt?" somebody said worriedly.

"Out of those vacant lots over close to school," Blackie said. "Nobody'd notice if we scraped it up."

I slapped T. J. on the shoulder. "Man, you had a wonderful idea," I said, and everybody grinned at him, remembering he had started it. "Our own private roof garden."

He grinned back. "It'll be ourn," he said. "All ourn." Then he looked thoughtful again. "Maybe I can lay my hands on some cotton seed, too. You think we could raise us some cotton?"

We'd started big projects before at one time or another, like any gang of kids, but they'd always petered out for lack of organization and direction. But this one didn't . . . somehow or other T. J. kept it going all through the winter months. He kept talking about the watermelons and the cotton we'd raise, come spring, and when even that wouldn't work he'd switch around to my idea of flowers and grass and trees, though he was always honest enough to add that it'd take a while to get any trees started. He always had it on his mind and he'd mention it in school, getting them lined up to carry dirt that afternoon, saying, in a casual way, that he reckoned a few more weeks ought to see the job through.

Our little area of private earth grew slowly. T. J. was smart enough to start in one corner of the building, heaping up the carried earth two or three feet thick, so that we had an immediate result to look at, to contemplate with awe. Some of the evenings T. J. alone was carrying earth up to the building, the rest of the gang distracted by other enterprises or interests, but T. J. kept plugging along on his own and eventually we'd all come back to him again, and then our own little acre would grow more rapidly.

He was careful about the kind of dirt he'd let us carry up there and more than once he dumped a sandy load over the parapet into the areaway below because it wasn't good enough. He found out the kinds of earth in all the vacant lots for blocks around. He'd pick it up and feel it and smell it, frozen though it was sometimes, and then he'd say it was good growing soil or it wasn't worth anything and we'd have to go on somewhere else.

Thinking about it now, I don't see how he kept us at it. It was hard work, lugging paper sacks and boxes of dirt all the way up the stairs of our own building, keeping out of the way of the grown-ups so they wouldn't catch on to what we were doing. They probably wouldn't have cared, for they didn't pay much attention to us, but we

wanted to keep it secret anyway. Then we had to go through the trapdoor to our roof, teeter over a plank to the fire escape, then climb two or three stories to the parapet and drop down onto the roof. All that for a small pile of earth that sometimes didn't seem worth the effort. But T. J. kept the vision bright within us, his words shrewd and calculated toward the fulfillment of his dream; and he worked harder than any of us. He seemed driven toward a goal that we couldn't see, a particular point in time that would be definitely marked by signs and wonders that only he could see.

The laborious earth just lay there during the cold months, inert and lifeless, the clods lumpy and cold under our feet when we walked over it. But one day it rained, and afterward there was a softness in the air and the earth was alive and giving again with moisture and warmth. That evening T. J. smelled the air, his nostrils dilating with the odor of the earth under his feet.

"It's spring," he said, and there was a gladness rising in his voice that filled us all with the same feeling. "It's mighty late for it, but it's spring. I'd just about decided it wasn't never gonna get here at all."

We were all sniffing at the air, too, trying to smell it the way that T. J. did, and I can still remember the sweet odor of the earth under our feet. It was the first time in my life that spring and spring earth had meant anything to me. I looked at T. J. then, knowing in a faint way the hunger within him through the toilsome winter months, knowing the dream that lay behind his plan. He was a new Antaeus,[2] preparing his own bed of strength.

---

2. **Antaeus:** a giant who drew strength from the earth

"Planting time," he said. "We'll have to find us some seed."

"What do we do?" Blackie said. "How do we do it?"

"First we'll have to break up the clods," T. J. said. "That won't be hard to do. Then we plant the seed, and after a while they come up. Then you got you a crop." He frowned. "But you ain't got it raised yet. You got to tend it and hoe it and take care of it and all the time it's growing and growing while you're awake and while you're asleep. Then you lay it by when it's growed and let it ripen and then you got you a crop."

"There's those wholesale seed houses over on Sixth," I said.

T. J. looked at the earth. "You-all seem mighty set on raising some grass," he said. "I ain't never put no effort into that. I spent all my life trying not to raise grass."

"But it's pretty," Blackie said. "We could play on it and take sunbaths on it. Like having our own lawn. Lots of people got lawns."

"Well," T. J. said. He looked at the rest of us, hesitant for the first time. He kept on looking at us for a moment. "I did have it in mind to raise some corn and vegetables. But we'll plant grass."

He was smart. He knew where to give in. And I don't suppose it made any difference to him, really. He just wanted to grow something, even if it was grass.

"Of course," he said, "I do think we ought to plant a row of watermelons. They'd be mighty nice to eat while we was a-laying on that grass."

We all laughed. "All right," I said. "We'll plant us a row of watermelons."

Things went very quickly then. Perhaps half the roof was covered with the earth, the half that wasn't broken by ventilators. T. J. showed us how to prepare the earth, breaking up the clods and smoothing it and sowing the grass seed. It looked rich and black now with moisture, receiving of the seed, and it seemed that the grass sprang up overnight, pale green in the early spring.

We couldn't keep from looking at it, unable to believe that we had created this delicate growth. We looked at T. J. with understanding now, knowing the fulfillment of the plan he had carried alone within his mind. We had worked without full understanding of the task, but he had known all the time.

We found that we couldn't walk or play on the delicate blades, as we had expected to, but we didn't mind. It was enough just to look at it, to realize that it was the work of our own hands, and each evening the whole gang was there, trying to measure the growth that had been achieved that day.

One time a foot was placed on the plot of ground . . . one time only, Blackie stepping onto it with sudden bravado. Then he looked at the crushed blades and there was shame in his face. He did not do it again. This was his grass, too, and not to be desecrated.[3] No one said anything, for it was not necessary.

T. J. had reserved a small section for watermelons and he was still trying to find some seed for it. The wholesale house didn't have any watermelon seed and we didn't know where we could lay our hands on them. T. J. shaped the earth into mounds, ready to receive them, three mounds lying in a straight line along the edge of the grass plot.

---

3. **desecrated:** treated or used without respect

Somewhere or other, T. J. got his hands on a seed catalog and brought it one evening to our roof garden.

"We can order them now," he said, showing us the catalog. "Look!"

We all crowded around, looking at the fat, green watermelons pictured in full color on the pages. Some of them were split open, showing the red tempting meat, making our mouths water.

"Now we got to scrape up some seed money," T. J. said, looking at us. "I got a quarter. How much you-all got?"

We made up a couple of dollars between us and T. J. nodded his head. "That'll be more than enough. Now we got to decide what kind to get. I think them Kleckley Sweets. What do you-all think?"

He was going into matters beyond our reach. We hadn't even known there were different kinds of melons. So we just nodded our heads and agreed that yes, we thought the Kleckley Sweets, too.

"I'll order them tonight," T. J. said. "We ought to have them in a few days."

Then an adult voice said behind us: "What are you boys doing up here?"

It startled us, for no one had ever come up here before, in all the time we had been using the roof of the factory. We jerked around and saw three men standing near the trapdoor at the other end of the roof. They weren't policemen, or night watchmen, but three men in plump business suits, looking at us. They walked toward us.

"What are you boys doing up here?" the one in the middle said again.

We stood still, guilt heavy among us, levied by the tone of voice, and looked at the three strangers.

The men stared at the grass flourishing behind us. "What's this?" the man said. "How did this get up here?"

"Sure is growing good, ain't it?" T. J. said conversationally. "We planted it."

The men kept looking at the grass as if they didn't believe it. It was a thick carpet over the earth now, a patch of deep greenness startling in the sterile industrial surroundings.

"Yes, sir," T. J. said proudly. "We toted that earth up here and planted that grass." He fluttered the seed catalog. "And we're just fixing to plant us some watermelon."

The man looked at him then, his eyes strange and faraway. "What do you mean, putting this on the roof of my building?" he said. "Do you want to go to jail?"

T. J. looked shaken. The rest of us were silent, frightened by the authority of his voice. We had grown up aware of adult authority, of policemen and night watchmen and teachers, and this man sounded like all the others. But it was a new thing to T. J.

"Well, you wan't using the roof," T. J. said. He paused a moment and added shrewdly, "So we just thought to pretty it up a little bit."

"And sag it so I'd have to rebuild it," the man said sharply. He turned away, saying to a man beside him, "See that all that junk is shoveled off by tomorrow."

"Yes, sir," the man said.

T. J. started forward. "You can't do that," he said. "We toted it up here and it's our earth. We planted it and raised it and toted it up here."

The man stared at him coldly. "But it's my building," he said. "It's to be shoveled off tomorrow."

"It's our earth," T. J. said desperately. "You ain't got no right!"

The men walked on without listening and descended clumsily through the trapdoor. T. J. stood looking after them, his body tense with anger, until they had disappeared. They wouldn't even argue with him, wouldn't let him defend his earth-rights.

He turned to us. "We won't let 'em do it," he said fiercely. "We'll stay up here all day tomorrow and the day after that and we won't let 'em do it."

We just looked at him. We knew that there was no stopping it. He saw it in our faces and his face wavered for a moment before he gripped it into determination.

"They ain't got no right," he said. "It's our earth. It's our land. Can't nobody touch a man's own land."

We kept on looking at him, listening to the words but knowing that it was no use. The adult world had descended on us even in our richest dream, and we knew there was no calculating the adult world, no fighting it, no winning against it.

We started moving slowly toward the parapet and the fire escape, avoiding a last look at the green beauty of the earth that T. J. had planted for us . . . had planted deeply in our minds as well as in our experience. We filed slowly over the edge and down the steps to the plank, T. J. coming last, and all of us could feel the weight of his grief behind us.

"Wait a minute," he said suddenly, his voice harsh with the effort of calling. We stopped and turned, held by the tone of his voice, and looked up at him standing above us on the fire escape.

"We can't stop them?" he said, looking down at us, his face strange in the dusky light. "There ain't no way to stop 'em?"

"No," Blackie said with finality. "They own the building."

We stood still for a moment, looking up at T. J., caught into inaction by the decision working in his face. He stared back at us and his face was pale and mean in the poor light.

"They ain't gonna touch my earth," he said fiercely. "They ain't gonna lay a hand on it! Come on."

He turned around and started up the fire escape again, almost running against the effort of climbing. We followed more slowly, not knowing what he intended. By the time we reached him, he had seized a board and thrust it into the soil, scooping it up and flinging it over the parapet into the areaway below. He straightened and looked us squarely in the face.

"They can't touch it," he said. "I won't let 'em lay a dirty hand on it!"

We saw it then. He stooped to his labor again and we followed it, the gusts of his anger moving in frenzied labor among us as we scattered along the edge of earth, scooping it and throwing it over the parapet, destroying with anger the growth we had nurtured with such tender care. The soil carried so laboriously upward to the light and the sun cascaded swiftly into the dark areaway, the green blades of grass crumpled and twisted in the falling.

It took less time than you would think . . . the task of destruction is infinitely easier than that of creation. We stopped at the end, leaving only a scattering of loose soil, and when it was finally over, a stillness stood among the group and over the factory building. We looked down at the bare sterility of black tar, felt the harsh texture of it under the soles of our shoes, and the anger had gone out of us, leaving only a sore aching in our minds like overstretched muscles.

T. J. stooped for a moment, his breathing slowing from anger and effort, caught into the same contemplation of destruction as all of us. He stooped slowly, finally, and picked up a lonely blade of grass left trampled under our feet, and put it between his teeth, tasting it, sucking the greenness out of it into his mouth. Then he started walking toward the fire escape, moving before any of us were ready to move, and disappeared over the edge while we stared after him.

We followed him but he was already halfway down to the ground, going on past the board where we crossed over, climbing down into the areaway. We saw the last section swing down with his weight and then he stood on the concrete below us, looking at the small pile of anonymous earth scattered by our throwing. Then he walked across the place where we could see him and disappeared toward the street without glancing back, without looking up to see us watching him.

They did not find him for two weeks. Then the Nashville police caught him just outside the Nashville freight yards. He was walking along the railroad track; still heading south, still heading home.

As for us, who had no remembered home to call us . . . none of us ever again climbed the escapeway to the roof.

About the Author

Borden Deal (1922–1985) wrote more than 100 short stories in addition to a large number of poems, articles, and novels. Many of his works have been adapted for movies, the stage, television, and radio. Born in Pontotoc, Mississippi, Deal traveled around the country as a young man, finding employment in a wide variety of jobs—circus performer, firefighter, and film company assistant—until he was able to support himself as a full-time writer. He published his first work at the age of 26 and went on to become a very successful writer. "Antaeus" is Deal's most famous short story. It has appeared in numerous anthologies and textbooks. Like T. J., many of Deal's characters come from or live in the South, the setting of most of the author's stories and novels.

Understand Key Ideas and Details. The following questions help you check your reading comprehension. Put an *x* in the box next to the correct answer.

1. "Antaeus" is mainly about
   - ☐ a. boys who plant a garden of grass on the roof of a factory.
   - ☐ b. how life in the North is different from life in the South.
   - ☐ c. the many problems between teenagers and adults.

2. What did T. J. and the gang need for their plan to succeed?
   - ☐ a. a great deal of money
   - ☐ b. permission from their parents
   - ☐ c. earth and seeds

3. The boys were unable to complete their project because
   - ☐ a. they kept quarreling among themselves.
   - ☐ b. T. J. became bored with the idea and went home.
   - ☐ c. the owner of the building forced them to leave.

4. The narrator states that "the task of destruction is infinitely easier than that of creation." This means that
   - ☐ a. most people are forced to lead difficult lives.
   - ☐ b. it is far easier to destroy than to build.
   - ☐ c. we should respect and admire great works of art.

Note New Vocabulary Words. The following questions check your vocabulary skills. Put an *x* in the box next to the correct answer. Each vocabulary word appears in the story.

1. Nobody challenged T. J. because his voice and manner were so resolute. The word *resolute* means
   - ☐ a. foolish or silly.
   - ☐ b. determined or firm.
   - ☐ c. violent or wild.

2. Nothing grew during the winter, when the earth was "inert and lifeless." Define the word *inert*.
   - ☐ a. without power to move or act
   - ☐ b. new or fresh
   - ☐ c. filled with beauty

3. "T. J. smelled the air, his nostrils dilating with the odor of the earth." What is the meaning of the word *dilating*?
   - ☐ a. becoming smaller
   - ☐ b. becoming weaker
   - ☐ c. becoming larger or wider

4. The idea of having their "own private domain" excited the boys. The word *domain* means
   - ☐ a. riches.
   - ☐ b. a tall building.
   - ☐ c. territory that is controlled by a person or a group of people.

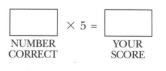

× 5 =

NUMBER CORRECT   YOUR SCORE

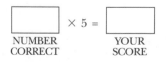

× 5 =

NUMBER CORRECT   YOUR SCORE

IDENTIFY STORY ELEMENTS. The following questions check your knowledge of story elements. Put an *x* in the box next to each correct answer.

1. Where is "Antaeus" *set*?
   - ☐ a. in a town in the South
   - ☐ b. on a farm somewhere in the United States
   - ☐ c. in a northern city

2. Which one of the following best *characterizes* T. J.?
   - ☐ a. T. J. was a stocky, soft-spoken boy who possessed leadership qualities.
   - ☐ b. T. J. had good ideas, but he was unable to influence others to try them.
   - ☐ c. T. J. was awkward and shy and was easily frightened by strangers.

3. Of these events, which happened first in the *plot* of the story?
   - ☐ a. T. J. scooped up soil and flung it over the wall.
   - ☐ b. The boys carried sacks of dirt onto the roof.
   - ☐ c. The boys looked at the three strangers.

4. What is the *mood* of the story?
   - ☐ a. joyous
   - ☐ b. mysterious
   - ☐ c. serious

THINK CRITICALLY ABOUT THE STORY. The following questions check your critical thinking skills. Put an *x* in the box next to each correct answer.

1. Evidence in the story suggests that the boys persisted in their project because
   - ☐ a. they had nothing else to do.
   - ☐ b. they thought it would be amusing to anger the owner of the building.
   - ☐ c. the project made them feel special and gave them a sense of accomplishment.

2. Which statement is *not* true?
   - ☐ a. The project advanced because of T. J.'s enthusiasm and direction.
   - ☐ b. Until the boys were forced to discontinue their work, they had been pleased with what they had achieved.
   - ☐ c. The task of planting grass was easy and took almost no time or effort.

3. We may infer that T. J. believed that
   - ☐ a. the building owner had the right to everything on the roof.
   - ☐ b. the boys were the sole owners of the land they had planted.
   - ☐ c. giving up the roof garden was not worth getting upset about.

4. It is fair to say that at the end of the story, the boys
   - ☐ a. were furious at T. J.
   - ☐ b. agreed with the building owner.
   - ☐ c. destroyed what might be considered "the fruits of their labor."

NUMBER CORRECT × 5 = YOUR SCORE

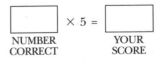

NUMBER CORRECT × 5 = YOUR SCORE

STUDY THE **W**RITER'S **C**RAFT. The following questions check your knowledge of skills related to the craft of writing. Put an *x* in the box next to each correct answer. You may refer to pages 4 and 5.

1. Antaeus was a giant who drew strength from the earth. By calling T. J. "a new Antaeus," the writer makes use of
   ☐ a. alliteration.
   ☐ b. science fiction.
   ☐ c. a literary allusion.

2. The statement "You get part of the bale offen your acre" illustrates
   ☐ a. standard English.
   ☐ b. highly poetic language.
   ☐ c. dialect.

3. "He was a new Antaeus" is
   ☐ a. a metaphor.
   ☐ b. a simile.
   ☐ c. an example of inner conflict.

4. The three strangers in business suits represent
   ☐ a. the power of authority.
   ☐ b. the need for change in the world.
   ☐ c. consideration and kindness.

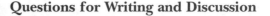

Questions for Writing and Discussion

- Although T. J. was a newcomer, the gang accepted him quickly and responded enthusiastically to his suggestions. Explain why.
- One of the boys called T. J. "a new Antaeus, preparing his own bed of strength." Why was T. J. "a new Antaeus," and what "bed of strength" was he preparing?
- Why did T. J. and the gang destroy the garden they had labored to create?
- Why did T. J. leave the city to return to his home after the roof garden was destroyed?

See additional questions for extended writing on pages 40 and 41.

Use the boxes below to total your scores for the exercises. Then record your scores on pages 198 and 199.

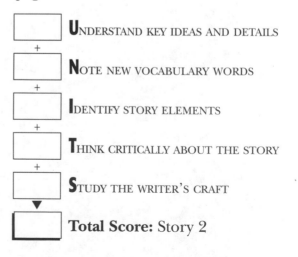

☐ **U**NDERSTAND KEY IDEAS AND DETAILS
+
☐ **N**OTE NEW VOCABULARY WORDS
+
☐ **I**DENTIFY STORY ELEMENTS
+
☐ **T**HINK CRITICALLY ABOUT THE STORY
+
☐ **S**TUDY THE WRITER'S CRAFT
▼
☐ **Total Score:** Story 2

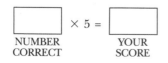

☐ × 5 = ☐

NUMBER   YOUR
CORRECT   SCORE

A great ad can sell just about anything. You'll read one of the best in . . .

This Farm for Sale

by Jesse Stuart

"This time we're goin' to sell this farm," Uncle Dick said to Aunt Emma. "I've just learned how to sell a farm. Funny, I never thought of it myself."

My cousins—Olive, Helen, Oliver, and Little Rick—all stopped eating and looked at one another and then looked at Uncle Dick and Aunt Emma. When Aunt Emma smiled, they smiled, too. Everybody seemed happy because Uncle Dick, who had just come from Blakesburg, had found a way to sell the farm. Everybody was happy but me. I was sorry Uncle Dick was going to sell the farm.

"This farm is just as good as sold!" Uncle Dick talked on. "I've got a real estate man, my old friend Melvin Spencer, coming here tomorrow to look the place over. He's goin' to sell it for me."

"I'd like to get enough for it to make a big payment on a fine house in Blakesburg," Aunt Emma said. "I've got the one picked out that I want. It's the beautiful Coswell house. I understand it's up for sale now and no one's livin' in it!"

"Gee, that will be wonderful," Cousin Olive said. "Right on the street and not any mud. We wouldn't have to wear galoshes all winter if we lived there!"

"I'll say it will be wonderful," Helen said, with a smile. "Daddy, I hope Mr. Spencer can sell this place."

I wanted to tell Aunt Emma the reason why no one was living in the Coswell house. Every time Big River rose to flood stage, the water got on the first floor in the house; and this was the reason why the Coswells had built a house on higher ground outside Blakesburg and had moved to it. And this was the reason why they couldn't keep a renter any longer than it took Big River to rise to flood stage. But this wasn't my business, so I didn't say anything.

"Mel Spencer will come here to look this farm over," Uncle Dick said. "Then he'll put an ad in the *Blakesburg Gazette.*"

"What will we do about the cows, horses, hogs, honeybees, hay in the barn lofts and

31

in the stacks, and corn in the bins?" Cousin Oliver asked.

"Sell them, too," Uncle Dick said. "When we sell, let's sell everything we have but our household goods."

It was ten o'clock the next day before Melvin Spencer came. Since he couldn't drive his car all the way to Uncle Dick's farm, he rode the mail truck to Red Hot. Red Hot is a store and post office on the Tiber River. And at Red Hot, Uncle Dick met him with an extra horse and empty saddle. So Melvin Spencer came riding up with Uncle Dick. And I'll never forget the first words he said when he climbed down from the saddle.

"Richard, it's a great experience to be in the saddle again," he said, breathing deeply of the fresh air. "All this reminds me of another day and time."

Oliver, Little Rick, and I followed Melvin Spencer and Uncle Dick as they started walking toward the Tiber bottoms.

"How many acres in this farm, Richard?" Melvin Spencer asked.

"The deed calls for three hundred, more or less," Uncle Dick said.

"How many acres of bottom land?" he asked Uncle Dick.

"I'd say about sixty-five," Uncle Dick replied.

We walked down the jolt-wagon road, where my cousins and I had often ridden Nell and Jerry to and from the field.

"What kind of land is this?" Melvin Spencer asked. He had to look up to see the bright heads of cane.

"It's limestone land," Uncle Dick bragged. "Never had to use fertilizer. My people have farmed these bottoms over a hundred years."

Then Uncle Dick showed Melvin Spencer the corn we had stored. It was August, and our growing corn was maturing. Melvin Spencer looked at the big cornfield. He was very silent. We walked on to the five acres of tobacco. Then we went down to the river.

"My farm comes to this river," Uncle Dick said. "I've often thought what a difference it would be if we had a bridge across this river. Then I could reach the Tiber road and go east to Blakesburg and west to Darter City. But we don't have a bridge; and until we go down the river seven miles to Red Hot where we can cross to the Tiber road, we'll always be in the mud. I've heard all my life that the county would build a bridge. My father heard it, too, in his lifetime."

"You *are* shut in here," Melvin Spencer agreed, as he looked beyond the Tiber River at the road.

"Now, we'll go to the house and get some dinner," Uncle Dick said. "Then I'll take you up on the hill this afternoon and show you my timber and the rest of the farm."

When we reached the big house, Melvin Spencer stopped for a minute and looked at the house and yard.

"You know, when I negotiate a piece of property, I want to look it over," he told Uncle Dick. "I want to know all about it and assess everything. How old is this house?"

"The date was cut on the chimney," Uncle Dick said.

Melvin Spencer looked over the big squat log house with the plank door, big stone steps, small windows, the moss-covered roof. Then we went inside, and he started looking again. That is, he did until Uncle Dick introduced him to Aunt Emma and Aunt Emma introduced him to a table that made him look some more.

"I've never seen anything like this since I was a boy," Melvin Spencer said, showing more interest in the loaded table than he had in the farm.

"All of this came from our farm here," Uncle Dick said.

I never saw a man eat like Melvin Spencer. He ate like I did when I first came to Uncle Dick's and Aunt Emma's each spring when school was over. He tried to eat something of everything on the table, but he couldn't get around to it all, as ravenous as he was.

"If I could sell this farm like you can prepare a meal, I'd get a whopping big price for it," he said with a chuckle as he looked at Aunt Emma.

"I hope you can," Aunt Emma said. "We're too far back here. Our children have to wade the winter mud to get to school. And we don't have electricity. We don't have the things that city people have. And I think every country woman wants them."

Melvin Spencer didn't listen to all that Aunt Emma said. He was much too busy eating. Uncle Dick, in evident enjoyment, looked at Aunt Emma and smiled.

"The old place is as good as sold," Uncle Dick said with a wink. "You're a-goin' to be out of the mud. We'll let some other woman slave around here and wear galoshes all winter. We'll be on the bright, clean streets wearin' well-shined shoes—every one of us. We'll have an electric washer, a radio where we won't have to have the batteries charged, a bathroom, and an electric stove. No more of this stove-wood choppin' for the boys and me."

When Uncle Dick said this, Olive and Helen looked at Aunt Emma and smiled. I looked at Oliver and Little Rick, and they were grinning. But Melvin Spencer never looked up from his plate.

When we got up from the table, Melvin Spencer thanked Aunt Emma, Cousin Olive, and Helen for the "best dinner" he'd had since he was a young man. Then he asked Aunt Emma for a picture of the house.

Aunt Emma sent Helen to get it. "If you can, just sell this place for us," Aunt Emma said to Melvin Spencer.

"I'll do my best," he promised her. "But as you ought to know, it will be a hard place to sell, located way back here and without a road."

"Are you a-goin' to put a picture of this old house in the paper?" Uncle Dick asked, as Helen came running with the picture.

"I might," Melvin Spencer said. "I never say much in an ad, since I have to make my words count. A picture means a sale sometimes. Of course, this expense will come from the sale of the property."

He said good-by to Aunt Emma, Olive, and Helen. Little Rick, Oliver, and I followed him and Uncle Dick out of the house and up the hill where the yellow poplars and the pines grow.

"Why hasn't this timber been cut long ago?" Melvin Spencer asked, looking up at the trees.

"Not any way to haul it out," Uncle Dick told him.

"That's right," Melvin Spencer said. "I'd forgot about the road. If a body doesn't have a road to his farm, Richard, he's not got much of a place."

"These old trees get hollow and blow down in storms," Uncle Dick said. "They should have been cut down a long time ago."

"Yes, they should have," Melvin Spencer agreed, as he put his hand on the bark of a yellow poplar. "We used to have trees like this in Pike County. But not any more."

While we walked under the beech grove, we came upon a drove of slender bacon hogs eating beechnuts.

"Old Skinny bacon hogs," Uncle Dick said, as they scurried past us. "They feed on the beeches and oaks, on saw-briar, greenbriar, and pine-tree roots, and on mulberries, persimmons, and pawpaws."

When we climbed to the top of a hill, a hawk circled lazily in the sky, and the land slanted in all directions.

"Show me from here what you own," Melvin Spencer said.

"It's very easy, Mel," Uncle Dick said. "The stream on the right and the one on the left are the left and right forks of Wolfe Creek. They are boundary lines. I own all the land between them. I own all the bottom land from where the forks join, down to that big bend in the Tiber. And I own down where the Tiber flows against those white limestone cliffs."

"You are fenced in by natural boundaries," Melvin Spencer said. "They're almost impossible to cross. This place is fairly inaccessible and will be hard to sell, Richard."

Then we went back down the hill, and Melvin and Uncle Dick climbed into the saddles and were off down the little narrow road toward Red Hot. Their horses went away at a gallop, because Melvin Spencer had to catch the mail truck, and he was already behind schedule.

On Saturday, Uncle Dick rode to Red Hot to get the paper. Since he didn't read very well, he asked me to read what Melvin Spencer had said about his house. When I opened the paper and turned to the picture of the house, everybody gathered around.

"Think of a picture of this old house in the paper," Aunt Emma said.

"But there are pictures of other houses for sale in the paper," Uncle Dick told her. "That's not anything to crow about."

"But it's the best-looking of the four," Cousin Olive said.

"It does look better than I thought it would," Aunt Emma sighed.

"Look, here's two columns all the way down the page," I said. "The other four places advertised here have only a paragraph about them."

"Read it, Shan," Uncle Dick said. "I'd like to know what Mel said about this place. Something good, I hope."

So I read this aloud:

Yesterday, I had a unique experience when I visited the farm of Mr. and Mrs. Richard Stone, which they have asked me to sell. I cannot write an ad about this farm. I must tell you about it.

I went up a winding road on horseback. Hazelnut bushes, with clusters of green hazelnuts bending their slender stems, swished across my face. Pawpaws, heavy with green clusters of fruit, grew along this road. Persimmons with bending boughs covered one slope below the road. Here are wild fruits and nuts of Nature's cultivation for the one who possesses land like this. Not any work but just to go out and gather the fruit. How many of you city dwellers would love this?

"What about him a-mentionin' the persimmons, pawpaws, and hazelnuts!" Uncle Dick broke in. "I'd never have thought of them. They're common things!"

When we put the horses in the big barn, Mr. Stone, his two sons, his nephew, and I walked down into his Tiber-bottom farm land. And, like the soil along the Nile River, this overflowed land, rich with limestone, never has to be fertilized. I saw cane as high as a giraffe, and as dark green as the waves of the Atlantic. It grew in long, straight rows with brown clusters of seed that looked to be up against the blue of the sky. I have never seen such dark clouds of corn grow out of the earth. Five acres of tobacco, with leaves as broad as a mountaineer's shoulders. Pleasant meadows with giant haystacks here and there. It is a land rich with fertility and abundant with crops.

"That sounds wonderful," Aunt Emma said, smiling.

This peaceful Tiber River, flowing dreamily down the valley, is a boundary to his farm. Here one can see to the bottoms of the deep holes, the water is so clear and blue. One can catch fish from the river for his next meal. Elder bushes, where they gather the berries to make the finest jelly in the world, grow along this riverbank as thick as ragweeds. The Stones have farmed this land for generations, have lived in the same house, have gathered elderberries for their jelly along the Tiber riverbanks, and fished in its sky-blue waters that long—and yet they will sell this land.

"Just a minute, Shan," Uncle Dick said as he got up from his chair. "Stop just a minute."

Uncle Dick pulled a handkerchief from his pocket and wiped the sweat from his forehead. His face seemed a bit flushed. He walked a little circle around the living room and then sat back down in his chair. But the sweat broke out on his face again when I started reading.

The proof of what a farm produces is at the farm table. I wish that whoever reads what I have written here could have seen the table prepared by Mrs. Stone and her two daughters. Hot fluffy biscuits with light-brown tops, brown-crusted cornbread, buttermilk, sweet milk (cooled in a freestone well), wild-grape jelly, wild-crabapple jelly, lean bacon that melted in my mouth, fresh apple pie, wild-blackberry cobbler, honey-colored sorghum from the limestone bottoms of the Tiber, and wild honey from the beehives.

"Oh, no one ever said that about a meal I cooked before," Aunt Emma broke in.

"Just a minute, Shan," Uncle Dick said, as he got up from his chair and with his handkerchief in his hand again.

This time Uncle Dick went a bit faster as he circled the living room. He wiped sweat from his face as he walked. He had a worried look on his face. I read on:

The house, eight rooms and two halls, would be a show place if close to some of our modern cities. The house itself would be worth the price I will later quote you on this farm. Giant yellow poplar logs with twenty- to thirty-inch facings, hewed smooth with broadaxes by the mighty hands of Stone pioneers, make the sturdy walls in this termite-proof house. Two planks make the broad doors in this house that is one-hundred-and-six years old. This beautiful home of pioneer architecture is without modern conveniences, but since a power line will be constructed up the Tiber River early next spring, a few modern conveniences will be possible.

"I didn't know that!" Aunt Emma was excited. "I guess it's just talk, like about the bridge across the Tiber."

After lunch I climbed a high hill to look at the rest of this farm. I walked through a valley of trees, where there were yellow poplars and pine sixty feet to the first limb. Beech trees with tops big enough to shade twenty-five head of cattle.

This Farm for Sale

Beechnuts streaming down like golden coins, to be gathered by the bacon hogs running wild. A farm with wild game and fowl, and a river bountiful with fish! And yet, this farm is for sale!

Uncle Dick walked over beside his chair. He looked as if he were going to fall over.

Go see for yourself roads not exploited by the county or state, where the horse's shoe makes music on the clay, where apple orchards with fruit are bending down, and barns and bins are full. Go see a way of life, a richness and fulfillment that make America great, that put solid foundation stones under America! This beautiful farm, fifty head of livestock, honeybees, crops old and new, and a home for only $22,000!

"Oh!" Aunt Emma screamed. I thought she was going to faint. "Oh, he's killed it with that price. It's unheard of, Richard! You couldn't get $6,000 for it."

Uncle Dick still paced the floor.

"What's the matter, Pa?" Oliver finally asked.

"I didn't know I had so much," Uncle Dick said. "I'm a rich man and didn't know it. I'm not selling this farm!"

"Don't worry, Richard," Aunt Emma said. "You won't sell it at that price!"

I never saw such disappointed looks as there were on my cousins' faces.

"But what will you do with Mr. Spencer?" Aunt Emma asked. "You've put the farm in his hands to sell."

"Pay him for his day and what he put in the paper," Uncle Dick told her. "I know we're not goin' to sell now, for it takes two to sign the deed. I'll be willing to pay Mel Spencer a little extra because he showed me what we have."

Then I laid the paper down and walked quietly from the room. Evening was coming on. I walked toward the meadows. I wanted to share the beauty of this farm with Melvin Spencer. I was never so happy.

About the Author

Jesse Stuart (1907–1984) was one of America's most beloved writers. Stuart was born in the Kentucky hill country and lived and worked on a farm similar to the one in "This Farm for Sale." Stuart bought the house in which he grew up, and he lived there for many years, writing and farming. During a long and distinguished career as a novelist, short-story writer, biographer, and poet, Stuart wrote nearly 500 short stories. One of his most popular books is an autobiographical novel, *The Thread That Runs So True,* in which the author draws on his experiences growing up in Kentucky and his early days as a teacher in Kentucky and Ohio.

UNDERSTAND KEY IDEAS AND DETAILS. The following questions help you check your reading comprehension. Put an *x* in the box next to the correct answer.

1. Which sentence best expresses the main idea of the story?
   - ☐ a. It is almost impossible to sell a farm without using a real estate agent.
   - ☐ b. A farmer learns to appreciate the many things he has taken for granted.
   - ☐ c. An old friend enjoys one of the best meals of his life.

2. Melvin Spencer stated that the farm would be difficult to sell because it
   - ☐ a. was far from a road.
   - ☐ b. had few animals or crops.
   - ☐ c. was not particularly beautiful.

3. What price did Melvin Spencer set for the farm and everything on it?
   - ☐ a. $22,000
   - ☐ b. $20,000
   - ☐ c. $6,000

4. As a result of Spencer's advertisement, Dick Stone
   - ☐ a. decided to ask for more money for the farm.
   - ☐ b. made a payment on a house in Blakesburg.
   - ☐ c. changed his mind about selling the farm.

NOTE NEW VOCABULARY WORDS. The following questions check your vocabulary skills. Put an *x* in the box next to the correct answer. Each vocabulary word appears in the story.

1. Before Melvin Spencer agreed to "negotiate a piece of property," he liked to look it over carefully. Which of the following best defines the word *negotiate*?
   - ☐ a. to visit
   - ☐ b. to read about
   - ☐ c. to arrange a selling price for

2. Mr. Spencer ate a tremendous amount of food because he was ravenous. What is the meaning of the word *ravenous*?
   - ☐ a. very wealthy
   - ☐ b. very thin
   - ☐ c. very hungry

3. The land was "fenced in by natural boundaries," making the farm quite inaccessible. The word *inaccessible* means
   - ☐ a. large.
   - ☐ b. hard to reach.
   - ☐ c. easy to get to.

4. Mr. Spencer wrote that the roads had not been "exploited by the county or state." As used here, the word *exploited* means
   - ☐ a. used by.
   - ☐ b. sold by.
   - ☐ c. forgotten by.

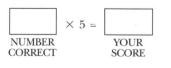

☐ × 5 = ☐
NUMBER CORRECT   YOUR SCORE

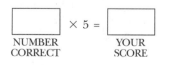

☐ × 5 = ☐
NUMBER CORRECT   YOUR SCORE

IDENTIFY STORY ELEMENTS. The following questions check your knowledge of story elements. Put an *x* in the box next to each correct answer.

1. What is the *setting* of the story?
   - ☐ a. a real estate office
   - ☐ b. a newspaper office
   - ☐ c. a farm

2. Which of the following is the best example of *character development*?
   - ☐ a. At first Mr. Stone was eager to sell the farm, but later he decided against doing that.
   - ☐ b. Shan thought that the farm was beautiful, and he hoped that the family would keep it.
   - ☐ c. Mr. Spencer said that the farm would be hard to sell, but he made it sound very attractive.

3. Who is the *narrator* of "This Farm for Sale"?
   - ☐ a. Shan
   - ☐ b. Uncle Dick
   - ☐ c. Melvin Spencer

4. Of these events, which happened last in the *plot* of the story?
   - ☐ a. Dick Stone asked Aunt Emma for a picture of the house.
   - ☐ b. The family listened to the description of the farm as portrayed in the newspaper.
   - ☐ c. Dick Stone and Melvin Spencer rode up to the farm.

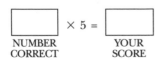

NUMBER CORRECT × 5 = YOUR SCORE

THINK CRITICALLY ABOUT THE STORY. The following questions check your critical thinking skills. Put an *x* in the box next to each correct answer.

1. We may infer that it would have been easier to sell the farm if the farm had
   - ☐ a. a bridge that crossed the Tiber River.
   - ☐ b. fewer trees on the land.
   - ☐ c. many more hills.

2. Which statement is *not* true?
   - ☐ a. Mr. Spencer made the farm more appealing by describing his experience there.
   - ☐ b. The advertisement suggested that the farm was beautiful but in poor condition.
   - ☐ c. Aunt Emma was shocked at the price Mr. Spencer asked for the farm.

3. We may conclude that Mr. Stone failed to appreciate that he had so much because he
   - ☐ a. did not like being a farmer.
   - ☐ b. was bored with country life.
   - ☐ c. had never stopped to think about all he had.

4. It is fair to say that Melvin Spencer
   - ☐ a. was sure that he would sell the farm in a day or two.
   - ☐ b. had little experience in selling real estate.
   - ☐ c. had a wonderful "way with words."

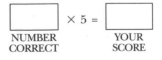

NUMBER CORRECT × 5 = YOUR SCORE

STUDY THE WRITER'S CRAFT. The following questions check your knowledge of skills related to the craft of writing. Put an *x* in the box next to each correct answer. You may refer to pages 4 and 5.

1. Shan noted that the "fine" Coswell house in Blakesburg often flooded. This is one way the author reveals that Shan
   ☐ a. hoped that the Stones would sell their farm.
   ☐ b. did not want the farm to be sold.
   ☐ c. did not care whether the family sold the farm.

2. Mr. Spencer wrote that he saw "cane as high as a giraffe" and "leaves as broad as a mountaineer's shoulders." This description contains
   ☐ a. a metaphor.
   ☐ b. two similes.
   ☐ c. a conflict with a force of nature.

3. "Hazlenut bushes, with clusters of green hazelnuts bending their slender stems, swished across my face" is an example of
   ☐ a. plot development.
   ☐ b. characterization.
   ☐ c. descriptive writing.

4. Mr. Spencer wrote, "This peaceful Tiber River, flowing dreamily down the valley, is a boundary to his farm." The words *peaceful* and *dreamily* are intended to
   ☐ a. create a favorable impression.
   ☐ b. make the reader feel sleepy.
   ☐ c. suggest that farmers are lazy.

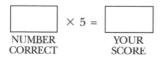

NUMBER CORRECT   × 5 =   YOUR SCORE

Questions for Writing and Discussion

● Describe in detail the Stone family's farm. Tell about the construction of their house and about the crops, plants, trees, and animals on the farm.
● At the story's conclusion, Dick Stone said, "I'm a rich man and didn't know it." Explain what he meant.
● Do you think that Mr. Stone was fair to his wife and children in deciding not to sell the farm? Give reasons for your answer.
● "This Farm for Sale" is a tribute to the power of the written word. Support this statement.

See additional questions for extended writing on pages 40 and 41.

Use the boxes below to total your scores for the exercises. Then record your scores on pages 198 and 199.

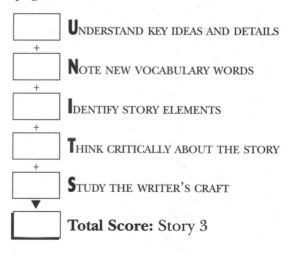

UNDERSTAND KEY IDEAS AND DETAILS
+
NOTE NEW VOCABULARY WORDS
+
IDENTIFY STORY ELEMENTS
+
THINK CRITICALLY ABOUT THE STORY
+
STUDY THE WRITER'S CRAFT
▼
Total Score: Story 3

Home

Questions for Discussion and Extended Writing

The following questions provide you with opportunities to express your thoughts and feelings about the selections in this unit. Your teacher may assign selected questions. When you write your responses, remember to state your point of view clearly and to support your position by presenting specific details—examples, illustrations, and references drawn from the story and, in some cases, from your life. Organize your writing carefully and check your work for correct spelling, capitalization, punctuation, and grammar.

1. The theme of this unit is "Home." Show how each story in the unit is related to this theme.

2. An old saying states, "Home is where the heart is." What is the meaning of this saying? Which character in the unit do you think would be most likely to agree with this saying? Support your opinion.

3. "American Sandwich" and "Antaeus" are set in cities. In which of these stories do you think that the setting is more important? Explain why.

4. Compare and contrast T. J. in "Antaeus" and Shan in "This Farm for Sale." In what ways are they similar? How are they different?

5. Young people are characters in each story in the unit. Which young person do you think exhibited the greatest leadership qualities? Support your answer.

6. Conflict is the struggle between opposing forces in a story. In which story do you think conflict plays the most important role? Identify the conflict or conflicts in the story you selected when you support your choice.

7. In Greek mythology, Antaeus was a powerful giant who drew his strength from the earth. Antaeus overpowered every stranger who entered his land. Antaeus was finally defeated by the mighty Hercules, who lifted Antaeus into the air. Show how this myth of victory and defeat can be applied to T. J.

8. Of the selections in this unit, descriptive language is most significant in "This Farm for Sale." Support this statement by referring to the story.

9. In "American Sandwich," Edite said, "More than anything I wanted to be like the others." Consider the following statement:

> Many young people wish "to belong." This is why they join clubs, dress in similar fashion, and identify with popular heroes. Being a member of a group is reassuring. Few people want to be "outsiders."

Explain why you agree or disagree with the statement above. Support your position in a carefully organized essay. The essay should have an introduction, a body, and a conclusion.

10. In each story in this unit, characters can take pride in an accomplishment or an achievement. Write about an accomplishment or achievement in which you take pride. Present specific details in your essay.

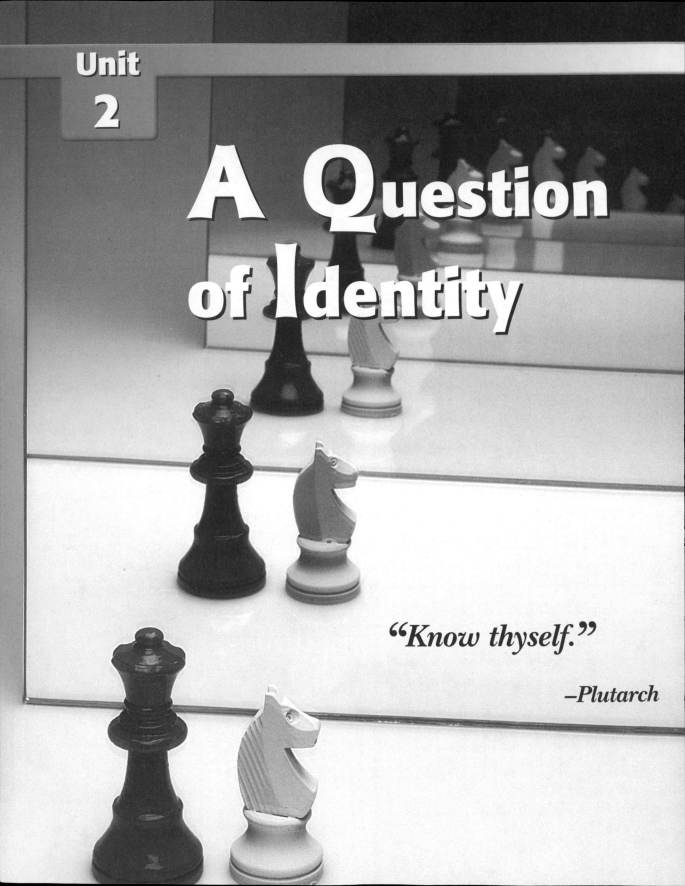

Unit 2

A Question of Identity

"Know thyself."

–Plutarch

Previewing the Unit

Who am I? What is my place in the world? What do I stand for, or represent? These are all questions that relate to identity, a subject that has fascinated—and baffled—human beings throughout history.

Almost 2,000 years ago the Greek essayist Plutarch advised, "Know thyself." In the stories in this unit, characters undertake a voyage of discovery to identify who they are.

RULES OF THE GAME Amy Tan's "Rules of the Game" deals largely with the relationship between a young girl (Meimei) who was born in America and her mother (Mrs. Jong), who grew up in China. Cultural conflicts between the two provide a framework for the story. But there is also, of course, a "generation gap"—the gap in age and ideas between the mother and the daughter. Meimei seeks to achieve independence, but she must accomplish this in an appropriate manner. The game of chess is a powerful symbol that runs through the story. To Meimei, "The chess board seemed to hold elaborate secrets waiting to be untangled." What are those "elaborate secrets" waiting to be solved? Perhaps they are associated with the process of growing up and finding one's identity.

TO SERVE MAN In the story "To Serve Man," we encounter some unusual visitors from another planet. They possess extraordinary powers, but some serious questions must be asked: Who are these creatures? What do they stand for? What can we learn about their true identity?

WHO AM I THIS TIME? In "Who Am I This Time?" we are introduced to Harry Nash, a clerk in a hardware store. In real life, Harry is scared, tongue-tied, and painfully shy. But on stage, Harry is instantly transformed, and he readily assumes the identity of any character he plays. Ultimately Harry meets Helene Shaw, who has her own problems in expressing emotion. Helene states, "When I meet somebody nice in real life, I feel as though I were in some kind of big bottle, as though I couldn't touch that person, no matter how hard I tried." How Harry and Helene deal with their identity issues is for the reader to discover.

We all have concerns related to identity. You will be interested in seeing how the characters in this unit handle theirs.

Life, like chess, was fascinating and complex. She had difficult decisions to make, and she had to play by the . . .

Rules of the Game

from *The Joy Luck Club*

by Amy Tan

I was six when my mother taught me the art of invisible strength. It was a strategy for winning arguments, respect from others, and eventually, though neither of us knew it at the time, chess games.

"Bite back your tongue," scolded my mother when I cried loudly, yanking her hand toward the store that sold bags of salted plums. At home, she said, "Wise guy, he not go against wind. In Chinese we say, Come from South, blow with wind—poom!—North will follow. Strongest wind cannot be seen."

The next week I bit back my tongue as we entered the store with the forbidden candies. When my mother finished her shopping, she quietly plucked a small bag of plums from the rack and put it on the counter with the rest of the items.

My mother imparted her daily truths so she could help my older brothers and me rise above our circumstances. We lived in San Francisco's Chinatown. Like most of the other Chinese children who played in the back alleys of restaurants and curio shops, I didn't think we were poor. My bowl was always full, three five-course meals every day, beginning with a soup full of mysterious things I didn't want to know the names of.

We lived on Waverly Place, in a warm, clean, two-bedroom flat that sat above a small Chinese bakery specializing in steamed pastries and dim sum.[1] In the early morning, when the alley was still quiet, I could smell fragrant red beans as they were cooked down to a pasty sweetness. By daybreak, our flat was heavy with the odor of fried sesame balls and sweet curried chicken crescents. From my bed, I would listen as my father got ready for work, then locked the door behind him, one-two-three clicks.

At the end of our two-block alley was a small sandlot playground with swings and slides well-shined down the middle with use. The play area was bordered by wood-slat benches where old-country people sat cracking roasted watermelon seeds with their golden teeth and scattering the husks to an impatient gathering of gurgling pigeons. The best playground, however, was the dark alley

itself. It was crammed with daily mysteries and adventures. My brothers and I would peer into the medicinal herb shop, watching Old Li dole out onto a stiff sheet of white paper the right amount of insect shells, saffron-colored seeds, and pungent[2] leaves for his ailing customers. It was said that he once cured a woman dying of an ancestral curse that had eluded the best of American doctors. Next to the pharmacy was a printer who specialized in gold-embossed wedding invitations and festive red banners.

Farther down the street was Ping Yuen Fish Market. The front window displayed a tank crowded with doomed fish and turtles struggling to gain footing on the slimy green-tiled sides. A hand-written sign informed tourists, "Within this store, is all for food, not for pet." Inside, the butchers with their bloodstained white smocks deftly gutted the fish while customers cried out their orders and shouted, "Give me your freshest," to which the butchers always protested, "All are freshest." On less crowded market days, we would inspect the crates of live frogs and crabs which we were warned not to poke, boxes of dried cuttlefish, and row upon row of iced prawns, squid, and slippery fish. The sanddabs made me shiver each time; their eyes lay on one flattened side and reminded me of my mother's story of a careless girl who ran into a crowded street and was crushed by a cab. "Was smash flat," reported my mother.

At the corner of the alley was Hong Sing's, a four-table café with a recessed stairwell in front that led to a door marked "Tradesmen." My brothers and I believed the bad people emerged from this door at

---

1. **dim sum:** shells of dough, usually filled with vegetables and meat

2. **pungent:** having a sharp or biting taste or smell

night. Tourists never went to Hong Sing's, since the menu was printed only in Chinese. A Caucasian man with a big camera once posed me and my playmates in front of the restaurant. He had us move to the side of the picture window so the photo would capture the roasted duck with its head dangling from a juice-covered rope. After he took the picture, I told him he should go into Hong Sing's and eat dinner. When he smiled and asked me what they served, I shouted, "Guts and duck's feet and octopus gizzards!" Then I ran off with my friends, shrieking with laughter as we scampered across the alley and hid in the entryway grotto of the China Gem Company, my heart pounding with hope that he would chase us.

My mother named me after the street that we lived on: Waverly Place Jong, my official name for important American documents. But my family called me Meimei, "Little Sister." I was the youngest, the only daughter. Each morning before school, my mother would twist and yank on my thick black hair until she had formed two tightly wound pigtails. One day, as she struggled to weave a hard-toothed comb through my disobedient hair, I had a sly thought.

I asked her, "Ma, what is Chinese torture?" My mother shook her head. A bobby pin was wedged between her lips. She wetted her palm and smoothed the hair above my ear, then pushed the pin in so that it nicked sharply against my scalp.

"Who say this word?" she asked without a trace of knowing how wicked I was being. I shrugged my shoulders and said, "Some boy in my class said Chinese people do Chinese torture."

"Chinese people do many things," she said simply. "Chinese people do business, do medicine, do painting. Not lazy like American people. We do torture. Best torture."

My older brother Vincent was the one who actually got the chess set. We had gone to the annual Christmas party held at the First Chinese Baptist Church at the end of the alley. The missionary ladies had put together a Santa bag of gifts donated by members of another church. None of the gifts had names on them. There were separate sacks for boys and girls of different ages.

One of the Chinese parishioners had donned a Santa Claus costume and a stiff paper beard with cotton balls glued to it. I think the only children who thought he was the real thing were too young to know that Santa Claus was not Chinese. When my turn came up, the Santa man asked me how old I was. I thought it was a trick question; I was seven according to the American formula and eight by the Chinese calendar. I said I was born on March 17, 1951. That seemed to satisfy him. He then solemnly asked if I had been a very, very good girl this year and did I believe in Jesus Christ and obey my parents. I knew the only answer to that. I nodded back with equal solemnity.

Having watched the other children opening their gifts, I already knew that the big gifts were not necessarily the nicest ones. One girl my age got a large coloring book of biblical characters, while a less greedy girl who selected a smaller box received a glass vial of lavender toilet water. The sound of the box was also important. A ten-year-old boy had chosen a box that jangled when he shook it. It was a tin globe of the world with a slit for inserting money. He must have thought it was full of dimes and nickels, because when he saw that it had just ten pennies, his face fell with such undisguised disappointment that his mother slapped the side of his head and led him out of the church hall, apologizing to the crowd for her son who had such bad manners he couldn't appreciate such a fine gift.

As I peered into the sack, I quickly fingered the remaining presents, testing their weight, imagining what they contained. I chose a heavy, compact one that was wrapped in shiny silver foil and a red satin ribbon. It was a twelve-pack of Life Savers and I spent the rest of the party arranging and rearranging the candy tubes in the order of my favorites. My brother Winston chose wisely as well. His present turned out to be a box of intricate plastic parts; the instructions on the box proclaimed that when they were properly assembled he would have an authentic miniature replica of a World War II submarine.

Vincent got the chess set, which would have been a very decent present to get at a church Christmas party, except it was obviously used and, as we discovered later, it was missing a black pawn and a white knight. My mother graciously thanked the unknown benefactor, saying, "Too good. Cost too much." At which point, an old lady with fine white, wispy hair nodded toward our family and said with a whistling whisper, "Merry, merry Christmas."

When we got home, my mother told Vincent to throw the chess set away. "She not want it. We not want it," she said, tossing her head stiffly to the side with a tight, proud smile. My brothers had deaf ears. They were already lining up the chess pieces and reading from the dog-eared instruction book.

I watched Vincent and Winston play during Christmas week. The chess board seemed to hold elaborate secrets waiting to be untangled. The chessmen were more powerful than Old Li's magic herbs that cured ancestral curses. And my brothers wore such serious faces that I was sure something was at stake that was greater than avoiding the tradesmen's door to Hong Sing's.

"Let me! Let me!" I begged between games when one brother or the other would sit back with a deep sigh of relief and victory, the other annoyed, unable to let go of the outcome. Vincent at first refused to let me play, but when I offered my Life Savers as replacements for the buttons that filled in for the missing pieces, he relented. He chose the flavors: wild cherry for the black pawn and peppermint for the white knight. Winner could eat both.

As our mother sprinkled flour and rolled out small doughy circles for the steamed dumplings that would be our dinner that night, Vincent explained the rules, pointing to each piece. "You have sixteen pieces and so do I. One king and queen, two bishops, two knights, two castles, and eight pawns. The pawns can only move forward one step, except on the first move. Then they can move two. But they can only take men by moving crossways like this, except in the beginning, when you can move ahead and take another pawn."

"Why?" I asked as I moved my pawn. "Why can't they move more steps?"

"Because they're pawns," he said.

"But why do they go crossways to take other men. Why aren't there any women and children?"

"Why is the sky blue? Why must you

always ask stupid questions?" asked Vincent. "This is a game. These are the rules. I didn't make them up. See. Here. In the book." He jabbed a page with a pawn in his hand. "Pawn. P-A-W-N. Pawn. Read it yourself."

My mother patted the flour off her hands. "Let me see book," she said quietly. She scanned the pages quickly, not reading the foreign English symbols, seeming to search deliberately for nothing in particular.

"This American rules," she concluded at last. "Every time people come out from foreign country, must know rules. You not know, judge say, Too bad, go back. They not telling you why so you can use their way go forward. They say, Don't know why, you find out yourself. But they knowing all the time. Better you take it, find out why yourself." She tossed her head back with a satisfied smile.

I found out about all the whys later. I read the rules and looked up all the big words in a dictionary. I borrowed books from the Chinatown library. I studied each chess piece, trying to absorb the power each contained.

I learned about opening moves and why it's important to control the center early on; the shortest distance between two points is straight down the middle. I learned about the middle game and why tactics between two adversaries are like clashing ideas; the one who plays better has the clearest plans for both attacking and getting out of traps. I learned why it is essential in the endgame[3] to have foresight, a mathematical under-standing of all possible moves, and patience; all weaknesses and advantages become evident to a strong adversary and are obscured to a tiring opponent. I discovered

---

3. **endgame:** the final stages of a chess game

that for the whole game one must gather invisible strengths and see the endgame before the game begins.

I also found out why I should never reveal "why" to others. A little knowledge withheld is a great advantage one should store for future use. That is the power of chess. It is a game of secrets in which one must show and never tell.

I loved the secrets I found within the sixty-four black and white squares. I carefully drew a handmade chessboard and pinned it to the wall next to my bed, where at night I would stare for hours at imaginary battles. Soon I no longer lost any games or Life Savers, but I lost my adversaries. Winston and Vincent decided they were more interested in roaming the streets after school in their Hopalong Cassidy cowboy hats.

On a cold spring afternoon, while walking home from school, I detoured through the playground at the end of our alley. I saw a group of old men, two seated across a fold-ing table playing a game of chess, others smoking pipes, eating peanuts, and watching. I ran home and grabbed Vincent's chess set, which was bound in a cardboard box with rubber bands. I also carefully selected two prized rolls of Life Savers. I came back to the park and approached a man who was observing the game.

"Want to play?" I asked him. His face widened with surprise and he grinned as he looked at the box under my arm.

"Little sister, been a long time since I play with dolls," he said, smiling benevolently. I quickly put the box down next to him on the bench and displayed my retort.

Lau Po, as he allowed me to call him, turned out to be a much better player than my brothers. I lost many games and many Life Savers. But over the weeks, with each diminishing roll of candies, I added new secrets. Lau Po gave me the names. The Double Attack from the East and West Shores. Throwing Stones on the Drowning Man. The Sudden Meeting of the Clan. The Surprise from the Sleeping Guard. The Humble Servant Who Kills the King. Sand in the Eyes of Advancing Forces. A Double Killing Without Blood.

There were also the fine points of chess etiquette. Keep captured men in neat rows, as well-tended prisoners. Never announce "Check" with vanity, lest someone with an unseen sword slit your throat. Never hurl pieces into the sandbox after you have lost a game, because then you must find them again, by yourself, after apologizing to all around you. By the end of the summer, Lau Po had taught me all he knew, and I had become a better chess player.

A small weekend crowd of Chinese people and tourists would gather as I played and defeated my opponents one by one. My mother would join the crowds during these outdoor exhibition games. She sat proudly on the bench, telling my admirers with proper Chinese humility, "Is luck."

A man who watched me play in the park suggested that my mother allow me to play in local chess tournaments. My mother smiled graciously, an answer that meant nothing. I desperately wanted to go, but I bit back my tongue. I knew she would not let me play among strangers. So as we walked home I said in a small voice that I didn't want to play in the local tournament. They would have American rules. If I lost, I would bring shame on my family.

"Is shame you fall down nobody push

you," said my mother.

During my first tournament, my mother sat with me in the front row as I waited for my turn. I frequently bounced my legs to unstick them from the cold metal seat of the folding chair. When my name was called, I leapt up. My mother unwrapped something in her lap. It was her *chang*, a small tablet of red jade which held the sun's fire. "Is luck," she whispered, and tucked it into my dress pocket. I turned to my opponent, a fifteen-year-old boy from Oakland. He looked at me, wrinkling his nose.

As I began to play, the boy disappeared, the color ran out of the room, and I saw only my white pieces and his black ones waiting on the other side. A light wind began blowing past my ears. It whispered secrets only I could hear.

"Blow from the South," it murmured. "The wind leaves no trail." I saw a clear path, the traps to avoid. The crowd rustled. "Shhh! Shhh!" said the corners of the room. The wind blew stronger. "Throw sand from the East to distract him." The knight came forward ready for the sacrifice. The wind hissed, louder and louder. "Blow, blow, blow. He cannot see. He is blind now. Make him lean away from the wind so he is easier to knock down."

"Check," I said, as the wind roared with laughter. The wind died down to little puffs, my own breath.

My mother placed my first trophy next to a new plastic chess set that the neighborhood Tao society had given to me. As she wiped each piece with a soft cloth, she said, "Next time win more, lose less."

"Ma, it's not how many pieces you lose," I said. "Sometimes you need to lose pieces to get ahead."

"Better to lose less, see if you really need."

At the next tournament, I won again, but it was my mother who wore the triumphant grin.

"Lost eight piece this time. Last time was eleven. What I tell you? Better off lose less!" I was annoyed, but I couldn't say anything.

I attended more tournaments, each one farther away from home. I won all games, in all divisions. The Chinese bakery downstairs from our flat displayed my growing collection of trophies in its window, amidst the dust-covered cakes that were never picked up. The day after I won an important regional tournament, the window encased a fresh sheet cake with whipped-cream frosting and red script saying, "Congratulations, Waverly Jong, Chinatown Chess Champion." Soon after that, a flower shop, headstone engraver, and funeral parlor offered to sponsor me in national tournaments. That's when my mother decided I no longer had to do the dishes. Winston and Vincent had to do my chores.

"Why does she get to play and we do all the work," complained Vincent.

"Is new American rules," said my mother. "Meimei play, squeeze all her brains out for win chess. You play, worth squeeze towel."

By my ninth birthday, I was a national chess champion. I was still some 429 points away from grand-master status, but I was touted as the Great American Hope, a child prodigy and a girl to boot. They ran a photo of me in *Life* magazine next to a quote in which Bobby Fischer said, "There will never be a woman grand master." "Your move, Bobby," said the caption.

The day they took the magazine picture I wore neatly plaited braids clipped with plastic barrettes trimmed with rhinestones. I was playing in a large high school auditorium that echoed with phlegmy coughs and the squeaky rubber knobs of chair legs sliding across freshly waxed wooden floors. Seated across from me was an American man, about the same age as Lau Po, maybe fifty. I remember that his sweaty brow seemed to weep at my every move. He wore a dark, malodorous suit. One of his pockets was stuffed with a great white kerchief on which he wiped his palm before sweeping his hand over the chosen chess piece with great flourish.

In my crisp pink-and-white dress with scratchy lace at the neck, one of two my mother had sewn for these special occasions, I would clasp my hands under my chin, the delicate points of my elbows poised lightly on the table in the manner my mother had shown me for posing for the press. I would swing my patent leather shoes back and forth like an impatient child riding on a school bus. Then I would pause, suck in my lips, twirl my chosen piece in midair as if undecided, and then firmly plant it in its new threatening place, with a triumphant smile thrown back at my opponent for good measure.

I no longer played in the alley of Waverly Place. I never visited the playground where the pigeons and old men gathered. I went to school, then directly home to learn new chess secrets, cleverly concealed advantages, more escape routes.

But I found it difficult to concentrate at home. My mother had a habit of standing over me while I plotted out my games. I think she thought of herself as my protective ally. Her lips would be sealed tight, and after each move I made, a soft "Hmmmmph" would escape from her nose.

"Ma, I can't practice when you stand there like that," I said one day. She retreated to the kitchen and made loud noises with the pots and pans. When the crashing stopped, I could see out of the corner of my eye that she was standing in the doorway. "Hmmmph!" Only this one came out of her tight throat.

My parents made many concessions to allow me to practice. One time I complained that the bedroom I shared was so noisy that I couldn't think. Thereafter, my brothers slept in a bed in the living room facing the street. I said I couldn't finish my rice; my head didn't work right when my stomach was too full. I left the table with half-finished bowls and nobody complained. But there was one duty I couldn't avoid. I had to accompany my mother on Saturday market days when I had no tournament to play. My mother would proudly walk with me, visiting many shops, buying very little. "This my daughter Wave-ly Jong," she said to whoever looked her way.

One day, after we left a shop I said under my breath, "I wish you wouldn't do that, telling everybody I'm your daughter." My mother stopped walking. Crowds of people with heavy bags pushed past us on the sidewalk, bumping into first one shoulder, then another.

"Aiii-ya. So shame be with mother?" She grasped my hand even tighter as she glared at me.

I looked down. "It's not that, it's just so obvious. It's just so embarrassing."

"Embarrass you be my daughter?" Her voice was cracking with anger.

"That's not what I meant. That's not what I said."

"What you say?"

I knew it was a mistake to say anything more, but I heard my voice speaking. "Why do you have to use me to show off? If you want to show off, then why don't you learn to play chess."

My mother's eyes turned into dangerous black slits. She had no words for me, just sharp silence.

I felt the wind rushing around my hot ears. I jerked my hand out of my mother's tight grasp and spun around, knocking into an old woman. Her bag of groceries spilled to the ground.

"Aii-ya! Stupid girl!" my mother and the woman cried. Oranges and tin cans careened down the sidewalk. As my mother stooped to help the old woman pick up the escaping food, I took off.

I raced down the street, dashing between people, not looking back as my mother screamed shrilly, "Meimei! Meimei!" I fled down an alley, past dark curtained shops and merchants washing the grime off their windows. I sped into the sunlight, into a large street crowded with tourists examining trinkets and souvenirs. I ducked into another dark alley, down another street, up another alley. I ran until it hurt and I realized I had nowhere to go, that I was not running from anything. The alleys contained no escape routes.

My breath came out like angry smoke. It was cold. I sat down on an upturned plastic pail next to a stack of empty boxes, cupping my chin with my hands, thinking hard. I imagined my mother, first walking briskly down one street or another looking for me, then giving up and returning home to await my arrival. After two hours, I stood up on creaking legs and slowly walked home.

The alley was quiet and I could see the yellow lights shining from our flat like two tiger's eyes in the night. I climbed the sixteen steps to the door, advancing quietly up each so as not to make any warning sounds. I turned the knob; the door was locked. I heard a chair moving, quick steps, the locks turning—click! click! click!—and then the door opened.

"About time you got home," said Vincent. "Boy, are you in trouble."

He slid back to the dinner table. On a platter were the remains of a large fish, its fleshy head still connected to bones swimming upstream in vain escape. Standing there waiting for my punishment, I heard my mother speak in a dry voice.

"We not concerning this girl. This girl not have concerning for us."

Nobody looked at me. Bone chopsticks clinked against the insides of bowls being emptied into hungry mouths.

I walked into my room, closed the door, and lay down on my bed. The room was dark, the ceiling filled with shadows from the dinnertime lights of neighboring flats.

In my head, I saw a chessboard with sixty-four black and white squares. Opposite me was my opponent, two angry black slits. She wore a triumphant smile. "Strongest wind cannot be seen," she said.

Her black men advanced across the plane, slowly marching to each successive level as a single unit. My white pieces screamed as they scurried and fell off the board one by one. As her men drew closer to my edge, I felt myself growing light. I rose up into the air and flew out the window. Higher and higher, above the alley, over the tops of tiled roofs, where I was gathered up by the wind and pushed up toward the night sky until everything below me disappeared and I was alone.

I closed my eyes and pondered my next move.

About the Author

Amy Tan (1952–) showed great literary promise early in life. At the age of eight, her article "What the Library Means to Me" won a writing contest and was published in a local newspaper. Born in Oakland, California, to Chinese immigrant parents, much of Tan's work deals with mother-daughter relationships within Chinese American families.

This selection is one of 16 related stories in Tan's award-winning first novel, *The Joy Luck Club.* Tan's other best-selling books include *The Kitchen God's Wife, The Hundred Secret Senses,* and *The Bonesetter's Daughter.* Tan's writing is clear, sensitive, and direct and combines a sense of humor with the ability to touch the reader's heart.

UNDERSTAND KEY IDEAS AND DETAILS. The following questions help you check your reading comprehension. Put an *x* in the box next to the correct answer.

1. "Rules of the Game" is mainly about the
   - ☐ a. difficulties experienced by people who immigrate to the United States.
   - ☐ b. relationship between a girl and her mother as the girl progresses in skill as a chess player.
   - ☐ c. strategies that one must employ to win at chess.

2. Meimei first played chess on a set that her brother received
   - ☐ a. at a church party.
   - ☐ b. as a gift from her family.
   - ☐ c. from a friend.

3. Meimei's brothers had to do her chores because
   - ☐ a. they could do them better than Meimei could.
   - ☐ b. she refused to do them.
   - ☐ c. she was devoting so much of her time to chess.

4. When Mrs. Jong showed Meimei off, the girl was
   - ☐ a. very pleased.
   - ☐ b. broken-hearted.
   - ☐ c. quite annoyed.

NOTE NEW VOCABULARY WORDS. The following questions check your vocabulary skills. Put an *x* in the box next to the correct answer. Each vocabulary word appears in the story.

1. An unknown benefactor contributed the gift. A *benefactor* is someone who
   - ☐ a. gives money, help, or some other gift.
   - ☐ b. asks for assistance.
   - ☐ c. is extremely intelligent.

2. Mrs. Jong was exhibiting humility when she stated that her daughter won by luck. Which of the following best defines the word *humility*?
   - ☐ a. great surprise
   - ☐ b. the quality of being humble
   - ☐ c. a secret desire

3. By her ninth birthday, Meimei was a chess champion, and she was considered "a child prodigy." The word *prodigy* means
   - ☐ a. a troublesome individual.
   - ☐ b. a marvel.
   - ☐ c. a fairly ordinary person.

4. Meimei's opponent had a sweaty brow, and his suit was malodorous. Since the prefix *mal-* means "bad," the word *malodorous* means
   - ☐ a. not expensive.
   - ☐ b. badly made.
   - ☐ c. having a bad smell.

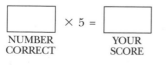

☐ × 5 = ☐

NUMBER CORRECT   YOUR SCORE

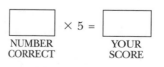

☐ × 5 = ☐

NUMBER CORRECT   YOUR SCORE

53

IDENTIFY STORY ELEMENTS. The following questions check your knowledge of story elements. Put an *x* in the box next to each correct answer.

1. Who is the *main character* in "Rules of the Game"?
   - ☐ a. Meimei
   - ☐ b. Mrs. Jong
   - ☐ c. Vincent

2. Of these events, which happened first in the *plot* of the story?
   - ☐ a. Lau Po agreed to play chess with Meimei.
   - ☐ b. Meimei let go of her mother's hand and ran.
   - ☐ c. Vincent showed Meimei the way that pawns moved.

3. Which of the following conflicts does *not* occur in the story?
   - ☐ a. a conflict between Meimei and her mother
   - ☐ b. a conflict between Meimei and a classmate
   - ☐ c. a conflict between Meimei and an opponent

4. Which statement best expresses the *theme* of the story?
   - ☐ a. Anyone who tries hard enough can be a national chess champion.
   - ☐ b. Members of a family should always agree with each other.
   - ☐ c. In life—as in chess—one must make difficult decisions.

THINK CRITICALLY ABOUT THE STORY. The following questions check your critical thinking skills. Put an *x* in the box next to each correct answer.

1. The story suggests that Meimei and her mother
   - ☐ a. always agreed with each other.
   - ☐ b. did not care about each other's feelings.
   - ☐ c. sometimes clashed because they grew up in different cultures.

2. Evidence in the story suggests that the "Rules" and the "Game" mentioned in the title refer to
   - ☐ a. the process of growing up.
   - ☐ b. decisions about which players may enter a tournament.
   - ☐ c. the laws of the United States.

3. We may infer that the Bobby Fischer quoted on page 50 in the story was
   - ☐ a. a photographer for *Life* magazine.
   - ☐ b. one of the world's great chess players.
   - ☐ c. a man who played chess in the playground near Meimei's home.

4. At the end of the story, Meimei imagined an opponent who "wore a triumphant smile." We may conclude that this opponent was
   - ☐ a. one of the chess players Meimei faced.
   - ☐ b. Meimei herself.
   - ☐ c. Meimei's mother.

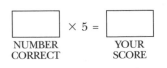

× 5 =

NUMBER CORRECT   YOUR SCORE

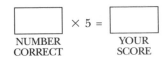

× 5 =

NUMBER CORRECT   YOUR SCORE

STUDY THE WRITER'S CRAFT. The following questions check your knowledge of skills related to the craft of writing. Put an *x* in the box next to each correct answer. You may refer to pages 4 and 5.

1. The statement "Life is a game of chess" is
   ☐ a. a simile.
   ☐ b. a metaphor.
   ☐ c. an example of foreshadowing.

2. Since some sections of the story are based on events in the author's life, "Rules of the Game" is
   ☐ a. a biography.
   ☐ b. autobiographical.
   ☐ c. a fable.

3. The sentence "I could see the yellow lights shining from our flat like two tiger's eyes in the night" contains
   ☐ a. an example of character development.
   ☐ b. a simile.
   ☐ c. conflict.

4. Which one of the following is true of Amy Tan's writing?
   ☐ a. She writes dialogue that is true-to-life.
   ☐ b. She does not seem to care about the characters she describes.
   ☐ c. She never creates passages that are descriptive.

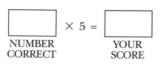

NUMBER CORRECT × 5 = YOUR SCORE

Questions for Writing and Discussion

- Although Mrs. Jong did not speak perfect English, she often gave her daughter very good advice. Discuss some good advice that Mrs. Jong offered Meimei.
- Meimei stated that chess "is a game of secrets in which one must show and never tell." What did Meimei mean by this?
- Discuss the reasons behind the clash that erupted between Meimei and her mother at the end of the story.
- At the conclusion of "Rules of the Game," Meimei pondered her next move. What might she be thinking?

See additional questions for extended writing on pages 78 and 79.

Use the boxes below to total your scores for the exercises. Then record your scores on pages 198 and 199.

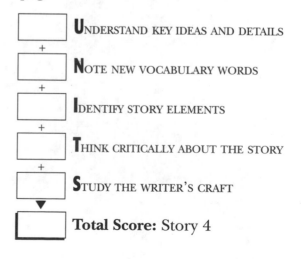

UNDERSTAND KEY IDEAS AND DETAILS

+

NOTE NEW VOCABULARY WORDS

+

IDENTIFY STORY ELEMENTS

+

THINK CRITICALLY ABOUT THE STORY

+

STUDY THE WRITER'S CRAFT

▼

Total Score: Story 4

The visitors from another planet were unattractive and strange. Still, no one could deny that they came to Earth . . .

To Serve Man

by Damon Knight

The Kanamit were not very pretty, it's true. They looked something like pigs and something like people, and that is not an attractive combination. Seeing them for the first time shocked you; that was their handicap. When a thing with the countenance[1] of a fiend comes from the stars and offers a gift, you are disinclined to accept.

I don't know what we expected interstellar visitors to look like—those who thought about it at all, that is. Angels, perhaps, or something too alien to be really awful. Maybe that's why we were all so horrified and repelled when they landed in their great ships and we saw what they really were like.

The Kanamit were short and very hairy—thick, bristly brown-gray hair all over their abominably plump bodies. Their noses were snoutlike and their eyes small, and they had thick hands of three fingers each. They wore green leather suspenders and green shorts, but I think the shorts were a concession to our notions of public decency. The garments were quite modishly[2] cut, with slash pockets and half-belts in the back. The Kanamit had a sense of humor, anyhow.

There were three of them at this session of the U.N.,[3] and I can't tell you how queer it looked to see them there in the middle of a solemn Plenary Session[4]—three fat piglike creatures in green suspenders and shorts, sitting at the long table below the podium, surrounded by the packed arcs of delegates from every nation. They sat correctly upright, politely watching each speaker. Their flat ears drooped over the earphones. Later on, I believe, they learned every human language, but at this time they knew only French and English.

They seemed perfectly at ease—and that, along with their humor, was a thing that tended to make me like them. I was in the minority; I didn't think they were trying to put anything over. They said quite simply that they wanted to help us and I believed it. As a U.N. translator, of course, my opinion didn't matter, but I thought they were the best thing that ever happened to Earth.

The delegate from Argentina got up and said that his government was interested by the demonstration of a new cheap power source, which the Kanamit had made at the previous session, but that the Argentine government could not commit itself as to its future policy without a much more thorough examination.

It was what all the delegates were saying, but I had to pay particular attention to Señor Valdes, because he tended to sputter and his diction was bad. I got through the translation all right, with only one or two momentary hesitations, and then switched to the Polish-English line to hear how Gregori was doing with Janciewicz. Janciewicz was the cross Gregori had to bear, just as Valdes was mine.

1. **countenance:** a look or expression

2. **modishly:** stylishly

3. **U.N.:** the United Nations, an organization of nations dedicated to cooperation and world peace

4. **Plenary Session:** a meeting for all of the members

Janciewicz repeated the previous remarks with a few ideological variations, and then the Secretary-General recognized the delegate from France, who introduced Dr. Denis Lévêque, the criminologist, and a great deal of complicated equipment was wheeled in.

Dr. Lévêque remarked that the question in many people's minds had been aptly expressed by the delegate from the U.S.S.R. at the preceding session, when he demanded, "What is the motive of the Kanamit? What is their purpose in offering us these unprecedented gifts, while asking nothing in return?"

The doctor then said, "At the request of several delegates and with the full consent of our guests, the Kanamit, my associates and I have made a series of tests upon the Kanamit with the equipment which you see before you. These tests will now be repeated."

A murmur ran through the chamber. There was a fusillade of flashbulbs, and one of the TV cameras moved up to focus on the instrument board of the doctor's equipment. At the same time, the huge television screen behind the podium lighted up, and we saw the blank faces of two dials, each with its pointer resting at zero, and a strip of paper tape with a stylus point resting against it.

The doctor's assistants were fastening wires to the temples of one of the Kanamit, wrapping a canvas-covered rubber tube around his forearm, and taping something to the palm of his right hand.

In the screen, we saw the paper tape begin to move while the stylus traced a slow zigzag pattern along it. One of the needles began to jump rhythmically; the other flipped over and stayed there, wavering slightly.

"These are the standard instruments for testing the truth of a statement," said Dr. Lévêque. "Our first object, since the physiology[5] of the Kanamit is unknown to us, was to determine whether or not they react to these tests as human beings do. We will now repeat one of the many experiments which was made in the endeavor to discover this."

He pointed to the first dial. "This instrument registers the subject's heart-beat. This shows the electrical conductivity of the skin in the palm of his hand, a measure of perspiration, which increases under stress. And this"—pointing to the tape-and-stylus device—"shows the pattern and intensity of the electrical waves emanating from his brain. It has been shown, with human subjects, that all these readings vary markedly depending upon whether the subject is speaking the truth."

He picked up two large pieces of cardboard, one red and one black. The red one was a square about a meter on a side; the black was a rectangle a meter and a half long. He addressed himself to the Kanama:

"Which of these is longer than the other?"

"The red," said the Kanama.

Both needles leaped wildly, and so did the line on the unrolling tape.

"I shall repeat the question," said the doctor. "Which of these is longer than the other?"

"The black," said the creature.

This time the instruments continued in their normal rhythm.

"How did you come to this planet?" asked the doctor.

---

5. **physiology:** the way that something living functions

"Walked," replied the Kanama.

Again the instruments responded, and there was a subdued ripple of laughter in the chamber.

"Once more," said the doctor, "how did you come to this planet?"

"In a spaceship," said the Kanama, and the instruments did not jump.

The doctor again faced the delegates. "Many such experiments were made," he said, "and my colleagues and myself are satisfied that the mechanisms are effective. Now," he turned to the Kanama, "I shall ask our distinguished guest to reply to the question put at the last session by the delegate of the U.S.S.R., namely, what is the motive of the Kanamit people in offering these great gifts to the people of Earth?"

The Kanama rose. Speaking this time in English, he said, "On my planet there is a saying, 'There are more riddles in a stone than in a philosopher's head.' The motives of intelligent beings, though they may at times appear obscure, are simple things compared to the complex workings of the natural universe. Therefore I hope that the people of Earth will understand, and believe, when I tell you that our mission upon your planet is simply this—to bring to you the peace and plenty which we ourselves enjoy, and which we have in the past brought to other races throughout the galaxy. When your world has no more hunger, no more war, no more needless suffering, that will be our reward."

And the needles had not jumped once.

The delegate from the Ukraine jumped to his feet, asking to be recognized, but the time was up and the Secretary-General closed the session.

I met Gregori as we were leaving the U.N.

chamber. His face was red with excitement. "Who promoted that circus?" he demanded.

"The tests looked genuine to me," I told him.

"A circus!" he said vehemently. "A second-rate farce! If they were genuine, Peter, why was debate stifled?"

"There'll be time for debate tomorrow surely."

"Tomorrow the doctor and his instruments will be back in Paris. Plenty of things can happen before tomorrow. In the name of sanity, man, how can anybody trust a thing that looks as if it ate the baby?"

I was a little annoyed. I said, "Are you sure you're not more worried about their politics than their appearance?"

He said, "Bah," and went away.

The next day reports began to come in from government laboratories all over the world where the Kanamit's power source was being tested. They were wildly enthusiastic. I don't understand such things myself, but it seemed that those little metal boxes would give more electrical power than an atomic pile, for next to nothing and nearly forever. And it was said that they were so cheap to manufacture that everybody in the world could have one of his own. In the early afternoon there were reports that seventeen countries had already begun to set up factories to turn them out.

The next day the Kanamit turned up with plans and specimens of a gadget that would increase the fertility of any arable land by sixty to one hundred percent. It speeded the formation of nitrates in the soil, or something. There was nothing in the headlines but the Kanamit any more. The day after that, they dropped their bombshell.

"You now have potentially unlimited power and increased food supply," said one of them. He pointed with his three-fingered hand to an instrument that stood on the table before him. It was a box on a tripod, with a parabolic reflector on the front of it. "We offer you today a third gift which is at least as important as the first two."

He beckoned to the TV men to roll their cameras into closeup position. Then he picked up a large sheet of cardboard covered with drawings and English lettering. We saw it on the large screen above the podium; it was all clearly legible.

"We are informed that this broadcast is being relayed throughout your world," said the Kanama. "I wish that everyone who has equipment for taking photographs from television screens would use it now."

The Secretary-General leaned forward and asked a question sharply, but the Kanama ignored him.

"This device," he said, "projects a field in which no explosive, of whatever nature, can detonate."[6]

There was an uncomprehending silence.

The Kanama said, "It cannot now be suppressed. If one nation has it, all must have it." When nobody seemed to understand, he explained bluntly. "There will be no more war."

That was the biggest news of the millennium, and it was perfectly true. It turned out that the explosives the Kanama was talking about included gasoline and Diesel explosions. They had simply made it impossible for anybody to mount or equip a modern army.

We could have gone back to bows and arrows, of course, but that wouldn't have satisfied the military. Not after having atomic bombs and all the rest. Besides, there wouldn't be any reason to make war. Every nation would soon have everything.

Nobody ever gave another thought to those lie-detector experiments, or asked the Kanamit what their politics were. Gregori was put out; he had nothing to prove his suspicions.

I quit my job with the U.N. a few months later, because I foresaw that it was going to die under me anyhow. U.N. business was booming at the time, but after a year or so there was going to be nothing for it to do. Every nation on Earth was well on the way to being completely self-supporting; they weren't going to need much arbitration.[7]

I accepted a position as translator with the Kanamit Embassy, and it was there that I ran into Gregori again. I was glad to see him, but I couldn't imagine what he was doing there.

"I thought you were on the opposition," I said. "Don't tell me you're convinced the Kanamit are all right."

He looked rather shamefaced. "They're not what they look, anyhow," he said.

It was as much of a concession as he could decently make, and I invited him down to the embassy lounge for a talk. It was an intimate kind of place, and he grew confidential.

"They fascinate me," he said. "I hate them instinctively on sight still—that hasn't changed, but I can evaluate it. You were right, obviously; they mean us nothing but

---

6. **detonate:** explode

7. **arbitration:** the process of settling disputes by using a judge or an individual trusted by both parties

good. But do you know"—he leaned across the table—"the question of the Soviet delegate was never answered."

I am afraid I snorted.

"No, really," he said. "They told us what they wanted to do—'to bring to you the peace and plenty which we ourselves enjoy.' But they didn't say *why*."

"Why do missionaries——"

"Hogwash!" he said angrily. "Missionaries have a religious motive. If these creatures have a religion, they haven't once mentioned it. What's more, they didn't send a missionary group, they sent a diplomatic delegation—a group representing the will and policy of their whole people. Now just what have the Kanamit, as a people or a nation, got to gain from our welfare?"

I said, "Cultural——"

"Cultural cabbage-soup! No, it's something less obvious than that, something obscure that belongs to their psychology and not to ours. But trust me, Peter, there is no such thing as a completely disinterested altruism.[8] In one way or another, they have something to gain."

"And that's why you're here," I said, "to try to find out what it is?"

"Correct. I wanted to get on one of the ten-year exchange groups to their home planet, but I couldn't; the quota was filled a week after they made the announcement. This is the next best thing. I'm studying their language, and you know that language reflects the basic assumptions of the people who use it. I've got a fair command of the spoken lingo already. It's not hard, really, and there are hints in it. Some of the idioms

are quite similar to English. I'm sure I'll get the answer eventually."

"More power," I said, and we went back to work.

I saw Gregori frequently from then on, and he kept me posted about his progress. He was highly excited about a month after that first meeting; said he'd got hold of a book of the Kanamit's and was trying to puzzle it out. They wrote in ideographs,[9] worse than Chinese, but he was determined to fathom it if it took him years. He wanted my help.

Well, I was interested in spite of myself, for I knew it would be a long job. We spent some evenings together, working with material from Kanamit bulletin-boards and so forth, and the extremely limited English-Kanamit dictionary they issued the staff. My conscience bothered me about the stolen book, but gradually I became absorbed by the problem. Languages are my field, after all. I couldn't help being fascinated.

We got the title worked out in a few weeks. It was "How to Serve Man," evidently a handbook they were giving out to new Kanamit members of the embassy staff. They had new ones in, all the time now, a shipload about once a month; they were opening all kinds of research laboratories, clinics and so on. If there was anybody on Earth besides Gregori who still distrusted those people, he must have been somewhere in the middle of Tibet.

It was astonishing to see the changes that had been wrought in less than a year. There were no more standing armies, no more shortages, no unemployment. When you

---

8. **disinterested altruism:** as used here, the phrase means "doing good without personal motives."

9. **ideographs:** symbols

picked up a newspaper you didn't see "H-BOMB" or "V-2"[10] leaping out at you; the news was always good. It was a hard thing to get used to. The Kanamit were working on human biochemistry, and it was known around the embassy that they were nearly ready to announce methods of making our race taller and stronger and healthier— practically a race of supermen—and they had a potential cure for heart disease and cancer.

I didn't see Gregori for a fortnight after we finished working out the title of the book; I was on a long-overdue vacation in Canada. When I got back, I was shocked by the change in his appearance.

"What on earth is wrong, Gregori?" I asked. "You look like the very devil."

"Come down to the lounge."

I went with him.

"Come on, man, what's the matter?" I urged.

"The Kanamit have put me on the passenger list for the next exchange ship,"

he said. "You, too, otherwise I wouldn't be talking to you."

"Well," I said, "but———"

"They're not altruists."[11]

I tried to reason with him. I pointed out they'd made Earth a paradise compared to what it was before. He only shook his head.

Then I said, "Well, what about those lie-detector tests?"

"A farce," he replied, without heat. "I said so at the time, you fool. They told the truth, though, as far as it went."

"And the book?" I demanded, annoyed. "What about that—'How to Serve Man'? That wasn't put there for you to read. They *mean* it. How do you explain that?"

"I've read the first paragraph of that book," he said. "Why do you suppose I haven't slept for a week?"

I said, "Well?" and he smiled a curious, twisted smile.

"It's a cookbook," he said.

---

10. **V-2:** a powerful rocket

11. **altruists:** people who do good for completely unselfish reasons

🌶

About the Author

Damon Knight (1922–2002) was born in Baker, Oregon. He became interested in science fiction when, as a boy, he first read "sci-fi" tales in the magazine *Amazing Stories.* He went on to become one of the leading science fiction writers of our day and was, in fact, the founding president of the Science Fiction Writers of America. Knight authored more than a dozen novels and numerous short story collections. He also edited many anthologies of science fiction stories. "To Serve Man" is one of the best-known episodes of *The Twilight Zone,* a popular TV series.

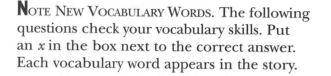

UNDERSTAND KEY IDEAS AND DETAILS. The following questions help you check your reading comprehension. Put an *x* in the box next to the correct answer.

1. Which sentence best states the main idea of the story?
   - ☐ a. It would be wonderful if there could be peace everywhere on Earth.
   - ☐ b. Creatures from another planet would surely be unfriendly.
   - ☐ c. Some visitors from space come to Earth for a very special purpose.

2. The tests that the Kanamit took appeared to show that they
   - ☐ a. had been lying about their motives for coming to Earth.
   - ☐ b. were telling the truth.
   - ☐ c. failed to answer the questions they had been asked.

3. At the U.N., the Kanamit declared that they intended to
   - ☐ a. rid the world of hunger and war.
   - ☐ b. decrease the food supply on Earth.
   - ☐ c. eventually take control of the planet.

4. At the end of the story, Gregori looked awful because he
   - ☐ a. had been working very hard.
   - ☐ b. had been attacked by the Kanamit.
   - ☐ c. had not slept since he discovered why the Kanamit came to Earth.

NOTE NEW VOCABULARY WORDS. The following questions check your vocabulary skills. Put an *x* in the box next to the correct answer. Each vocabulary word appears in the story.

1. At the U.N., a representative offered some ideological remarks. Which of the following best defines the word *ideological?*
   - ☐ a. intended to be humorous
   - ☐ b. difficult to understand
   - ☐ c. related to political statements or opinions

2. The Kanamit's gifts were unprecedented —and the Kanamit didn't ask for anything in return. The word *unprecedented* means
   - ☐ a. never done before.
   - ☐ b. unimportant.
   - ☐ c. very harmful.

3. The room was filled to capacity with photographers; there was a "fusillade of flashbulbs." What is the meaning of the word *fusillade?*
   - ☐ a. a lack
   - ☐ b. a rapid outburst
   - ☐ c. a question

4. The Kanamit planned to increase the productivity, or output, of all arable land. Land that is *arable* is
   - ☐ a. foreign.
   - ☐ b. very small.
   - ☐ c. able to be plowed.

× 5 =

NUMBER
CORRECT

YOUR
SCORE

× 5 =

NUMBER
CORRECT

YOUR
SCORE

IDENTIFY **S**TORY **E**LEMENTS. The following questions check your knowledge of story elements. Put an *x* in the box next to each correct answer.

1. Which statement best *characterizes* the Kanamit?
   - ☐ a. They were ineffective in pursuing their goals.
   - ☐ b. They were self-serving.
   - ☐ c. They were altruists—those who do good just for the sake of helping others.

2. Of these events, which happened last in the *plot* of the story?
   - ☐ a. The Kanamit took lie-detector tests.
   - ☐ b. Gregori read the first paragraph of "How to Serve Man."
   - ☐ c. Peter quit his job at the U.N.

3. The Kanamit's *motive* for coming to Earth was to
   - ☐ a. gain the trust of the people and later use them for food.
   - ☐ b. improve the quality of life of people everywhere.
   - ☐ c. gain knowledge that they could later use on their own planet.

4. The author's main *purpose* in writing the story was to
   - ☐ a. make the reader feel sad.
   - ☐ b. shock or surprise the reader.
   - ☐ c. inform the reader about scientific data, or facts.

THINK **C**RITICALLY **A**BOUT THE **S**TORY. The following questions check your critical thinking skills. Put an *x* in the box next to each correct answer.

1. We may infer that the book "How to Serve Man" was filled with
   - ☐ a. recipes.
   - ☐ b. suggestions for enriching the lives of people on Earth.
   - ☐ c. diagrams and plans for increasing power sources around the world.

2. Evidence in the story suggests that the Kanamit wanted to eliminate war on Earth because
   - ☐ a. they cared deeply about the welfare of human beings.
   - ☐ b. that would assure a greater supply of food for the Kanamit.
   - ☐ c. they believed that war was foolish and uncivilized.

3. Which statement is *not* true?
   - ☐ a. Peter was silly to question the Kanamit's motives.
   - ☐ b. Gregori's suspicions about the Kanamit proved to be well founded.
   - ☐ c. The Kanamit had the knowledge to improve conditions on Earth.

4. It is likely that the Kanamit thought that taller, stronger, and healthier people
   - ☐ a. might overpower the Kanamit.
   - ☐ b. would be able to give the Kanamit helpful advice.
   - ☐ c. would be tastier than other people.

NUMBER CORRECT   × 5 =   YOUR SCORE

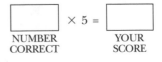

NUMBER CORRECT   × 5 =   YOUR SCORE

STUDY THE WRITER'S CRAFT. The following questions check your knowledge of skills related to the craft of writing. Put an *x* in the box next to each correct answer. You may refer to pages 4 and 5.

1. "To Serve Man" is an example of
   ☐ a. a detective story.
   ☐ b. an autobiographical story.
   ☐ c. science fiction.

2. Gregori asks, "How can anybody trust a thing that looks as if it ate the baby?" This is
   ☐ a. the author's picturesque way of saying that the Kanamit were ugly.
   ☐ b. a metaphor.
   ☐ c. an illustration of inner conflict.

3. As a result of the Kanamit's work, Earth was paradise. This sentence contains
   ☐ a. a moral.
   ☐ b. alliteration.
   ☐ c. a metaphor.

4. Which one of the following features is found in the story?
   ☐ a. flashback
   ☐ b. symbolism
   ☐ c. a surprise ending

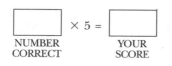

NUMBER CORRECT × 5 = YOUR SCORE

Questions for Writing and Discussion

- The title of the story is a pun—a play on words in which two meanings for a word or phrase are intended. Explain how the title of the story is a pun.
- "To Serve Man" makes clear that the Kanamit were intelligent, clever, and destructive. Support this statement by offering specific references in the story.
- What changes did the Kanamit bring about on Earth? What did the Kanamit think their real reward would be for these changes?
- How do we know Peter and Gregori are among those to be saved?

See additional questions for extended writing on pages 78 and 79.

Use the boxes below to total your scores for the exercises. Then record your scores on pages 198 and 199.

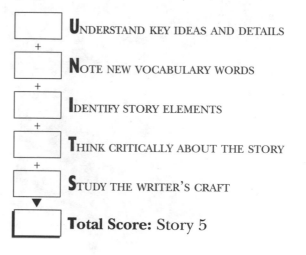

UNDERSTAND KEY IDEAS AND DETAILS
+
NOTE NEW VOCABULARY WORDS
+
IDENTIFY STORY ELEMENTS
+
THINK CRITICALLY ABOUT THE STORY
+
STUDY THE WRITER'S CRAFT
▼
Total Score: Story 5

Harry was the best actor in town—and he never turned down a role.
Whenever he was asked to play a part, he just responded . . .

Who Am I This Time?

by Kurt Vonnegut Jr.

The North Crawford Mask and Wig Club, an amateur theater company I belong to, voted to do Tennessee Williams' *A Streetcar Named Desire* for the spring play. Doris Sawyer, who always directs, said she couldn't direct this time because her mother was so sick. And she said the club ought to develop some other directors anyway, because she couldn't live forever, even though she'd made it safely to seventy-four.

So I got stuck with the directing job, even though the only thing I'd ever directed before was the installation of combination aluminum storm windows and screens I'd sold. That's what I am, a salesman of storm windows and doors, and here and there a bathtub enclosure. As far as acting goes, the highest rank I ever held on stage was either butler or policeman, whichever's higher.

I made a lot of conditions before I took the directing job, and the biggest one was that Harry Nash, the only real actor the club has, had to take the Marlon Brando[1] part in the play. To give you an idea of how versatile Harry is, inside of one year he was Captain Queeg in *The Caine Mutiny Court Martial,* then Abe Lincoln in *Abe Lincoln in Illinois* and then the young architect in *The Moon is Blue.* The year after that, Harry Nash was Henry the Eighth in *Anne of the Thousand Days* and Doc in *Come Back Little Sheba,* and I was after him for the Marlon Brando part in *A Streetcar Named Desire.* Harry wasn't at the meeting to say whether he'd take the part or not. He never came to meetings. He was too shy. He didn't stay away from meetings because he had something else to do. He wasn't married, didn't go out with women—didn't have any close men friends either. He stayed away from all kinds of gatherings because he never could think of anything to say or do without a script.

So I had to go down to Miller's Hardware Store, where Harry was a clerk, the next day and ask him if he'd take the part. I stopped off at the telephone company to complain about a bill I'd gotten for a call to Honolulu, I'd never called Honolulu in my life.

And there was this beautiful woman I'd never seen before behind the counter at the phone company, and she explained that the company had put in an automatic billing machine and that the machine didn't have all the bugs out of it yet. It made mistakes. "Not only did I not call Honolulu," I told her, "I don't think anybody in North Crawford ever has or will."

So she took the charge off the bill, and I asked her if she was from around North

Crawford. She said no. She said she just came with the new billing machine to teach the local people how to take care of it. After that, she said, she would go with some other machine to someplace else. "Well," I said, "as long as people have to come along with the machines, I guess we're all right."

"What?" she said.

"When machines start delivering themselves," I said, "I guess that's when the people better start really worrying."

"Oh," she said. She didn't seem very interested in that subject, and I wondered if she was interested in anything. She seemed kind of numb, almost a machine herself, an automatic phone-company politeness machine.

"How long will you be in town here?" I asked her.

"I stay in each town eight weeks, sir," she said. She had pretty blue eyes, but there sure wasn't much hope or curiosity in them. She told me she had been going from town to town like that for two years, always a stranger.

And I got it in my head that she might make a good Stella for the play. Stella was the wife of the Marlon Brando character, the wife of the character I wanted Harry Nash to play. So I told her where and when we were going to hold tryouts, and said the club would be very happy if she'd come.

She looked surprised, and she warmed up a little. "You know," she said, "that's the first time anybody ever asked me to participate in any community thing."

"Well," I said, "there isn't any other way to get to know a lot of nice people faster than to be in a play with 'em."

She said her name was Helene Shaw. She said she might just surprise me—and herself. She said she just might come.

---

1. **Marlon Brando:** the actor who played Stanley Kowalski in the play and the movie *A Streetcar Named Desire.* Brando's performances were so powerful that the part continues to be associated with his name.

Who Am I This Time?

You would think that North Crawford would be fed up with Harry Nash in plays after all the plays he'd been in. But the fact was that North Crawford probably could have gone on enjoying Harry forever, because he was never Harry on stage. When the maroon curtain went up on the stage in the gymnasium of the Consolidated Junior-Senior High School, Harry, body and soul, was exactly what the script and the director told him to be.

Somebody said one time that Harry ought to go to a psychiatrist so he could be something important and colorful in real life, too—so he could get married anyway, and maybe get a better job than just clerking in Miller's Hardware Store. But I don't know what a psychiatrist could have turned up about him that the town didn't already know. The trouble with Harry was he'd been left on the doorstep of a church when he was a baby, and he never did find out who his parents were.

When I told him there in Miller's that I'd been appointed director, that I wanted him in my play, he said what he always said to anybody who asked him to be in a play—and it was kind of sad, if you think about it.

"Who am I this time?" he said.

So I held the tryouts where they're always held—in the meeting room on the second floor of the North Crawford Public Library. Doris Sawyer, the woman who usually directs, came to give me the benefit of all her experience. The two of us sat upstairs, while the people who wanted parts waited below. We called them upstairs one by one.

Harry Nash came to the tryouts, even though it was a waste of time. I guess he wanted to get that little bit more acting in.

For Harry's pleasure, and our pleasure, too, we had him read from the scene where he gets really violent. It was a play in itself, the way Harry did it, and Tennessee Williams hadn't written it all either. Tennessee Williams didn't write the part, for instance, where Harry, who weighs about one hundred forty-five, who's about five feet eight inches tall, added fifty pounds to his weight and four inches to his height by just picking up a playbook. He had a short little double-breasted suit coat on and a dinky little red tie with a horsehead on it. He took off the coat and tie, opened his collar, then turned his back to Doris and me, getting up steam for the part. There was a great big rip in the back of his shirt, and it looked like a fairly new shirt too. He'd ripped it on purpose, so he could be that much more like Marlon Brando, right from the first.

When he faced us again, he was huge and handsome and conceited and cruel. Doris read the part of Stella, the wife, and I read the lines of Blanche, her sister in the play. Harry was so dynamic, he practically scared the life out of both of us.

And then, while Doris and I were getting over our emotional experiences, like people coming out from under ether,[2] Harry put down the playbook, put on his coat and tie, and turned into the bland hardware-store clerk again.

"Was—was that all right?" he said, and he seemed pretty sure he wouldn't get the part.

"Well," I said, "for a first reading, that wasn't too bad."

"Is there a chance I'll get the part?" he said. I don't know why he always had to pretend there was some doubt about his getting a part, but he did.

"I think we can safely say we're leaning powerfully in your direction," I told him.

---

2. **ether:** a liquid sometimes used to cause sleep in a patient during a medical operation

He was very pleased. "Thanks! Thanks a lot!" he said, and he shook my hand.

"Is there a pretty new girl downstairs?" I said, meaning Helene Shaw.

"I didn't notice," said Harry.

It turned out that Helene Shaw *had* come for the tryouts, and Doris and I had our hearts broken. We thought the North Crawford Mask and Wig Club was finally going to put a really good-looking, really young girl on stage, instead of one of the somewhat elderly women who generally have to play the role of girls.

But Helene Shaw couldn't act for sour apples. No matter what we gave her to read, she was the same girl with the same smile for anybody who had a complaint about his phone bill.

Doris tried to coach her some, to make her understand that Stella in the play was a very passionate girl who loved a brute, but Helene just read the lines the same way again. I don't think a volcano could have stirred her up.

"Dear," said Doris, "I'm going to ask you a personal question."

"All right," said Helene.

"Have you ever been in love?" said Doris. "The reason I ask," she said, "remembering some old love might help you put more warmth in your acting."

Helene frowned and thought hard. "Well," she said, "I travel a lot, you know. And practically all the men in the different companies I visit are married and I never stay anyplace long enough to know many people who aren't."

"What about school?" said Doris. "What about puppy love and all the other kinds of love in school?"

So Helene thought hard about that, and then she said, "Even in school I was always moving around a lot. My father was a construction worker, following jobs around, so

I was always saying hello or good-by to someplace, without anything in between."

"Um," said Doris.

"Would movie stars count?" said Helene. "I don't mean in real life. I never knew any. I just mean up on the screen."

Doris looked at me and rolled her eyes. "I guess that's love of a kind," she said.

And then Helene got a little enthusiastic. "I used to sit through movies over and over again," she said, "and pretend I was married to whoever the man movie star was. They were the only people who came with us. No matter where we moved, movie stars were there."

"Uh huh," said Doris.

"Well, thank you, Miss Shaw," I said. "You go downstairs and wait with the rest. We'll let you know."

So we tried to find another Stella. And there just wasn't one, not one woman in the club with the dew still on her.[3] "All we've got are Blanches," I said, meaning all we had were faded women who could play the part of Blanche, Stella's faded sister. "That's life, I guess—twenty Blanches to one Stella."

"And when you find a Stella," said Doris, "it turns out she doesn't know what love is."

Doris and I decided there was one last thing we could try. We could get Harry Nash to play a scene along with Helene. "He just might make her bubble the least little bit," I said.

"That girl hasn't got a bubble in her," said Doris.

So we called down the stairs for Helene to come back on up, and we told somebody to go find Harry. Harry never sat with the rest of the people at tryouts—or at rehearsals either. The minute he didn't have a part to play, he'd

---

3. **with the dew still on her:** a phrase meaning "young"

disappear into some hiding place where he could hear people call him, but where he couldn't be seen. At tryouts in the library he generally hid in the reference room, passing the time looking at flags of different countries in the front of the dictionary.

Helene came back upstairs, and we were very sorry and surprised to see that she'd been crying.

"Oh, dear," said Doris. "Oh, my—now what on earth's the trouble, dear?"

"I was terrible, wasn't I?" said Helene, hanging her head.

Doris said the only thing anybody can say in an amateur theater company when somebody cries. She said, "Why, no dear—you were marvelous."

"No, I wasn't," said Helene. "I'm a walking icebox, and I know it."

"Nobody could look at you and say that," said Doris.

"When they get to know me, they can say it," said Helene. "When people get to know me, that's what they do say." Her tears got worse. "I don't want to be the way I am," she said. "I just can't help it, living the way I've lived all my life. The only experiences I've had have been in crazy dreams of movie stars. When I meet somebody nice in real life, I feel as though I were in some kind of big bottle, as though I couldn't touch that person, no matter how hard I tried." And Helene pushed on air as though it were a big bottle all around her.

"You ask me if I've ever been in love," she said to Doris. "No—but I want to be. I know what this play's about. I know what Stella's supposed to feel and why she feels it. I—I—I—" she said, and her tears wouldn't let her go on.

"You what, dear?" said Doris gently.

"I—" said Helene, and she pushed on the imaginary bottle again. "I just don't know how to begin," she said.

There was heavy clumping on the library stairs. It sounded like a deep-sea diver coming upstairs in his lead shoes. It was Harry Nash, turning himself into Marlon Brando. In he came, and he was so much in character that the sight of a weeping woman made him sneer.

"Harry," I said, "I'd like you to meet Helene Shaw. Helene—this is Harry Nash. If you get the part of Stella, he'll be your husband in the play." Harry didn't offer to shake hands. He put his hands in his pockets, and he hunched over, and he looked straight into her eyes. He kept on looking at her. Her tears stopped right then and there.

"I wonder if you two would play the fight scene," I said, "and then the reunion scene right after it."

"Sure," said Harry, his eyes still on her. "Sure," he said, "if Stell's game."

"What?" said Helene. She'd turned the color of cranberry juice.

"Stell—Stella," said Harry. "That's you. Stell's my wife."

I handed the two of them playbooks. Harry snatched his from me without a word of thanks. Helene's hands weren't working very well, and I had to kind of mold them around the book.

"I'll want something I can throw," said Harry.

"What?" I said.

"There's one place where I throw a radio out a window," said Harry. "What can I throw?"

So I said an iron paperweight was the radio, and I opened the window wide.

Helene Shaw looked scared to death.

"Where you want us to start?" said Harry, and he rolled his shoulders like a prizefighter warming up.

"Start a few lines back from where you throw the radio out the window," I said.

"O.K., O.K.," said Harry, warming up, warming up. He scanned the stage directions. "Let's see," he said, "after I throw the radio, she runs off stage, and I chase her."

"Right," I said.

"O.K., baby," Harry said to Helene, his eyelids drooping. "On your mark," said Harry. "Get ready, baby. Go!"

When the scene was over, Helene Shaw was limp. She sat down with her mouth open and her head hanging to one side. She wasn't in any bottle any more. There wasn't any bottle to hold her up and keep her safe and clean. The bottle was gone.

"Do I get the part or don't I?" Harry snarled at me.

"You'll do," I said.

"You said a mouthful!" he said. "I'll be going now. . . . See you around, Stella," he said to Helene, and he left. He slammed the door behind him.

"Helene?" I said. "Miss Shaw?"

"Me?" she said.

"The part of Stella is yours," I said. "You were great!"

"I was?" she said.

"I had no idea you had that much fire in you, dear," Doris said to her.

"Fire?" said Helene. She didn't know if she was afoot or on horseback.

"Skyrockets! Pinwheels! Fireworks!" said Doris.

"Me," said Helene. And that was all she said. She looked as though she were going to sit in the chair with her mouth open forever.

"Stella," I said.

"Huh?" she said.

"You have my permission to go."

So we started having rehearsals four nights a week on the stage of the Consolidated School. And Harry and Helene set such a pace that everybody in the production was half crazy with excitement and exhaustion before we'd rehearsed four times. Usually a director has to beg people to learn their lines, but I had no such trouble. Harry and Helene were working so well together that everybody else in the cast regarded it as a duty and an honor and a pleasure to support them.

I was certainly lucky—or thought I was. Things were going so well so early in the game that I had to say to Harry and Helene after one love scene, "Hold a little something back for the actual performance, would you please? You'll burn yourselves out."

I said that at the fourth or fifth rehearsal, and Lydia Miller, who was playing Blanche, the faded sister, was sitting next to me in the audience. In real life, she's the wife of Verne Miller. Verne owns Miller's Hardware Store. Verne was Harry's boss.

"Lydia," I said to her, "have we got a play or have we got a play?"

"Yes," she said, "you've got a play, all right." She made it sound as though I'd committed some kind of crime, done something just terrible. "You should be very proud of yourself."

"What do you mean by that?" I said.

Before Lydia could answer, Harry yelled at me from the stage, asked if I was through with him, asked if he could go home. I told him he could and, still Marlon Brando, he left, kicking furniture out of his way and slamming doors. Helene was left all alone on the stage, sitting on a couch with the same gaga look she'd had after the tryouts. That girl was drained.

I turned to Lydia again and I said, "Well—until now, I thought I had every reason to be happy and proud. Is there something going on I don't know about?"

"Do you know that girl's in love with Harry?" said Lydia.

"In the play?" I said.

"What play?" said Lydia. "There isn't any play going on now, and look at her up there." She gave a sad cackle. "You aren't directing this play."

"Who is?" I said.

"Mother Nature at her worst," said Lydia. "And think what it's going to do to that girl when she discovers what Harry really is." She corrected herself. "What Harry really isn't," she said.

I didn't do anything about it, because I didn't figure it was any of my business. I heard Lydia try to do something about it, but she didn't get very far.

"You know," Lydia said to Helene one night, "I once played Ann Rutledge, and Harry was Abraham Lincoln."

Helene clapped her hands. "That must have been heaven!" she said.

"It was, in a way," said Lydia. "Sometimes I'd get so worked up, I'd love Harry the way I'd love Abraham Lincoln. Then I'd have to come back to earth and remind myself that he was just a clerk in my husband's hardware store."

"He's the most marvelous man I ever met," said Helene.

"Of course. One thing you have to get set for, when you're in a play with Harry," said Lydia, "is what happens after the last performance."

"What are you talking about?" said Helene.

"Once the show's over," said Lydia, "whatever you thought Harry was just evaporates into thin air."

"I don't believe it," said Helene.

"I admit it's hard to believe," said Lydia.

Then Helene got a little sore. "Anyway, why tell *me* about it?" she said. "Even if it is true, what do I care?"

"I—I don't know," said Lydia, backing away. "I—I just thought you might find it interesting."

"Well, I don't," said Helene.

And Lydia slunk away, feeling about as frowzy and unloved as she was supposed to feel in the play. After that nobody said anything more to Helene to warn her about Harry, not even when word got around that she'd told the telephone company that she didn't want to be moved around anymore, that she wanted to stay in North Crawford.

So the time finally came to put on the play. We ran it for three nights—Thursday, Friday, and Saturday—and we murdered those audiences. They believed every word that was said on stage.

On Thursday night some folks at the telephone company sent Helene a dozen red roses. When Helene and Harry were taking a curtain call together, I passed the roses over the footlights to her. She came forward for them, took one rose from the bouquet to give to Harry. But when she turned to give Harry the rose in front of everybody, Harry was gone. The curtain came down on that extra little scene—that girl offering a rose to nothing and nobody.

I went backstage, and I found her still holding that one rose. She'd put the rest of the bouquet aside. There were tears in her eyes. "What did I do wrong?" she said to me, stupefied. "Did I insult him some way?"

"No," I said. "He always does that after a performance. The minute it's over, he clears out as fast as he can."

"And tomorrow he'll disappear again?"

"Without even taking off his makeup."

"And Saturday?" she said. "He'll stay for the cast party on Saturday, won't he?"

"Harry never goes to parties," I said. "When the curtain comes down on Saturday, that's the last anybody will see of him till he goes to work on Monday."

"How sad," she said.

Helene's performance on Friday night wasn't nearly so good as Thursday's. She seemed to be thinking about other things. She watched Harry take off after curtain call. She didn't say a word.

On Saturday she put on the best performance yet. Ordinarily it was Harry who set the pace. But on Saturday Harry had to work to keep up with Helene.

When the curtain came down on the final curtain call, Harry wanted to get away, but he couldn't. Helene wouldn't let go his hand. The rest of the cast and the stage crew and a lot of well-wishers from the audience were all standing around Harry and Helene, and Harry was trying to get his hand back.

"Well," he said, "I've got to go."

"Where?" she said.

"Oh," he said, "home."

"Won't you please take me to the cast party?" she said.

He got very red. "I'm afraid I'm not much on parties," he said. All the Marlon Brando in him was gone. He was tongue-tied, he was scared, he was shy—he was everything Harry was famous for being between plays.

"All right," she said. "I'll let you go—if you promise me one thing."

"What's that?" he said, and I thought he would jump out a window if she let go of him then.

"I want you to promise to stay here until I get you your present," she said.

"Present?" he said, getting even more panicky.

"Promise?" she said.

He promised. It was the only way he could get his hand back. And he stood there miserably while Helene went down to the ladies' dressing room for the present. While he waited, a lot of people congratulated him on being such a fine actor. But congratulations never made him happy. He just wanted to get away.

Helene came back with the present. It turned out to be a little blue book with a big red ribbon for a place marker. It was a copy of *Romeo and Juliet*. Harry was very embarrassed. It was all he could do to say "Thank you."

"The marker marks my favorite scene," said Helene.

"Um," said Harry.

"Don't you want to see what my favorite scene is?" she said.

So Harry had to open the book to the red ribbon.

Helene got close to him, and read a line of Juliet's. "'How cam'st thou hither, tell me, and wherefore?'" she read. "'The orchard walls are high and hard to climb, and the place death, considering who thou art, if any of my kinsmen find thee here.'" She pointed to the next line. "Now, look what Romeo says," she said.

"Um," said Harry.

"Read what Romeo says," said Helene.

Harry cleared his throat. He didn't want to read the line, but he had to. "'With love's light wings did I o'erperch[4] these walls,'" he read out loud in his everyday voice. But then a change came over him. "'For stony limits cannot hold love out,'" he read, and he straightened up, and eight years dropped away from him, and he was brave and happy, and adoring. "'And what love can do, that dares love attempt,'" he read, "'therefore thy kinsmen are no obstacle to me.'"

"'If they do see thee they will murder thee,'" said Helene.

"'Alack!'" said Harry, "'there lies more peril in thine eye than twenty of their swords.'" Helene led him toward the backstage exit. "'Look thou but sweet,'" said Harry, "'and I am proof against their enmity.'"[5]

"'I would not for the world they saw thee here,'" said Helene, and that was the last we heard. The two of them were out the door and gone.

They never did show up at the cast party. One week later they were married.

---

4. **o'erperch:** fly over

5. **proof against their enmity:** protected from their attacks

They seem very happy, although they're kind of strange from time to time, depending on which play they're reading to each other at the time.

I dropped into the phone company office the other day, on account of the billing machine was making dumb mistakes again. I asked her what plays she and Harry'd been reading lately.

"In the past week," she said, "I've been married to Macbeth and have been in love with Hamlet. Wouldn't you say I was the luckiest girl in town?"

I said I thought so, and I told her most of the women in town thought so too.

"They had their chance," she said.

"Most of 'em couldn't stand the excitement," I said. And I told her I'd been asked to direct another play. I asked if she and Harry would be available for the cast. She gave me a big smile and said, "Who are we this time?"

About the Author

Kurt Vonnegut Jr. (1922–) is one of America's most distinguished authors. Born in Indianapolis, Indiana, Vonnegut has written novels, short stories, plays, and essays. Probably his best-known novels are *Cat's Cradle* and *Slaughterhouse Five*. Most of Vonnegut's works deal with serious issues such as human values, war and peace, and the future of society. Although many of Vonnegut's themes may seem grim, he has the ability to treat them with his own special brand of charm, irony, and humor. These qualities may be seen in "Who Am I This Time?" which is taken from *Welcome to the Monkey House,* a collection of Vonnegut's short fiction.

UNDERSTAND KEY IDEAS AND DETAILS. The following questions help you check your reading comprehension. Put an *x* in the box next to the correct answer.

1. This story is mainly about
   ☐ a. an amateur theater company's difficulties in putting on a production.
   ☐ b. two people who are far better at expressing their emotions on stage than in real life.
   ☐ c. what life is like in a town named North Crawford.

2. The narrator hoped that Helene would try out for the part of Stella because
   ☐ a. the narrator wanted Helene and Harry to fall in love.
   ☐ b. the narrator knew at once that Helene would be a fine actress.
   ☐ c. Helene, like the character she was to play, was young and beautiful.

3. Why was Lydia worried about what might happen when the show was over?
   ☐ a. She realized that Helene had fallen in love with Harry.
   ☐ b. She didn't know what play the company was going to put on next.
   ☐ c. She was afraid that Harry would give up acting.

4. Helene was successful in initiating a romance with Harry by
   ☐ a. telling him that he was a great actor.
   ☐ b. giving him numerous gifts.
   ☐ c. having him play Romeo to her Juliet.

NOTE NEW VOCABULARY WORDS. The following questions check your vocabulary skills. Put an *x* in the box next to the correct answer. Each vocabulary word appears in the story.

1. Harry was so versatile that he could play any role he was offered. The word *versatile* means
   ☐ a. idle.
   ☐ b. pleasant.
   ☐ c. able to do many things well.

2. His performance was so dynamic that he nearly "scared the life" out of the directors. What is the meaning of the word *dynamic?*
   ☐ a. terrible
   ☐ b. forceful
   ☐ c. weak

3. Lydia felt frowzy and uncomfortable— the way she "was supposed to feel in the play." Define the word *frowzy.*
   ☐ a. untidy and sloppy looking
   ☐ b. adored
   ☐ c. very cheerful

4. There were tears in Helene's eyes as she said, stupefied, "What did I do wrong?" The word *stupefied* means
   ☐ a. shocked.
   ☐ b. frightened.
   ☐ c. pleased.

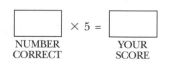

NUMBER CORRECT × 5 = YOUR SCORE

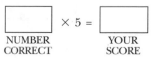

NUMBER CORRECT × 5 = YOUR SCORE

IDENTIFY STORY ELEMENTS. The following questions check your knowledge of story elements. Put an *x* in the box next to each correct answer.

1. Who is the *narrator* of the story?
   - ☐ a. Harry Nash
   - ☐ b. Helene Shaw
   - ☐ c. the director of the play

2. Of these events, which happened first in the *plot* of the story?
   - ☐ a. Helene Shaw tried out for a role in *A Streetcar Named Desire.*
   - ☐ b. Harry and Helene got married.
   - ☐ c. Helene gave Harry a copy of *Romeo and Juliet.*

3. Which statement best illustrates *character development?*
   - ☐ a. Although Harry always insisted on trying out for a role, everyone knew he would get the part.
   - ☐ b. At first Helene had trouble expressing her emotions, but later she found a way to convey them.
   - ☐ c. After the final performance of the play, Harry was—as usual—tongue-tied and shy.

4. The *climax* of the story occurs when
   - ☐ a. Helene meets Harry, as Marlon Brando, and falls in love.
   - ☐ b. Helene turns to give Harry a rose and discovers that he is gone.
   - ☐ c. the audience cheers enthusiastically after the final performance.

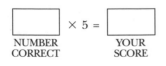

NUMBER CORRECT   × 5 =   YOUR SCORE

THINK CRITICALLY ABOUT THE STORY. The following questions check your critical thinking skills. Put an *x* in the box next to each correct answer.

1. It is fair to say that Helene did not really fall in love with Harry but fell in love with
   - ☐ a. the character Harry was playing.
   - ☐ b. acting—being on stage.
   - ☐ c. the companionship of the members of the company.

2. Which of the following confirms that Helene had fallen in love?
   - ☐ a. She agreed to attend a tryout at the North Crawford Public Library.
   - ☐ b. She told the telephone company that she wanted to stay in North Crawford.
   - ☐ c. She said that movie stars were the only people for whom she felt "love of a kind."

3. We may infer that Romeo and Juliet were characters who
   - ☐ a. fell in love at first sight.
   - ☐ b. fought frequently with each other.
   - ☐ c. had difficulty showing their feelings.

4. Probably the best way for Harry and Helene to maintain a happy marriage is
   - ☐ a. to stay at home with each other day after day.
   - ☐ b. to read a book about how to establish successful relationships.
   - ☐ c. to play roles on stage in which they are in love with each other.

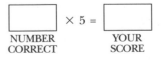

NUMBER CORRECT   × 5 =   YOUR SCORE

STUDY THE WRITER'S CRAFT. The following questions check your knowledge of skills related to the craft of writing. Put an *x* in the box next to each correct answer. You may refer to pages 4 and 5.

1. Helene complained, "I'm a walking ice-box." This sentence contains
   ☐ a. onomatopoeia.
   ☐ b. a metaphor.
   ☐ c. a simile.

2. What image does the author use to illustrate Helene's inability to project her emotions?
   ☐ a. a bathtub enclosure
   ☐ b. a large bottle
   ☐ c. a billing machine

3. References to plays such as *Romeo and Juliet, Macbeth,* and *Hamlet* are examples of the author's use of
   ☐ a. poetic language.
   ☐ b. alliteration.
   ☐ c. allusions.

4. Lydia stated that when a play was over, "whatever you thought Harry was just evaporates into thin air." This is the writer's way of saying that following a performance,
   ☐ a. Harry's stage personality disappears immediately.
   ☐ b. Harry becomes angry and unpleasant.
   ☐ c. Harry feels ill and stops eating for a while.

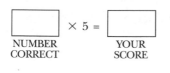

NUMBER CORRECT   × 5 =   YOUR SCORE

Questions for Writing and Discussion

● The director agreed to direct the play—on the condition that Harry Nash would play the main role. Explain why.
● When it came to expressing emotion, how were Helene and Harry similar? How were they different?
● On stage, Harry Nash was never truly himself. Do you agree or disagree with this statement? Tell why.
● *Romeo and Juliet* is a love story that has an unhappy ending. Do you think that Helene and Harry's love will last? Give reasons for your answer.

See additional questions for extended writing on pages 78 and 79.

Use the boxes below to total your scores for the exercises. Then record your scores on pages 198 and 199.

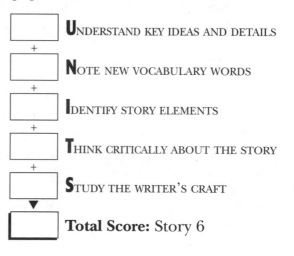

UNDERSTAND KEY IDEAS AND DETAILS

+

NOTE NEW VOCABULARY WORDS

+

IDENTIFY STORY ELEMENTS

+

THINK CRITICALLY ABOUT THE STORY

+

STUDY THE WRITER'S CRAFT

▼

Total Score: Story 6

A Question of Identity

Questions for Discussion and Extended Writing

The following questions provide you with opportunities to express your thoughts and feelings about the selections in this unit. Your teacher may assign selected questions. When you write your responses, remember to state your point of view clearly and to support your position by presenting specific details—examples, illustrations, and references drawn from the story and, in some cases, from your life. Organize your writing carefully and check your work for correct spelling, capitalization, punctuation, and grammar.

1. The theme of this unit is "A Question of Identity." Show how each story in the unit is related to that theme.

2. "Rules of the Game" and "Who Am I This Time?" are stories in which characters change as they relate to each other. Select one character from each story and indicate why those characters changed and how.

3. An old saying states, "Things are not always what they seem." Using two stories from the unit, demonstrate that things may not be what they seem to be.

4. To a certain extent, the way we feel about ourselves helps to define our identity. Select two characters in the unit and describe in detail how they felt about themselves.

5. In many ways, "To Serve Man" is different from the other stories in the unit. Do you agree or disagree with this statement? Support your position by referring to the selections.

6. In which story do you think conflict plays the most important role? Identify the conflict in the story you have selected when you support your choice.

7. Draw upon material found in one of the selections to write a descriptive essay. Possibilities include San Francisco's Chinatown in "Rules of the Game" and the Kanamit in "To Serve Man." Give your essay a title.

8. At the end of each story, one or more characters must embark on a journey. Which character or characters do you think will have the brightest future? State your point of view clearly and give reasons for your answer.

9. Which character in the unit do you most admire or care about? Explain why.

10. In "Rules of the Game," Meimei's life was dramatically changed by the chess set her brother received. Write an essay about a gift that is meaningful to you. Be sure to indicate what the gift is, who gave the gift to you, and why the gift is significant. If you prefer, write in detail about a special gift you would like to receive. Give reasons for your choice. Your essay should have an introduction, a body, and a conclusion.

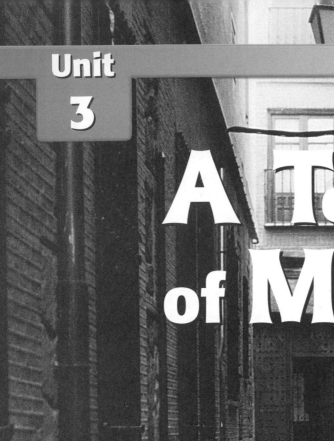

A Touch of Mystery

"I love to lose myself in a mystery."

–Thomas Browne

Previewing the Unit

According to an old saying, "Everybody loves a good mystery." In fact, more than 300 years ago Thomas Browne wrote, "I love to lose myself in a mystery." If that's true, fasten your seat belt. You're in for a wild ride!

In this unit, you will meet two of the world's most famous fictional detectives—and a girl who proves she's no slouch when it comes to being a sleuth.

KIM'S GAME Let's start with Nora, who becomes an amateur detective when she finds herself unwillingly involved in a murder mystery. You'll like Nora. It's easy enough to say that she's *real*—and she is—but she possesses qualities that set her apart. The title "Kim's Game" refers to a game in which players have fifteen seconds to view an assortment of items. Later, the player who remembers the most items wins. Do you think you would be good at Kim's Game? As you might guess, Nora is.

THE PRESIDENT REGRETS "The President Regrets" features Ellery Queen. Queen is one of the best-known detectives that American fiction has produced. He has appeared in hundreds of stories. In this one, Ellery makes up a puzzle—or mystery—for the Puzzle Club to solve. When the members of the Club pause to eat dinner, you—and they—will have all the facts necessary to work out the answer to the puzzle. Stop at that point and try to figure out the solution.

THE ADVENTURE OF THE SPECKLED BAND And now for the star of the show, the master detective, Sherlock Holmes. Holmes is probably the most famous detective that has ever been created, and he is one of the most popular characters in literature. Sherlock Holmes clubs exist all over the world. You might be surprised at how many people believe that Sherlock Holmes really lived. Holmes—to the never-ending delight and amazement of his devoted friend Dr. Watson—uses the process of *deduction* (reaching conclusions by reasoning) to solve the mysteries. Therefore, the Sherlock Holmes tales are always filled with clues. "The Adventure of the Speckled Band" is one of Arthur Conan Doyle's greatest stories. In it you will see Sherlock Holmes at his best.

As you read the stories, watch for clues that will help you unravel each mystery that lies ahead.

It's hard to get away with murder when you must
confront someone who's a master at playing . . .

Kim's Game

by M. D. Lake

"**N**ora, are you sure you wouldn't like to play Kim's Game with us?" Miss Bowers called to her from over by the great stone fireplace.

"I'm sure, thank you," Nora replied politely, glancing up and then dropping her nose back into her book. Outside, she could hear the rain falling on the sloping roof of the lodge. It had rained steadily ever since they arrived at camp.

She was at the far end of the room, curled up on a sofa, her feet tucked under her, as far away from the other girls as she could get. It wasn't that she didn't like them exactly; it was just that, after being cooped up with them for three days, they didn't interest her very much. None of them liked to read, and they all seemed to have seen the same television shows and movies. As a result, she couldn't understand half of what they were talking about or, if she could, why they got so excited about it.

"Nora's not very good at Kim's Game," she heard one of the girls say, in a high, clear voice that was meant to carry.

"She beat us all yesterday," another one pointed out.

"Twice. The first two times. Beginner's luck. She lost the third game and then she quit."

Nora smiled to herself. She'd never played Kim's Game, never even heard of it, until she got to summer camp and the counselors were forced to come up with indoor activities because of the cold weather and rain. But after she'd won the first two games, she discovered it was too easy for her, and so she decided to have fun with the third game. She put down on her list things that weren't there—silly things, but the other girls didn't notice that—and left out obvious things that were—the teakettle, the butcher knife—and so, of course, she lost. Even

83

then she didn't lose by much, because the other girls weren't very observant.

They didn't have to be, Nora supposed, in their lives. That thought went through her like a sharp knife and she realized she was suddenly close to tears. She straightened her back and put her feet firmly down on the floor and told herself she was glad she was so observant. It was a lot more important to notice things with your eyes than to cry with them.

She hadn't wanted to come to summer camp. She'd wanted to stay home, where she could keep an eye on her parents. She knew that something was wrong between them—worse than usual, a lot worse—and she thought that if she were there, she'd at least be able to figure out the meaning of all the little things she'd noticed and heard; her father's angry speech sometimes; the tears she'd seen in her mother's eyes; the abrupt changes of subject when she came into the room when her mother was entertaining friends; and the quarrels between her parents that got more and more frequent, when they thought she was in bed and asleep.

Usually they didn't insist that she do anything except homework and chores, but this year they'd insisted that she go to camp. She wondered what she'd find when she returned home. She wondered if both of her parents would still be living in the house and, if not, which one of them would be gone.

The main door of the lodge opened and a wet figure in a raincoat and hat came in. It was Miss Schaefer.

She hung her coat and hat on a peg and stepped into the room, looked around, and saw the girls standing in a circle over by the fireplace. They were staring with great

concentration at objects scattered on a blanket, with Cathy Bowers standing behind them timing them with her watch.

Kim's Game! Lydia Schaefer had never liked it, thought it was stupid. She didn't have the kind of memory you need to be good at games like that, either.

She nodded to Cathy Bowers and crossed the room to the far corner, with its comfortable overstuffed chairs and a sofa and coffee table littered with books and old magazines. She sat down in one of the chairs, and picked up a magazine. She took her reading glasses out of a case and put the case back in her shirt pocket. As she did, she noticed a girl on the sofa opposite her sitting up straight, her pointy nose buried in a book. She looked as though she'd been crying, or wanted to cry. Lydia Schaefer smiled and said, "I was always rotten at Kim's Game, too, when I was your age. Don't let it bother you."

Nora glanced up, as if surprised she was no longer alone. Her eyes met Miss Schaefer's without expression. She didn't like Miss Schaefer because she knew Miss Schaefer didn't like her—and not just her either: Miss Schaefer didn't like children period. Nora wondered why she was a camp counselor. Then she shrugged and decided it didn't matter. She had enough adults to try to figure out without adding another one to the list.

"What's your name?" Miss Schaefer persisted, somewhat uneasy under the child's stare. She also didn't like getting a shrug for a response. Hadn't she tried to console the child for being no good at a game?

"Nora." It wasn't just objects on a blanket Miss Schaefer wasn't able to remember.

"I'd probably be rotten at Kim's Game now, too," Miss Schaefer went on. "Oh, well, I'm sure you and I have inner lives that are much more interesting than theirs. Don't we?"

"I guess so," Nora said, wanting to get back to her book.

"It's probably why we wear glasses," Miss Schaefer went on, as if determined to make friends with Nora. "We don't need outer reality as much as other people, so our eyes—"

Before she could finish what Nora already knew was going to be a dumb sentence, a voice interrupted. "Could I see you in my office, Lydia?" Miss Schaefer turned quickly and looked over her shoulder, startled at the officious tone of voice. It was Ruth Terrill, the head counselor.

"Sure, Ruth," she said, trying to keep her voice normal. "Now?"

"Please," Ruth said.

Nora watched the two women disappear into the hallway. She'd known they hadn't liked each other for most of the three days she'd been at camp, but until that moment she hadn't known Miss Schaefer was afraid of Miss Terrill. She wondered why, then shrugged again. These adults, and the things going on between them, weren't her problem. Quickly she dipped her nose back into her book.

Over by the fireplace, the other girls were playing another round of Kim's Game. *You'd think they'd have just about every small object in the lodge memorized by now,* Nora thought.

She would have.

That night, when she first heard the voices, she thought she was at home and in her own bed, because they sounded the way her parents did when they thought she was asleep and wouldn't be able to hear them discussing whatever it was that was wrong between them that they were keeping from her. Then, seeing the log beams in the darkness above her and hearing the rain dripping from the eaves, she remembered where she was. She could hear the quiet sounds the girls around her made in their sleep and the sound of the wind in the forest outside. She hated the wind this summer, a sickly, menacing noise that never seemed to stop.

The voices were those of the camp counselors in the main room of the lodge. Just as she did at home when her parents' voices woke her up, she slipped out of bed and went to listen. She tiptoed down the row of sleeping girls, then down the dark hall to the door to the main room. It wasn't closed all the way, which was why she'd been able to hear the voices.

Lydia Schaefer was describing how, just a little while ago, she'd been hurrying up to the lodge from her cabin. She'd heard sudden rustling in the forest next to the path, and then a man had grabbed her from behind. He had a knife, she said, and he threatened her with it, but she managed to tear herself away from him and run back to the lodge. She was still out of breath. Nora could hear that.

One of the other counselors asked Miss Schaefer why she hadn't shouted for help. She said she was too frightened at first and then, when she saw the lights of the lodge and knew the man wasn't going to catch up to her, she didn't want to scare the girls by making a lot of noise. The head counselor, Ruth Terrill, asked her if she could describe the man. It was so dark, Miss Schaefer answered, and it happened so fast that she didn't get a good look at him. But she thought he was tall—and he was wearing glasses, she was certain of that.

Miss Terrill said that she was going to call the sheriff, and they all agreed not to worry the girls with it.

That's what adults were always trying to do, Nora thought, as she tiptoed back down the hall to bed. *They don't want to worry the girls! My mom and dad are breaking up, but they don't want me to know about it!*

Adults are a lot more childish than children in a lot of ways, she thought.

She was barely awake, trying to identify every creaking noise the old building made in the night, when she heard a car driving up the dirt road to the lodge. A car door shut quietly and, as she fell asleep, she could hear the voices again in the main room, a man's voice among them now. She dreamed of the forest and of a man waiting for her among the trees.

The next morning, Nora looked up from her book and saw through the big front window, a police car pull up in front of the lodge and a large man in a brown uniform climb out. Miss Terrill and Miss Schaefer must have been watching for him too, for they met him before he could come inside. They stood on the wide porch, out of the rain, talking in voices too low for Nora to hear.

She wondered if it was the same man who'd come when Miss Terrill called the police the night before. *The other girls probably wouldn't have paid any attention to him even if he'd come in,* Nora thought. *They were all sitting at the dining-room table, writing letters home, probably complaining about the lack of television and shopping malls and anything fun to do.* Nora wasn't going to give her parents the satisfaction of complaining about anything. Besides, she didn't know which of them would be there to read whatever she wrote.

The weather was clearing up and they were supposed to go horseback riding the next day. Maybe, on account of the man in the forest, they'd stay indoors. She hoped so.

After all the other girls were asleep that night, she lay in bed and thought about the man in the forest with the knife. She had a good imagination and could see the knife blade and the lenses of his glasses glittering in the moonlight as he watched the lodge from the darkness, watched and waited for somebody to come down the path alone. What would Miss Terrill do, she wondered, if he tried to come into the lodge, tried to kidnap one of the girls? Miss Terrill always slept in the lodge with them. The other counselors had small cabins of their own, two to a cabin except for Miss Schaefer, who had a cabin all to herself, farthest down the path. Apparently, none of the other counselors wanted to share a cabin with Miss Schaefer, or else she didn't like any of them. Nora was glad she didn't have to sleep in one of those cabins, alone in the forest with the darkness and the sick wind in the pines that never stopped—and the man in the trees.

Then she heard a noise—it sounded like the start of a shout—coming from the lodge's main room, and then the sound of something falling. She sat up and strained to hear more, but there wasn't anything more— only the quiet breathing of the sleeping girls in the room with her, and the wind. She stared at the door to the main room, waited for it to open and for a tall man wearing glasses to come through, but nothing happened.

Maybe she'd been asleep and dreaming. Maybe it had been her imagination. But she couldn't stand it, here any more than at home. She had to know.

She slipped out of bed and crept silently down the dark hall on her bare feet. She opened the door a crack, very slowly, and peered into the room. At first she thought it was empty except for the moonlight, but then she saw something on the floor by the fireplace, a huddled figure. She forgot the man in the forest with the knife. She forgot to be scared. She went across the room to see who it was.

It was Miss Terrill. She was lying on her back, staring up at the ceiling, the wooden handle of a knife protruding from her.

Nora stared for a long moment, seeing everything there was to see—Miss Terrill's brown leather bag on the floor by her hand and the things that had spilled from it, some of them in the slowly spreading blood and some where the blood didn't reach.

A sound, a flicker of movement, made her look up. Miss Schaefer was coming through the front door.

"What are you doing out of bed, child? You get—Ruth!" She rushed over to Miss Terrill and knelt by her, saw what Nora had seen, and scrambled back to her feet.

"Did you see what happened?" she asked.

"No. I just heard something, so I—"

"You can't stay here," Miss Schaefer said. "Come with me." She took Nora by the hand and, instead of taking her back to the dormitory, almost dragged her across the room and down the hall to the kitchen.

"What's your name again?"

"Nora."

"Oh, yes, Nora," Miss Schaefer said. "The little girl who likes to read. You stay here until I come back. You'll be all right. Whoever did that to poor Ruth is gone now." She pushed Nora down onto a chair. "I'm going to call the police. Don't go back to the dorm—you might wake the other girls, and we don't want to scare them, do we? Promise?"

Nora promised and Miss Schaefer turned and went quickly down the hall.

Nora didn't like it in the kitchen. The clock on the wall made an ominous humming noise, like the wind outside. It was almost one A.M. There were knives on the drying board by the sink that the cook used to cut meat and vegetables, sharp and glittery in the moonlight pouring through the window, with handles like the one on the knife in Miss Terrill. The man from the forest might have been here, might be here now, hiding in the pantry or the closet or in the darkness over by the stove.

A sudden noise behind her made her jump up and spin around, but nothing moved in the kitchen's shadows. It was probably a mouse. Nora didn't like that thought either, because she wasn't wearing shoes.

She didn't care what she'd promised Miss Schaefer. She ran back to the main room. She meant to cross the door to the fireplace, run to the room where the telephone was and Miss Schaefer, but when she got to Miss Terrill's body, she couldn't help it—she stopped to look again.

What she saw this time terrified her.

"I told you to stay in the kitchen," Miss

Schaefer said, so close that Nora jumped and almost screamed. Her voice was soft and cold with anger—the worst kind—and she took Nora in her hard grip.

"I got scared," Nora said, trying not to tremble. They were alone with the body, the two of them, and the hallway door was closed. The other children slept soundly; the other counselors were far away.

"Scared? Of what?"

Then Nora blurted out, so suddenly it surprised her, "Of *him!*"

"Who?" In spite of herself, Miss Schaefer straightened up and looked quickly around the room.

"A man," Nora said. "He was looking at me through the kitchen window!"

"What did he look like?" Miss Schaefer sounded as surprised as Nora.

"He was big," Nora told her. "Tall—and he had dark hair. Miss Schaefer, what if he comes back?"

"I locked the door," Miss Schaefer said. "He can't get in now, nobody can." And then she asked, "How could you see him through the window, Nora? It's dark outside."

"Because," Nora said, and hesitated, trying desperately to think of an explanation, feeling Miss Schaefer's cold eyes on her and remembering the knives in the kitchen that glittered in the moonlight. "Because the *moon* was so bright, I could see it glittering in his glasses!"

Miss Schaefer thought about that for a moment and then she exhaled and relaxed her grip on Nora's arm. She almost smiled. "I called the police," she said. "They'll be here soon. I don't think you have anything to be afraid of now."

Nora didn't think so either.

The police arrived, and the sheriff, the man she'd seen talking to Miss Terrill and Miss Schaefer that morning. The other counselors came too, staring down in horror at Ruth Terrill. One of them took Nora by the arm and led her over to the couch by the front windows, away from the body. She said that wasn't anything for a girl her age to see, but since she'd found the body, she'd have to talk to the policemen. Nora almost laughed at how dumb that sounded. She could see the heads of some of the other girls, crowded in the entryway to the dorm, their eyes big. A counselor was standing in front of them to keep them from seeing too much.

Miss Schaefer explained to the other counselors that she'd been afraid to go outside and down the path to tell them what had happened—not with a killer on the loose—and of course she hadn't wanted to leave Nora and the rest of the children alone either. After all, he'd attacked her too, out there in the forest, but she'd been lucky—luckier than Ruth Terrill—she'd managed to get away from him.

The sheriff asked her why she'd come up to the lodge in the first place. She told him she'd left her book there, the one she wanted to read in bed before going to sleep. "I had my flashlight," she said, "and I ran all the way." Then she called over to Nora, as if anxious to turn attention away from herself. "Tell the sheriff about the man you saw at the window in the kitchen, Nora."

"I didn't see anybody," Nora answered. "But I saw something else—over by Miss Terrill's body."

"What did you see?" the sheriff asked. "Come over here and tell me."

"No. You go over by Miss Terrill's body."

"Go—" The sheriff hesitated, gave her a

puzzled look, and then he did as she asked. Something in her voice made him do that.

"What's this all about?" Miss Schaefer wanted to know. "You told me, Nora—"

Nora didn't pay any attention to her, only looked to make sure one of the policemen was standing between her and Miss Schaefer. "You just tell me if I'm right about the things scattered around Miss Terrill," she called to the sheriff.

"Nora," Miss Schaefer said and tried hard to laugh, "we're not playing Kim's Game now."

"What's Kim's Game?" the sheriff asked.

"It's a game we play sometimes," Nora told him, "when we have to be indoors on account of the weather. Miss Bowers gives us about fifteen seconds to look at a lot of things she's put on a blanket on the floor and then we have to go to another part of the room and write down everything we remember. Whoever remembers the most things wins."

"Nora's just like me, sheriff," Miss Schaefer said. "She's not very good at it." Her laugh had the same sickly sound as the wind had in the forest, but the forest was quiet now.

Nora looked back at the sheriff and said, "There's a pen and a little tube of sun cream and a pocketknife with a red handle. There's a change purse too. It's brown."

"That's right," the sheriff said, glancing across the room at her. She was staring straight ahead, with her eyes wide open. The sheriff had a daughter too, but when she tried hard to remember things, she screwed her eyes tight shut.

"There're some keys on a ring," Nora went on, "in the middle of the blood, and there's a box of Band-Aids and a comb next to them. There's money too. Two quarters and some dimes—three dimes, I think."

"Is that all?" the sheriff asked.

"That's all there is *now*," Nora said. "But when I found Miss Terrill, there was a glasses case, and the glasses were still in it. It was blue and red—plaid—and part of it was in the blood. You can still see where it was, if you look—I could, anyway, when I came back in here, after Miss Schaefer took me to the kitchen and left me there alone. There's a kind of notch in the blood where the glasses case was. The blood must have run up against it and then had to go around."

The sheriff looked and said, "The notch is still there, Nora, in the blood. Do you know where the case is now?"

"No," she said.

"Do you know who has a glasses case like that?"

"Yes," she said, in a very small voice, but forcing herself to look at Miss Schaefer.

"You have a plaid glasses case, Lydia," Miss Bowers said to Miss Schaefer.

Miss Schaefer ran out of the lodge, but she didn't get far. Maybe she didn't try very hard; maybe she didn't want to be alone in the forest.

"I should have cut your little throat when I had the chance," she said to Nora when one of the policemen brought her back into the lodge. She was smiling when she said it, but it wasn't the nicest smile Nora had ever seen.

The glasses case had fallen out of Miss Schaefer's jacket pocket as she killed Miss Terrill. She didn't notice it was gone until she started down the path to her cabin, but when she came back to get it, Nora was there. After she took Nora to the kitchen, she went back and got the case, wiped off the blood, and then put it back in her pocket before she called the sheriff.

Why had she killed Miss Terrill? Nora never found out, and she didn't care anyway. It had to do with something that happened between the two women a long time ago—probably before Nora was even born—the kind of thing adults fight over, not really caring who gets hurt. It was the kind of thing kids aren't supposed to know about, so Nora only got bits and pieces of the story.

When they heard about the murder, some of the parents drove up the mountain and took their daughters home. For a while there was a regular parade of cars arriving and departing with little girls. Some of the cars had one parent in them, and some had both.

The sun was shining and Nora was getting ready to go horseback riding with the girls who were left when Miss Bowers came out and told her that her mother was on the phone and wanted to know if she wanted to go home.

Her horse had huge eyes, like brown marbles, with curiosity in them. Nora wondered what it would be like to ride a horse like that.

"Tell Mom I'm fine," she said to Miss Bowers, "and that I'm having a good time. Tell her to say hello to Dad for me too, and give him a big kiss if she can."

The man in charge of the horses showed the girls how to mount them, and when they were all ready, they rode into the forest together.

About the Author

M. D. Lake is the pen name of a former professor of Scandinavian literature at the University of Minnesota. Lake is married and has—in the order of their appearance—two children, two cats, and three grandchildren. Lake is the author of a series of mysteries in which the main character is Peggy O'Neill, a campus cop. The third book in the series, *Poisoned Ivy,* won an American Mystery Award in 1993, and "Kim's Game" won an Agatha Award—an award named for Agatha Christie, the great English mystery writer—in 1994.

UNDERSTAND KEY IDEAS AND DETAILS. The following questions help you check your reading comprehension. Put an *x* in the box next to the correct answer.

1. "Kim's Game" is mainly about
   - ☐ a. adults who "protect" children by hiding unpleasant information from them.
   - ☐ b. some campers who enjoy watching television shows and movies.
   - ☐ c. a girl who solves a crime by using the methods employed in a game.

2. Although Nora didn't dislike the other girls, they
   - ☐ a. didn't interest her very much.
   - ☐ b. all played Kim's Game very well.
   - ☐ c. hated Nora.

3. Which one of the following details was the most important in solving the crime?
   - ☐ a. Nora realized that Miss Schaefer was afraid of Miss Terrill.
   - ☐ b. Nora realized that the glasses case had been removed.
   - ☐ c. Nora realized that Miss Schaefer didn't like children.

4. At the end of the story, Nora decided to
   - ☐ a. return home at once.
   - ☐ b. complain to her mother.
   - ☐ c. stay at camp and go horseback riding with some of the girls.

NOTE NEW VOCABULARY WORDS. The following questions check your vocabulary skills. Put an *x* in the box next to the correct answer. Each vocabulary word appears in the story.

1. To do well at Kim's Game, it was necessary to be observant. Which of the following best defines the word *observant*?
   - ☐ a. to be young and active
   - ☐ b. to possess a good sense of humor
   - ☐ c. to notice and remember things well

2. Miss Schaefer was upset because the head counselor spoke to her in an "officious tone of voice." Someone who is *officious*
   - ☐ a. meddles in other people's business.
   - ☐ b. never cares about what other people say or do.
   - ☐ c. is usually quiet and shy.

3. A knife was protruding from Miss Terrill. The word *protruding* means
   - ☐ a. sticking out.
   - ☐ b. next to.
   - ☐ c. far from.

4. When Nora realized that she was alone and in danger, the situation seemed ominous. What is the meaning of the word *ominous*?
   - ☐ a. exciting
   - ☐ b. threatening
   - ☐ c. unusual

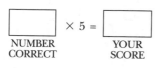

NUMBER CORRECT × 5 = YOUR SCORE

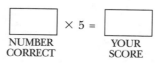

NUMBER CORRECT × 5 = YOUR SCORE

IDENTIFY STORY ELEMENTS. The following questions check your knowledge of story elements. Put an *x* in the box next to each correct answer.

1. What is the *setting* of "Kim's Game"?
   ☐ a. a farm that had horses
   ☐ b. a small hotel in the country
   ☐ c. a summer camp

2. Who is the *main character* in the story?
   ☐ a. Lydia Schaefer
   ☐ b. Ruth Terrill
   ☐ c. Nora

3. Which of the following best illustrates *foreshadowing*?
   ☐ a. Early in the story, Miss Schaefer took her reading glasses out of a case.
   ☐ b. Nora asked Miss Bowers to tell her Mom that she was having a good time.
   ☐ c. Miss Schaefer was wearing a wet raincoat when she first entered the lodge.

4. Of these events, which happened last in the *plot* of the story?
   ☐ a. Nora realized that Miss Schaefer was afraid of Miss Terrill.
   ☐ b. Nora listed the things she saw near Miss Terrill's body.
   ☐ c. Miss Schaefer told Nora to wait in the kitchen.

THINK CRITICALLY ABOUT THE STORY. The following questions check your critical thinking skills. Put an *x* in the box next to each correct answer.

1. Nora probably saved her life by having said that she
   ☐ a. was not good at Kim's Game.
   ☐ b. saw a man looking at her through the kitchen window.
   ☐ c. liked to read.

2. When she saw Miss Terrill's body a second time, Nora became terrified. Why?
   ☐ a. She suddenly felt sorry for Miss Terrill.
   ☐ b. She was upset by the bloody scene.
   ☐ c. She realized that the glasses case was missing.

3. We may conclude that Nora
   ☐ a. believed that the other girls were fascinating.
   ☐ b. could easily have won the third game of Kim's Game if she wanted to.
   ☐ c. thought that adults always acted in appropriate ways.

4. Evidence in the story suggests that Nora
   ☐ a. was upset by the problems that her parents were experiencing.
   ☐ b. was smart but could not think quickly enough when the situation required it.
   ☐ c. seriously considered going home after the murder occurred.

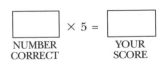

NUMBER CORRECT   × 5 =   YOUR SCORE

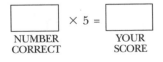

NUMBER CORRECT   × 5 =   YOUR SCORE

STUDY THE **W**RITER'S **C**RAFT. The following questions check your knowledge of skills related to the craft of writing. Put an *x* in the box next to each correct answer. You may refer to pages 4 and 5.

1. One of the most striking things about the way the story is constructed is that
   - ☐ a. the murder is, in effect, solved by playing a variation of Kim's Game.
   - ☐ b. the murderer has no motive for killing her victim.
   - ☐ c. young people and adults are characters in the story.

2. A thought suddenly went through Nora like a sharp knife. This sentence contains
   - ☐ a. a metaphor.
   - ☐ b. a simile.
   - ☐ c. inner conflict.

3. Which fact foreshadows the possibility that danger lies ahead?
   - ☐ a. Nora thought that the girls were writing letters filled with complaints.
   - ☐ b. Nora won the first two games of Kim's Game that she played.
   - ☐ c. Miss Terrill spoke sharply to Miss Schaefer, and Miss Schaefer reacted with fear.

4. Which of the following images is most important in the story?
   - ☐ a. books
   - ☐ b. cars
   - ☐ c. knives

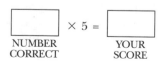

NUMBER CORRECT × 5 = YOUR SCORE

Questions for Writing and Discussion

- What character traits does Nora possess that would make her a good detective?
- At the beginning of the story, Miss Schaefer attempted to engage Nora in conversation, but Nora declined. Explain why.
- What lie did Nora tell Miss Schaefer? Why did Nora tell that lie? Why did Nora make sure that "one of the policemen was standing between her and Miss Schaefer"?
- Explain in detail how Nora solved the crime.

See additional questions for extended writing on pages 118 and 119.

Use the boxes below to total your scores for the exercises. Then record your scores on pages 198 and 199.

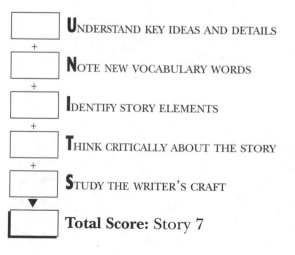

UNDERSTAND KEY IDEAS AND DETAILS

+

NOTE NEW VOCABULARY WORDS

+

IDENTIFY STORY ELEMENTS

+

THINK CRITICALLY ABOUT THE STORY

+

STUDY THE WRITER'S CRAFT

▼

Total Score: Story 7

The President Regrets

by Ellery Queen

The Puzzle Club is a group of very important people drawn together by one common passion—to mystify one another. Their pleasure, in short, is puzzles.

Application is by invitation only, and membership must be won, the applicant having to submit to the Ordeal by Puzzle. If the applicant survives the test, he or she gains automatic admission to the Club.

Shortly after Ellery became the Puzzle Club's sixth member, it was proposed and unanimously voted to invite the president of the United States to apply for membership.

This was no frivolous matter because the members took their puzzles seriously, and the president was known to love mysteries of all kinds. Besides, the Club's famous founder and first member, millionaire oil man Syres, had been friendly with the occupant of the White House since their boyhood days.

The invitation went to Washington, and rather to Ellery's surprise the president promptly accepted the challenge. Out of respect for the president's busy schedule, he was urged to designate his own date, which he did. But when Ellery arrived at Syres's Park Avenue penthouse on the appointed evening to find the membership assembled, he was greeted with gloomy news. The president regretted that he could not make it after all. A Secret Service man, just departed, had brought the message that a new crisis in the Middle East had caused a last-minute cancellation of the president's flight to New York.

"What shall we do now?" asked Darnell, the famous criminal lawyer.

"There's no point in wasting the puzzle we've prepared for the president," said Dr. Vreeland, the well-known psychiatrist. "Let's save it for whenever he can get here."

"It's too bad Dr. Arkavy is still attending that conference in Moscow," said Emmy Wandermere, the poet. Dr. Arkavy was the Nobel Prize-winning biochemist. "He has such a quick mind, he can always come up with something on the spur of the moment."

"Maybe our newest member can help us out," said their host, Syres. "What do you say, Queen? You must have a hundred problems at your fingers' ends, from your long experience as a writer and a detective."

"Let me think." Ellery cogitated. Then he chuckled. "All right. Give me a few minutes to work out the details . . ." It took him far less. "I'm ready. I suggest we work together, to begin with. Since this is going to be a murder mystery, we will obviously require a victim. Any suggestions?"

"A woman, of course," the poet said at once.

"A very glamorous one," said the psychiatrist.

"That," said the criminal lawyer, "would seem to call for a Hollywood movie star."

"Good enough," Ellery said. "And a glamorous star of the screen calls for a glamorous name. Let's call her . . . oh, Valetta Van Buren. Agreed?"

"Valetta Van Buren." Miss Wandermere considered. "Yes. That's perfect, Mr. Queen."

"Well, Valetta is in New York to attend the opening of her latest picture and to do the circuit of TV appearances in promotion of it," Ellery went on. "But this hasn't proved an ordinary publicity tour. In fact, Valetta has had a frightening experience. It shook her up so much that she wrote me an agitated letter about it which, by the magic of coincidence, I received just this morning."

"In which," Dr. Vreeland pressed, "she said—"

"That during this New York visit she permitted herself to be escorted about town by four men—"

"Who are all, naturally, in love with her?" asked the poet.

"You guessed it, Miss Wandermere. She identified the four in her letter. One is that notorious playboy, John Thrushbottom Taylor the Third—and if you haven't heard of Mr. Taylor, it's because I just made him up. The second is that fabulously successful Wall Street money manager named . . . well, let's call him A. Palmer Harrison. The third, of course, is the extremely popular artist Leonardo Price. And the last of the quartet is—let's see—Biff Wilson, the professional football player."

"A likely story," grinned oil man Syres.

"Now," Ellery said, "having named the four men for me, Valetta went on to say that yesterday all four proposed marriage to her —each of them, on the same day. Unhappily, Valetta felt nothing for any of them—nothing permanent, at any rate. She rejected all four. It was a busy day for Miss Van Buren, and she would have enjoyed it except for one thing."

"One of them," said the criminal lawyer, "turned ugly."

"Exactly, Darnell. Valetta wrote me that three of them took their turndowns with grace. But the fourth flew into a homicidal rage and threatened to kill her. She was terrified that he would try to carry out his threat and asked me to get in touch with her at once. She felt reluctant to go to the police, she wrote, because of the bad publicity it would bring her."

"What happened then?" asked Syres.

"I phoned, of course," Ellery replied, "as soon as I finished reading her letter. Would you believe it? I was too late. She was murdered last night, a short time after she must have mailed the letter."

"How," asked Darnell, "was the foul deed done?"

Ellery said, "The nature of the weapon is unimportant and irrelevant. However, I will say this: Valetta *was* murdered by the admirer who threatened her life."

"And is that all?" asked the oil man.

"No, I've saved the most important part for last, Mr. Syres. Valetta's letter gave me one clue. In writing about the four men, she said that she'd noticed *she had something in common with three of the four,* and that the *fourth* was the one who had threatened her."

"Oh," said Dr. Vreeland. "Then all we have to establish is the thing they had in common. The three sharing it with Valetta would be innocent. By elimination, therefore, the one left over has to be the guilty man."

Ellery nodded. "And now—are there any questions?"

"I take it," the poet murmured, "that we may disregard the obvious possibilities of connection—that Valetta and three of the men were of the same age, or had the same color hair, or came from the same town or state, or attended the same college—that sort of thing?"

Ellery laughed. "Yes, you may disregard those."

"Social position?" the millionaire ventured.

"Three of the men you described—Playboy John Something Taylor, Wall Street man A. Palmer Harrison, Artist Price—did they all come from high society? That probably wouldn't be true of the pro football player, What's-His-Name."

"It just happened," Ellery informed them, "that Price was born in a Greenwich Village loft. And Valetta came from the slums of Chicago."

They pondered.

"Had three of the four men ever served with Valetta," asked Darnell suddenly, "on the same jury?"

"No."

"As speakers on a TV show?" asked the poet quickly.

"No, Miss Wandermere."

Miss Wandermere suddenly said, "It isn't anything like that. Am I right, Mr. Queen, in assuming that all the facts necessary to solve the puzzle were given to us in your story?"

"I wondered when someone was going to ask that." Ellery chuckled. "That's exactly so, Miss Wandermere. There's really no need to ask any more questions at all."

"Then I for one need more time," said the oil tycoon, Syres. "What about the rest of you? I suggest we eat the exquisite dinner I've arranged before we solve Queen's puzzle."

Miss Wandermere's eyes suddenly sparkled as she thought of the answer during the appetizer. Darnell suddenly smiled and was filled with elation while he was finishing his soup. Dr. Vreeland uttered, "Ah, yes!" at the serving of the lobster. And their host, Syres, muttered, "Aha, I see it now!" during dessert. But no one uttered a word until they were seated in the living room again.

"I detect from your looks," Ellery said, "that

none of you encountered any real difficulty with my little puzzle."

"It's too bad the president had to miss this," Syres roared. "It was made to order, Queen, for his type of mind! He would really have loved it! Are you all quite ready?"

There was a universal nod.

"In that case," Ellery said, "which of Valetta's four admirers murdered her?"

"Ladies first," said Dr. Vreeland with a gallant nod to Miss Wandermere.

"The key to the puzzle," said the poet promptly, "consists in the fact, Mr. Queen, that you really told us just one thing about Valetta *and* her four admirers. It follows that whatever she and three of the four men had in common must relate to that thing."

"A logic I can't dispute," murmured Ellery. "And what was that thing?"

Darnell grinned. "What thinking about the president's visit here tonight must have suggested to your mind when we asked you for a puzzle. Their names."

"You named the movie star Valetta Van Buren," said Syres. *"Van Buren—the name of a president of the United States."*

"Then Playboy John Thrushbottom Taylor

the Third," said Dr. Vreeland. "You hid that one, Queen! But of course Taylor is the name of a president of the United States, too— Zachary Taylor."

"And the Wall Street man, A. Palmer Harrison," the lawyer said. "William Henry Harrison was a president of the United States. Also Benjamin Harrison. He was a president, too."

"And professional football player Biff Wilson." Miss Wandermere's eyes twinkled. "That 'Biff' was masterly, Mr. Queen. But—of course, Wilson, for Woodrow Wilson."

"And that leaves one character whose name," said the oil man, "is not the name of a president—Leonardo Price. So Price, the artist, murdered Valetta. You almost had me fooled, Queen. *Taylor, Van Buren, Harrison!* That was tricky, picking the less well-known presidents."

"You could hardly expect me to name one of my characters Eisenhower,"[1] Ellery grinned. "Which reminds me. Here's to our absent president—and may he turn out to be the Puzzle Club's next member!"

---

1. **Eisenhower:** Dwight D. Eisenhower, the 34th president of the United States

About the Authors

Frederic Dannay (1905–1982) and Manfred B. Lee (1905–1971) The great fictional detective Ellery Queen was the brainchild of Frederic Dannay and Manfred B. Lee, cousins who were born the same year in Brooklyn, New York. One day, while having lunch together, the cousins decided to enter a writing contest sponsored by a magazine. They won easily by creating Ellery Queen, considered by many to be America's greatest detective. Dannay and Lee wrote more than thirty novels, dozens of books, and countless radio scripts, all starring Ellery Queen. Queen also appeared in many movies and TV series. Interestingly, for many years, people did not know that the stories were written by *two* men. When the author was asked to lecture, one cousin or the other appeared—always wearing a mask.

UNDERSTAND KEY IDEAS AND DETAILS. The following questions help you check your reading comprehension. Put an *x* in the box next to the correct answer.

1. "The President Regrets" is mainly about
   □ a. the reason that a movie star is murdered.
   □ b. a mystery that is solved by members of the Puzzle Club.
   □ c. various presidents of the United States of America.

2. The president could not attend the meeting of the Puzzle Club because
   □ a. there was a new crisis in the Middle East.
   □ b. he had to go to a conference in Moscow.
   □ c. he had business to take care of in New York.

3. According to Ellery Queen, three of the four men who admired Valetta
   □ a. were the same age.
   □ b. attended the same college.
   □ c. had something in common with her.

4. The man who murdered Valetta
   □ a. worked on Wall Street.
   □ b. was born in Chicago.
   □ c. did not have the same name as a president of the United States.

NOTE NEW VOCABULARY WORDS. The following questions check your vocabulary skills. Put an *x* in the box next to the correct answer. Each vocabulary word appears in the story.

1. Inviting the president was not a "frivolous matter, because the members took puzzles seriously." The word *frivolous* means
   □ a. unimportant or silly.
   □ b. agreeable or pleasant.
   □ c. significant or meaningful.

2. The president agreed to designate the date he would attend the meeting. What is the meaning of the word *designate*?
   □ a. ask about or question
   □ b. indicate or state
   □ c. alter or change

3. Ellery cogitated briefly before making up the puzzle. The word *cogitated* means
   □ a. worried about.
   □ b. quickly gave up.
   □ c. thought about.

4. The weapon she was killed with was "unimportant and irrelevant." Define the word *irrelevant*.
   □ a. not to the point or off the subject
   □ b. powerful or forceful
   □ c. taken into custody

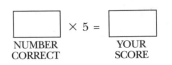

× 5 =

NUMBER CORRECT   YOUR SCORE

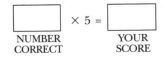

× 5 =

NUMBER CORRECT   YOUR SCORE

IDENTIFY STORY ELEMENTS. The following questions check your knowledge of story elements. Put an *x* in the box next to each correct answer.

1. Of these events, which happened first in the *plot* of "The President Regrets"?
   ☐ a. The members of the Puzzle Club ate dinner.
   ☐ b. Ellery Queen said that he had received a letter from Valetta Van Buren.
   ☐ c. Syres stated the name of the man who murdered Valetta.

2. "Since this is going to be a murder mystery, we will obviously require a victim." Who uttered this line of *dialogue?*
   ☐ a. Dr. Vreeland
   ☐ b. Ellery Queen
   ☐ c. Miss Wandermere

3. The story is *set*
   ☐ a. at the home of a movie star in Hollywood, California.
   ☐ b. at a fancy apartment in New York City.
   ☐ c. in the president's office in Washington, D.C.

4. The author's *purpose* in writing the story was to
   ☐ a. amuse or entertain.
   ☐ b. convince or persuade.
   ☐ c. teach or instruct.

THINK CRITICALLY ABOUT THE STORY. The following questions check your critical thinking skills. Put an *x* in the box next to each correct answer.

1. The conclusion to the story proves that the Puzzle Club members
   ☐ a. went to the meetings primarily to enjoy good food.
   ☐ b. deserved membership in the Club.
   ☐ c. were jealous of each other.

2. We may infer that Ellery Queen
   ☐ a. possessed a lively imagination.
   ☐ b. did not have much experience as a writer or detective.
   ☐ c. knew that the president would be unable to attend the meeting.

3. It is fair to say that if Valetta had been poisoned, that fact would have
   ☐ a. helped the members greatly in solving the mystery.
   ☐ b. had no effect, or bearing, on the problem's solution.
   ☐ c. changed the way that the story ended.

4. In years to come, which of the following would have the greatest impact on this story?
   ☐ a. changes in the way in which presidents are elected
   ☐ b. increased security provided for Hollywood stars
   ☐ c. the election of a president whose last name was Price

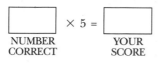

NUMBER CORRECT × 5 = YOUR SCORE

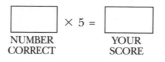

NUMBER CORRECT × 5 = YOUR SCORE

99

STUDY THE WRITER'S CRAFT. The following questions check your knowledge of skills related to the craft of writing. Put an *x* in the box next to each correct answer. You may refer to pages 4 and 5.

1. Which of the following is most important to the solution of the mystery?
   ☐ a. an important clue
   ☐ b. how the crime was committed
   ☐ c. knowledge of the personality of Valetta Van Buren

2. The description "the famous founder and first member" contains
   ☐ a. a very powerful image.
   ☐ b. a simile.
   ☐ c. alliteration.

3. Syres told Ellery, "You must have a hundred problems at your fingers' ends." This is figurative language that suggests that Ellery
   ☐ a. had written a hundred problems.
   ☐ b. has many personal problems.
   ☐ c. often gave puzzles to his friends.

4. "The President Regrets" is an example of "a story within a story" because
   ☐ a. the story appears in a book that contains other stories.
   ☐ b. the story is part of a unit on mystery stories.
   ☐ c. one of the characters in the story tells a story to the other characters.

Questions for Writing and Discussion

- What is the meaning of the phrase "Ordeal by Puzzle"? How do you think "the ordeal" worked?
- What was the most important thing that the members of the Club had to figure out to solve the puzzle?
- At the conclusion of the story Ellery stated, "You could hardly expect me to name one of my characters Eisenhower." Why *didn't* Ellery give one of his characters that name?
- What are three names that Ellery could not have given to the murderer in the mystery? What are some other possible names he might have given the other suspects?

See additional questions for extended writing on pages 118 and 119.

Use the boxes below to total your scores for the exercises. Then record your scores on pages 198 and 199.

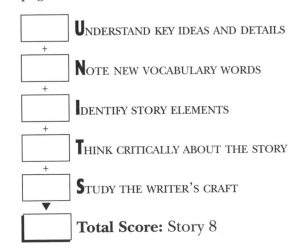

☐ **U**NDERSTAND KEY IDEAS AND DETAILS
  +
☐ **N**OTE NEW VOCABULARY WORDS
  +
☐ **I**DENTIFY STORY ELEMENTS
  +
☐ **T**HINK CRITICALLY ABOUT THE STORY
  +
☐ **S**TUDY THE WRITER'S CRAFT
  ▼
☐ **Total Score:** Story 8

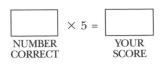

☐ × 5 = ☐

NUMBER   YOUR
CORRECT   SCORE

Sherlock Holmes faces one of the most difficult challenges of his career when he tries to solve . . .

The Adventure of the Speckled Band

by Arthur Conan Doyle

In glancing over my notes of the more than seventy cases solved by my friend Sherlock Holmes, I find many tragic, some comic, a large number strange, but none ordinary. Of these varied cases, however, I cannot find any more unusual than "The Adventure of the Speckled Band."

It began early one April morning when I woke to find Sherlock Holmes standing, fully dressed, by the side of my bed. He was a late riser as a rule, and, as the clock on the mantelpiece showed me that it was only a quarter past seven, I blinked up at him in some surprise, and perhaps just a little resentment, for I was myself regular in my habits.

101

"Very sorry to wake you up Watson," said he, "but I was awakened early myself."

"What is it, then? A fire?"

"No, a client. It seems that a young lady has arrived in a considerable state of excitement, who insists upon seeing me. She is waiting now in the sitting-room. When young ladies wander about the metropolis at this hour of the morning, and wake sleepy people up out of their beds, I presume that it is something very pressing which they have to communicate. Should it prove to be an interesting case, you would, I am sure, wish to follow it from the outset. I thought, at any rate, that I should call you and give you the chance."

"My dear fellow, I would not miss it for anything."

I had no keener pleasure than in following Holmes in his professional investigations, and in admiring the rapid deductions, always founded on a logical basis, with which he unravelled the problems which were submitted to him. I rapidly threw on my clothes, and was ready in a few minutes to accompany my friend down to the sitting-room. A lady dressed in black and heavily veiled, who had been sitting near the window, rose as we entered.

"Good morning, madam," said Holmes cheerily. "My name is Sherlock Holmes. This is my good friend and associate, Dr. Watson, before whom you can speak as freely as before myself. Ah, I am glad to see that Mrs. Hudson has had the good sense to light the fireplace. Please draw up a chair to it, for I observe that you are shivering."

"It is not cold which makes me shiver," said the woman in a low voice, changing her seat as requested.

"What then?"

"It is fear, Mr. Holmes. It is terror." She raised her veil as she spoke, and we could see that she was indeed in a pitiable state of agitation, her face all drawn and grey, with restless, frightened eyes, like those of some hunted animal.

"You must not fear," said Holmes soothingly. "We shall soon set matters right, I have no doubt. You have come in by train this morning, I see."

"You know me, then?"

"No, but I observe the second half of a return ticket in the palm of your left glove. You must have started early, and yet you had a good, long drive in a dog-cart,[1] along heavy roads, before you reached the station."

The lady gave a violent start, and stared in bewilderment at my companion.

"There is no mystery, my dear madam," said he, smiling. "The left arm of your jacket is spattered with mud in no less than seven places. The marks are perfectly fresh. There is no vehicle except a dog-cart which throws up mud in that way, and then only when you sit on the left-hand side of the driver."

"Whatever your reasons may be, you are perfectly correct," said she. "I started from home before six, reached Leatherhead at twenty past, and came in by the first train to Waterloo. Sir, I can stand this strain no longer, I shall go mad if it continues. I have no one to turn to—none, except only one, who cares for me, and he, poor fellow, can be of little aid. I have heard of you from Mrs. Farintosh, whom you helped in the hour of her need. It was from her that I had your address. Do you think you could help me too, and at least throw a little light through the dense darkness which surrounds

---

1. **dog-cart:** a small, open, horse-drawn wagon

me? At present it is out of my power to reward you for your services, but in a month or two I shall be married, and shall have my own income, and then you shall not find me ungrateful."

"Farintosh," said he. "Ah, yes, I recall the case. It was before your time, Watson. I can only say, madam, that I shall be happy to devote the same care to your case as I did to that of your friend. As to reward, my profession is its reward, but you are at liberty to defray whatever expenses I may be put to, at the time which suits you best. And now I beg that you will tell us everything that may help us in forming an opinion upon the matter."

"My name is Helen Stoner, and I am living with my stepfather, who is the last survivor of one of the oldest Saxon families in England, the Roylotts of Stoke Moran, on the western border of Surrey."

Holmes nodded his head. "The name is familiar to me," said he.

"The family was at one time among the richest in England, and the estate extended over the borders into Berkshire in the north, and Hampshire in the west. In the last century, however, four successive heirs were so completely wasteful that the family fortune was eventually ruined. Nothing is left today but a few acres of ground and a two-hundred-year-old house. My stepfather went to India, where, by his professional skill and his force of character, he became a doctor and established a large practice.

"When Dr. Roylott was in India he married my mother, Mrs. Stoner. My sister Julia and I were twins, and we were only two years old at the time of my mother's remarriage. She had a considerable sum of money, and all of this she bequeathed to Dr. Roylott. The will had a provision that a certain sum of money—a large sum, I believe—should be given to each of us when we married. Shortly after our return to England my mother died—she was killed eight years ago in a railway accident. Dr. Roylott then took us to live with him in the ancestral house at Stoke Moran. The money which my mother had left was enough for all our wants, and there seemed no obstacle to our happiness.

"But a terrible change came over our stepfather about this time. Instead of making friends and exchanging visits with our neighbors, who had at first been overjoyed to see a Roylott of Stoke Moran back in the old family seat, he shut himself up in his house, and seldom came out except to indulge in ferocious quarrels with whoever might cross his path. A series of disgraceful brawls took place, two of which ended in the police-court, until at last he became the terror of the village, and the folks would fly at his approach, for he is a man of immense strength, and absolutely uncontrollable in his anger.

"He has no friends at all except some wandering vagabonds, and he lets them camp on the few acres of land which represent the family estate. He has a passion also for animals from India, which are sent to him from that country, and he has at this moment a cheetah and a baboon, which wander freely over his grounds and are feared by the villagers almost as much as is their master.

"You can imagine from what I say that my poor sister Julia and I had no great pleasure in our lives. No servant would stay with us, and for a long time we did all the work of the house. She was only thirty at the time of her death, and yet her hair had already begun to turn white."

"Your sister is dead, then?"

"She died just two years ago, and it is of her death that I wish to speak to you. You can understand that, living the life which I have described, we were not likely to see anyone of our own age and position. We had, however, an aunt, and we were occasionally allowed to pay short visits at this lady's house. Julia went there at Christmas two years ago, and met there a man, to whom she became engaged. My stepfather learned of the engagement when my sister returned, and offered no objection to the marriage; but within a fortnight of the day which had been fixed for the wedding, the terrible event occurred which has deprived me of my only companion."

Sherlock Holmes looked closely at his visitor.

"Please be precise as to the details," said he.

"It is easy for me to be so, for every event of that dreadful time is seared into my memory. The house is, as I have already said, very old, and only one wing[2] is now inhabited. The bedrooms in this wing are on the ground floor of the building. Of these bedrooms, the first is Dr. Roylott's, the second my sister's, and the third my own. They are all side by side, though there are no doors between them, but they all open out into the same corridor. Do I make myself plain?"

"Perfectly so."

"The windows of the three rooms open out upon the lawn. That fatal night Dr. Roylott had gone to his room early,

---

2. **wing:** Here, the word means "part of a building."

though we knew that he had not gone to sleep, for my sister was troubled by the smell of the Indian cigars which it was his custom to smoke. She left her room, therefore, and came into mine, where she sat for some time, chatting about her approaching wedding. At eleven o'clock she rose to leave me, but she paused at the door and looked back.

"'Tell me, Helen,' said she, 'have you ever heard anyone whistle in the dead of the night?'

"'Never.' said I.

"'I suppose that you could not possibly whistle yourself in your sleep?'

"'Certainly not. But why?'

"'Because during the last few nights I have always, about three in the morning, heard a low clear whistle. I am a light sleeper, and it has awakened me. I cannot tell where it came from—perhaps from the next room, perhaps from the lawn. I thought that I would just ask you whether you had heard it.'

"'No, I have not. It must be those vagabonds.'

"'Very likely. And yet, I wonder that you did not hear it also.'

"'Ah, but I sleep more heavily than you.'

"'Well, it is of no great consequence, at any rate,' she smiled back at me, closed my door, and a few moments later I heard her key turn in the lock."

"Indeed," said Holmes. "Was it your custom always to lock yourselves in at night?"

"Always."

"And why?"

"I think that I mentioned to you that the Doctor kept a cheetah and a baboon. We had no feeling of security unless our doors were locked."

"Quite so. Please proceed with your statement."

"I could not sleep that night. A vague feeling of impending misfortune bothered me. It was a wild night. The wind was howling outside, and the rain was beating and splashing against the windows. Suddenly, amidst all the hubbub of the gale, there burst forth the wild scream of a terrified woman. I knew that it was my sister's voice. I sprang from my bed, wrapped a shawl round me, and rushed into the corridor. As I opened my door I seemed to hear a low whistle, such as my sister described, and a few moments later a clanging sound, as if something made of metal had fallen. As I ran down the passage, I saw that my sister's door was unlocked. By the light of the corridor lamp I saw my sister appear at the opening, her face filled with terror, her hands groping for help, her whole figure swaying to and fro. I ran to her and threw my arms round her, but at that moment her knees seemed to give way and she fell to the ground. She writhed as one who is in terrible pain.

"At first I thought that she had not recognized me, but as I bent over her she suddenly shrieked out in a voice which I shall never forget, 'Helen! It was the band! The speckled band!' There was something else that she wanted to say, and she stabbed with her finger into the air in the direction of the doctor's room, and fell to the floor. I rushed out, calling loudly for my stepfather, and I met him hastening from his room. When he reached my sister's side she was unconscious. Though he tried to revive her, and sent for medical aid from the village, all efforts were in vain, for she slowly sank and died without having recovered her consciousness. Such was the dreadful end of my beloved sister."

"One moment," said Holmes; "are you sure about this whistle and the sound of metal? Could you swear to it?"

"It is my strong impression that I heard it, and yet among the crash of the gale, and the creaking of an old house, I may possibly have been deceived."

"And what conclusions did the police come to?"

"They investigated the case with great care, for Dr. Roylott's conduct had long been notorious in the county, but they were unable to find any satisfactory cause of death. Her door had been locked from the inside, and the windows were blocked by old-fashioned shutters with broad iron bars, which were locked every night. The walls and the floor were also shown to be solid. It is certain, therefore, that my sister was quite alone when she met her end. Besides, there were no marks of any violence upon her."

"How about poison?"

"The doctors examined her for it, but without success."

"What do you think that this unfortunate lady died of, then?"

"It is my belief that she died of pure fear and nervous shock, though what it was which frightened her I cannot imagine."

"Ah, and what did you gather she meant by 'the band—the speckled band'?"

"I do not know. It may refer to a band of people—vagabonds who camp on our land. Some of them wear spotted handkerchiefs over their heads."

Holmes shook his head like a man who is far from being satisfied.

He said, "Please go on with your story."

"Two years have passed since then, and my life has been until lately lonelier than ever. A month ago, however, a dear friend, whom I have known for many years, has done me the honor to ask my hand in marriage, and we are to be married in the spring. Two days ago some repairs were started in the wing of the building, so that I have had to move into the room in which my sister died, and to sleep in the very bed in which she slept. Imagine, then, my terror when last night, as I lay awake, thinking about her terrible fate, I suddenly heard in the silence of the night the low whistle which had been the herald of her own death. I sprang up and lit the lamp, but nothing was to be seen in the room. I was too shaken to go to bed again, however, so I dressed and as soon as it was daylight I slipped down, got a dog-cart at the Crown Inn, and drove to Leatherhead, from whence I have come on this morning, with the one object of seeing you and asking your advice."

"You have done wisely," said my friend. "There are a thousand details which I should desire to know before I decide upon our course of action. Yet we have not a moment to lose. If we were to come to Stoke Moran today, would it be possible for us to see these rooms without the knowledge of your stepfather?"

"As it happens, he spoke of coming into town today upon some most important business. It is probable that he will be away all day, and that there would be nothing to disturb you."

"Excellent. You are not opposed to this trip, Watson?"

"By no means."

"Then we shall both come. What are you going to do yourself?"

"I have one or two things which I would wish to do now that I am in town. But I shall return by the twelve o'clock train, so as to be there in time for your arrival."

"And you may expect us early in the afternoon. I have myself some small business matters to attend to. Will you not wait and breakfast?"

"No, I must go. My heart is lightened already since I have confided my trouble to you. I shall look forward to seeing you again this afternoon." She dropped her thick black veil over her face, and glided from the room.

"And what do you think of it all, Watson?" asked Sherlock Holmes, leaning back in his chair.

"It seems to me to be a most dark and sinister business."

"Dark enough and sinister enough."

"Yet if the lady is correct in saying that the flooring and walls are solid, and that the door and windows were locked, then her sister must have been undoubtedly alone when she met her mysterious end."

"What becomes, then, of those whistles in the night, and what of the very peculiar words of the dying woman?"

"I cannot imagine."

"We have every reason to believe that the doctor has an interest in preventing his stepdaughter's marriage. It is precisely for that reason that we are going to Stoke Moran this day. I want to see whether—but what, in the name of . . . !"

Our door had been suddenly thrown open, and a huge man framed himself in the doorway. He was wearing a black hat and a long dark coat. So tall was he that his hat actually brushed the top of the doorway. His large face turned from one to the other of us, while his eyes blazed with hatred.

"Which of you is Holmes?" asked this figure.

"My name, sir, but you have the advantage over me," said my companion quietly.

"I am Dr. Grimesby Roylott, of Stoke Moran."

"Indeed, Doctor," said Holmes. "Please take a seat."

"I will do nothing of the kind. My stepdaughter has been here. What has she been saying to you?"

"It is a little cold for the time of the year," said Holmes.

"What has she been saying to you?" screamed the man furiously.

"But I have heard that the flowers should do well," continued my companion calmly.

"Ha! You put me off, do you?" said our new visitor, taking a step forward, and shaking his fist. "I know you, you scoundrel! I have heard of you before. You are Holmes the meddler."

My friend smiled.

"Holmes the busybody!"

Holmes chuckled heartily. "Your conversation is most entertaining," said he. "When you go out close the door, for I feel a draft."

"I will go when I have had my say. Don't you dare to meddle with my affairs. I know that Miss Stoner has been here—I traced her! I am a dangerous man to fall foul of. See here!" He stepped swiftly forward, to the fireplace, seized the poker, and bent it into a curve with his huge hands.

"See that you keep yourself out of my grip," he snarled, and hurling the twisted poker into the fireplace, he strode out of the room.

"He seems a very charming and amiable person," said Holmes, laughing. "I am not quite so bulky, but if he had remained I might have shown him that my grip was not much more feeble than his own." As he spoke, Holmes picked up the steel poker, and with a sudden twist straightened it out.

"And now, Watson, we shall order breakfast, and afterwards I shall walk down to the courthouse, where I hope to get some data which may help us in this matter."

It was nearly one o'clock when Sherlock Holmes returned from his excursion. He held in his hand a sheet of blue paper, scrawled over with notes and figures.

"I have seen Mrs. Stoner's will," said he. "Each daughter can claim a very large income on the day she marries. It is evident, therefore, that Dr. Roylott has the very strongest motives for standing in the way of anything of the sort. And now, Watson, this is too serious to waste any time, especially as the man is aware that we are interested in his affairs, so if you are ready we shall call a cab and drive to Waterloo. I should be very much obliged if you would slip your revolver into your pocket. It is an excellent argument with gentlemen who can twist steel pokers into knots. That and a toothbrush are, I think, all that we need."

At Waterloo we were fortunate in catching a train for Leatherhead, where we hired a cab at the station inn, and drove for four or five miles through the lovely Surrey lanes. It was a perfect day, with a bright sun and a few fleecy clouds in the heavens. The trees and flowers were just throwing out their first green shoots, and the air was full of the pleasant smell of the moist earth. My companion sat in front, his arms folded, his hat pulled down over his eyes, buried in the deepest thought. Suddenly, however, he tapped me on the shoulder, and pointed over the meadows.

"Look there!" said he.

A heavily timbered park stretched up in a gentle slope. Then we saw the high roof of a very old mansion.

"Stoke Moran?" said he.

"Yes, sir, that is the house of Dr. Grimesby Roylott," remarked the driver.

We got off, paid our fare, and the cab rattled back on its way to Leatherhead.

"Good afternoon, Miss Stoner. You see that we have been as good as our word."

Our client of the morning had seen us from the window and hurried forward to meet us with a face which spoke her joy. "I have been waiting so eagerly for you," she cried, shaking hands with us warmly. "All has turned out splendidly. Dr. Roylott has gone to town, and it is unlikely that he will be back before evening."

"We have had the pleasure of making the Doctor's acquaintance," said Holmes, and in a few words he sketched out what had occurred.

She cried out, "He has followed me, then!"

"So it appears."

"He is so cunning that I never know when I am safe from him. What will he say when he returns?"

"He must guard himself, for he may find that there is someone more cunning than himself upon his track. Now, we must make the best use of our time, so kindly take us at once to the rooms which we are to examine."

We were quickly led to the three rooms which stood side by side.

"This, I take it, is the room in which you used to sleep, the center one your sister's, and the one next to it Dr. Roylott's?" said Holmes.

"Exactly so. But I am now sleeping in the middle one."

"I understand. By the way, there does not seem to be any very pressing need for repairs in this wing."

"I believe that it was an excuse to move me from my room."

"As you both locked your doors at night, it was impossible to enter your rooms from that side. Now, would you have the kindness to go into your room, and to lock the shutters."

Miss Stoner did so, and Holmes endeavored in every way to force the shutter open, but without success.

"Hmm," said he, scratching his chin, "no one could pass through these shutters if they were bolted. Well, we shall see if anything here throws any light upon the matter."

Holmes examined the chamber in which Miss Stoner was now sleeping, and in which her sister had met her fate. It was a little room, with a low ceiling and a gaping fireplace, after the fashion of old country houses. A brown chest of drawers stood in one corner, a narrow bed in another, and a dressing-table on the left-hand side of the window. These articles, with two small chairs, made up all the furniture in the room, except for a square of carpet in the center. Holmes pulled one of the chairs into a corner and sat silent, while his eyes travelled round and round and up and down, taking in every detail of the apartment.

"Where does that bell go?" he asked at last, pointing to a thick bell rope which hung down beside the bed. The end of it was actually lying upon the pillow.

"It goes to the housekeeper's room. We can ring it to call her."

"It looks newer than the other things."

"Yes, it was only put there a couple of years ago."

"Your sister asked for it, I suppose?"

"No, I never heard of her using it. We used always to get what we wanted for ourselves."

"Indeed, then it seems unnecessary to put a bell rope there. You will excuse me for a few minutes while I satisfy myself as to this floor." He threw himself down upon his face with his magnifying glass in his hand, and crawled swiftly backwards and forwards, examining carefully the cracks between the boards. Finally he walked over to the bed and spent some time in staring at it, and in running his eye up and down the wall. Finally he took the bell rope in his hand and gave it a brisk tug.

"Why, it's a dummy," said he.

"Won't it ring?"

"No, it is not even attached. This is very interesting. You can see now that it is fastened to a hook just above where the little opening of the air ventilator is."

"How very absurd! I never noticed that before," said Miss Stoner.

"Very strange!" muttered Holmes, pulling at the rope. "There are one or two very unusual points about this room. For example, what a fool a builder must be to put an air ventilator in another room, when, with the same trouble, he might have built it so that it would reach the fresh air outside!"

"That is also quite modern," said the lady.

"Done about the same time as the bell rope," remarked Holmes.

"Yes, there were several little changes carried out about that time."

"They seem to have been of a most interesting character—dummy bell ropes and ventilators which do not ventilate. With your permission, Miss Stoner, we shall now carry our research into Dr. Roylott's room."

Dr. Grimesby Roylott's chamber was larger than that of his stepdaughter, but was as plainly furnished. A bed, a small wooden shelf full of books, an armchair beside the bed, a plain wooden chair against the wall, a round table, and a large iron safe were the principal things which met the eye. Holmes walked slowly round and examined each and all of them with the keenest interest.

"What's in here?" he asked, tapping the safe.

"My stepfather's business papers."

"Oh! you have seen inside, then?"

"Only once, some years ago. I remember that it was full of papers."

"There isn't a cat in it, for example?"

"No. What a strange idea!"

"Well, look at this!" He pointed to a small saucer of milk which stood on the top of it.

"No; we don't keep a cat. But there is a cheetah and a baboon."

"Ah, yes, of course! Well, a cheetah is just a big cat, and yet a saucer of milk does not go very far in satisfying its wants, I daresay. There is one point which I should wish to determine." He squatted down in front of the wooden chair, and examined the seat of it with the greatest attention.

"Thank you. That is quite settled," said he, rising. "Hello! Here is something interesting!"

The object which had caught his eye was a small dog leash hung on one corner of the bed. The leash, however, was curled upon itself, and tied so as to make a small, tight loop at the end.

"What do you think about that, Watson?"

"It's a common enough leash. But I don't know why it should be looped at the end."

"That is not quite so common, is it? Ah, me! it's a wicked world, and when a clever man turns his brain to crime it is the worst of all. I think that I have seen enough now, Miss Stoner, and, with your permission, we shall walk out upon the lawn."

I had never seen my friend's face so grim, or his brow so dark, as it was when we turned from the scene of this investigation.

"It is essential, Miss Stoner," said he, finally, "that you should absolutely follow my advice in every respect."

"I shall most certainly do so."

"The matter is too serious for any hesitation. Your life may depend upon it. In the first place, both my friend and I must spend the night in your room."

Both Miss Stoner and I gazed at him in astonishment.

"Yes, it must be so. Let me explain. I believe that that is the village inn over there?"

"Yes, that is the Crown Inn."

"Very good. Your windows would be visible from there?"

"Certainly."

"You must confine yourself to your room, on the pretense of a headache, when your stepfather comes back. Then when you hear him retire for the night, you must open the shutters of your window, put your lighted lamp there as a signal to us, and then leave at once and go into the room which you used to occupy. I have no doubt that, in spite of the repairs, you could manage there for one night."

"Oh, yes, easily."

"The rest you will leave in our hands."

"But what will you do?"

"We shall spend the night in your room, and we shall investigate the cause of this noise which has disturbed you."

"I believe, Mr. Holmes, that you have already made up your mind," said Miss Stoner.

"Perhaps I have."

"Then for pity's sake tell me what was the cause of my sister's death."

"I should prefer to have clearer proof before I speak."

"You can at least tell me whether my own thought is correct, and if she died from some sudden fright."

"No, I do not think so. I think that there was probably some more tangible cause. And now, Miss Stoner, we must leave you, for if Dr. Roylott returned and saw us, our journey would be in vain. Good-bye, and be brave, for if you will do what I have told you, you may rest assured that we shall soon drive away the dangers that threaten you."

Sherlock Holmes and I had no difficulty in engaging a room at the Crown Inn. It was on the top floor, and from our window we could command a good view of Stoke Moran. At dusk we saw Dr. Grimesby Roylott drive past, his huge form looming up beside the little figure of the lad who drove him. The boy had some slight difficulty in undoing the heavy iron gates, and we heard the hoarse roar of the Doctor's voice, and saw the fury with which he shook his clenched fists at him. A few minutes later we saw a sudden light spring up in one of the rooms.

"Do you know, Watson," said Holmes, as we sat together in the gathering darkness, "I really have some concern about your coming with me tonight. There is a distinct element of danger."

"Can I be of assistance?"

"Your presence might be of the greatest value."

"Then I shall certainly come."

"It is very kind of you."

"You speak of danger. You have evidently seen more in those rooms than was visible to me."

"No, but I fancy that I may have deduced a little more. I imagine that you saw all that I did."

"I saw nothing remarkable except the bell rope, although what purpose that could serve, I confess, is more than I can imagine."

"You saw the ventilator, too?"

"Yes, but I do not think that it is such a very unusual thing to have a small opening between two rooms. It was so small that a rat could hardly pass through."

"I knew that we should find a ventilator before ever we came to Stoke Moran."

"My dear Holmes!"

"Oh, yes, I did. You remember in her statement she said that her sister could smell Dr. Roylott's cigar. Now, of course that suggests at once that there must be a common opening between the two rooms. It could only be a very small one, or it would have been discovered by the police. I deduced a ventilator."

"But what harm can there be in that?"

"Well, it is very curious, Watson. A ventilator is made, a bell cord is hung, and a lady who sleeps in the bed dies. Does not that strike you?"

"I cannot as yet see any connection."

"Did you observe anything very peculiar about that bed?"

"No."

"It was nailed to the floor. Did you ever see a bed fastened like that before?"

"I cannot say that I have."

"The lady could not move her bed. It must always be in the same relative position

to the ventilator and the rope—for so we may call it, since it was clearly never meant to be a bell pull."

"Holmes," I cried. "I seem to see dimly what you are hinting at. We are only just in time to prevent some subtle and horrible crime."

"Subtle enough and horrible enough. I think, Watson, that we shall have horrors enough before the night is over, so let us turn our minds for a few hours to something more cheerful."

About nine o'clock the light in the room was extinguished, and all was dark in the direction of Stoke Moran. Two hours passed slowly away, and then, suddenly, just at the stroke of eleven, a single bright light shone out right in front of us.

"That is our signal," said Holmes, springing to his feet; "it comes from the middle window."

A moment later we were out on the dark road, a chill wind blowing in our faces, and one yellow light twinkling in front of us through the gloom to guide us on our somber errand.

Making our way among the trees, we reached the lawn, crossed it, and were about to enter through the window, when out from a clump of bushes there darted what seemed to be a hideous and distorted child, who threw itself on the grass, and then ran swiftly across the lawn into the darkness.

"Holmes," I whispered, "did you see that? What was that?"

Holmes broke into a low laugh, and put his lips to my ear.

"This is a strange household," he murmured. "That is the baboon."

I had forgotten the strange pets which

the Doctor kept. There was a cheetah, too; perhaps we might find it upon our shoulders at any moment. I looked nervously about. A large hawk-like bird soared past the mansion. I confess I felt easier in my mind when we found ourselves inside the bedroom. My companion noiselessly closed the door, moved the lamp onto the table, and cast his eyes round the room. All was as we had seen it in the daytime. Then creeping up to me, he whispered into my ear again so gently that it was all that I could do to distinguish the words:

"The least sound would be fatal to our plans."

I nodded to show that I had heard.

"We must sit without a light. He would see it through the ventilator."

I nodded again.

"Do not go to sleep. Your very life may depend upon it. Have your pistol ready in case we should need it. I will sit on the side of the bed, and you in that chair."

I took out my revolver and laid it on the corner of the table.

Holmes had brought up a long thin cane, and this he placed upon the bed beside him. By it he laid the box of matches and the stump of candle. Then he turned down the lamp and we were left in darkness.

How shall I ever forget that dreadful vigil? I could not hear a sound, not even the drawing of a breath, and yet I knew that my companion sat open-eyed, within a few feet of me, in the same state of nervous tension in which I was myself. We waited in absolute darkness. From outside came the occasional cry of a night-bird, and once, a long drawn cat-like whine, which told us that the cheetah was wandering about. Far away we could hear the deep tones of the church clock, which boomed out every quarter of an hour. How long they seemed, those quarters! Twelve o'clock, and one, and two, and three o'clock, and still we sat waiting silently for whatever might befall.

Suddenly there was the momentary gleam of a light up in the direction of the ventilator, which vanished immediately, but was followed by a strong smell of burning oil and heated metal. Someone in the next room had lit a lantern. I heard a gentle sound of movement, and then all was silent once more, though the smell grew stronger. For half an hour I sat with straining ears. Then suddenly another sound became audible—a very gentle, soothing sound, like that of a small jet of steam escaping continually from a kettle. The instant that we heard it, Holmes sprang from the bed, struck a match, and lashed furiously with his cane at the bell pull.

"You see it, Watson?" he yelled. "You see it?"

But I saw nothing. I had heard a low clear whistle, but could not tell what it was at which my friend lashed so savagely. I could, however, see that his face was deadly pale, and was filled with horror and loathing.

He had ceased to strike, and was gazing up at the ventilator, when suddenly there broke from the silence of the night the most horrible cry to which I have ever listened. It swelled up louder and louder, a hoarse yell of pain and fear and anger all mingled in the one dreadful shriek. They say that down in the village, that cry woke sleepers from their beds. It struck cold to our hearts, and I stood gazing at Holmes, and he at me, until the last echoes of it had died away into the silence from which it rose.

"What can it mean?" I gasped.

"It means that it is all over," Holmes answered. "And perhaps, after all, it is for the best. Take your pistol, and we shall enter Dr. Roylott's room."

With a grave face he lit the lamp, and led the way down the hall. Twice he struck at the chamber door without any reply from within. Then he turned the handle and entered, I at his heels, with the pistol in my hand.

It was a strange sight which met our eyes. On the table stood a dark lantern, throwing a brilliant beam of light upon the iron safe, the door of which was ajar. Beside this table, on the wooden chair, sat Dr. Grimesby Roylott. Across his lap lay the dog leash which we had noticed during the day. His chin was pointed upwards, and his eyes were staring at the corner of the ceiling. Twisted tightly around his forehead was a yellow band with brownish speckles. As we entered he made neither sound nor motion.

"The band! the speckled band!" whispered Holmes.

I took a step forward. In an instant his strange head-band began to move. There arose the diamond-shaped head and puffed neck of a snake.

It is a swamp adder! cried Holmes—"the deadliest snake in India. Dr. Roylott died within ten seconds of being bitten. Let us get this creature back into its den. Then we can alert Miss Stoner, and let the police know what has happened."

As he spoke he drew the dog leash swiftly from the dead man's lap. He threw the noose round the snake's neck, pulled it sharply, and, carrying it at arm's length, thrust it into the iron safe, which he closed upon it.

Such are the facts of the death of Dr. Grimesby Roylott, of Stoke Moran. What I had not yet learned of the case was told me by Sherlock Holmes as we travelled back.

"It became clear to me," said Holmes in the cab, "that whatever danger threatened an occupant of the room could not come either from the window or the door. My attention was speedily drawn, as I have already remarked to you, to the ventilator, and to the bell rope which hung down to the bed. The discovery that this was a dummy, and that the bed was nailed to the floor, instantly gave rise to the suspicion that the rope was there as a bridge for something passing through the hole, and coming to the bed. The idea of a snake instantly occurred to me, and when I coupled it with my knowledge that the Doctor was furnished with a supply of animals from India, I felt that I was probably on the right track. Dr. Roylott was a clever and ruthless man. He knew the snake's poison takes effect immediately and could not possibly be discovered by any chemical test. And it was not likely that anyone would notice the two tiny dark holes where the snake's poisonous fangs had done their work.

"Then I thought of the whistling sound of which both sisters had spoken. Of course, he must call back the snake before the morning light. He had trained it, probably by the use of the milk which we saw, to return to him when he whistled. He would put the snake through the ventilator at the hour that he thought best, with the certainty that it would crawl down the rope, and land on the bed. It might or might not bite the occupant. Perhaps she might escape every night for a week, but sooner or later she must fall a victim.

113

The Adventure of the Speckled Band

"I had come to these conclusions before I ever entered his room. An inspection of his chair showed me that he had been in the habit of standing on it, which, of course, would be necessary in order that he should reach the ventilator. The sight of the safe, the saucer of milk, and the dog leash with the loop convinced me I was right. The sound of banging metal heard by Miss Stoner was obviously caused by her stepfather hastily closing the door of his safe upon the snake. Having once made up my mind, you know the steps which I took in order to put the matter to the proof. I heard the creature hiss, as I have no doubt that you did also, and I instantly lit the light and attacked it with the cane."

"With the result of driving it back through the ventilator."

"And also with the result of causing it to turn upon its master at the other side. Some of the blows of my cane roused its temper, so that it struck the first person it saw. In this way I am no doubt indirectly responsible for Dr. Grimesby Roylott's death, but I cannot say that it is likely to weigh very heavily upon my conscience."

About the Author

Sir Arthur Conan Doyle (1859–1930) was born in Edinburgh, Scotland. He studied medicine at the University of Edinburgh, where he was a student of Dr. Joseph Bell, who used deductive principles (reasoning to draw conclusions) in treating diseases. When Conan Doyle created Sherlock Holmes, generally considered the world's greatest and most famous detective, he had his character Holmes employ the deductive principles that had so impressed Conan Doyle. It is hard to overstate the popularity of Sherlock Holmes. He has appeared in more than fifty short stories and four novels by Conan Doyle, and in stage plays and numerous movies and television programs. When Conan Doyle "killed off" his character Holmes in a story, there was such an uproar by the public that the author was forced to bring Holmes back to life. Many people do not believe that Sherlock Holmes was an imaginary sleuth. They think that he actually lived and that he resided at 221B Baker Street, his home in the stories. Sherlock Holmes is truly one of the most beloved characters in detective fiction.

UNDERSTAND KEY IDEAS AND DETAILS. The following questions help you check your reading comprehension. Put an *x* in the box next to the correct answer.

1. "The Adventure of the Speckled Band" is mainly about
   - ☐ a. the lives of Sherlock Holmes and his devoted friend, Dr. Watson.
   - ☐ b. why a young woman fears for her life.
   - ☐ c. how Sherlock Holmes solves an unusual case.

2. When confronting Holmes and Watson, Dr. Roylott demonstrated that he was
   - ☐ a. both angry and powerful.
   - ☐ b. interested in his stepdaughter's welfare.
   - ☐ c. willing to listen to reason.

3. Holmes dealt with the swamp adder by
   - ☐ a. tying it down while it was drinking milk from a saucer.
   - ☐ b. shooting it with Dr. Watson's revolver.
   - ☐ c. throwing it into an iron safe.

4. Which of the following is *not* an important clue to the solution of the case?
   - ☐ a. a whistling sound
   - ☐ b. a small wooden shelf full of books
   - ☐ c. a bell rope that did not work

NOTE NEW VOCABULARY WORDS. The following questions check your vocabulary skills. Put an *x* in the box next to the correct answer. Each vocabulary word appears in the story.

1. Sherlock Holmes was willing to let Helen Stoner defray his expenses at some time in the future. The word *defray* means
   - ☐ a. pay.
   - ☐ b. be relieved of.
   - ☐ c. ask about.

2. Helen Stoner's mother bequeathed a large sum of money to Dr. Roylott. What is the meaning of the word *bequeathed*?
   - ☐ a. borrowed from
   - ☐ b. desperately needed
   - ☐ c. left or gave to someone in a will

3. Helen was troubled by a feeling of impending doom. Which of the following expressions best defines the word *impending*?
   - ☐ a. unlikely or not probable
   - ☐ b. strangely fascinating
   - ☐ c. about to happen

4. Holmes and Watson never forgot the night of their "dreadful vigil." What is a *vigil*?
   - ☐ a. a remarkable adventure that has an unhappy ending
   - ☐ b. a period of time, often during sleeping hours, when one watches carefully
   - ☐ c. a very dangerous animal

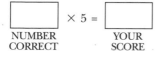

NUMBER CORRECT × 5 = YOUR SCORE

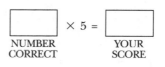

NUMBER CORRECT × 5 = YOUR SCORE

IDENTIFY STORY ELEMENTS. The following questions check your knowledge of story elements. Put an *x* in the box next to each correct answer.

1. Who is the *narrator* of "The Adventure of the Speckled Band"?
   ☐ a. Sherlock Holmes
   ☐ b. Dr. Watson
   ☐ c. Helen Stoner

2. Which of the following statements best *characterizes* Sherlock Holmes?
   ☐ a. Holmes was very intelligent, but he was weak and rather sickly.
   ☐ b. Holmes relied on Dr. Watson to protect him in dangerous situations.
   ☐ c. Holmes had extraordinary powers of observation and the ability to draw accurate conclusions.

3. What was Dr. Roylott's *motive* for murdering Julia Stoner?
   ☐ a. money
   ☐ b. revenge
   ☐ c. hatred

4. The *mood* of the story is best described as
   ☐ a. suspenseful.
   ☐ b. joyous.
   ☐ c. sad.

THINK CRITICALLY ABOUT THE STORY. The following questions check your critical thinking skills. Put an *x* in the box next to each correct answer.

1. If Helen Stoner had not consulted Sherlock Holmes, she most likely would have
   ☐ a. been married in the spring as planned.
   ☐ b. suffered the same terrible fate that her sister experienced.
   ☐ c. managed to block her stepfather's plans.

2. We may infer from this story that Dr. Watson
   ☐ a. followed, and perhaps even studied, the cases of Sherlock Holmes.
   ☐ b. had the same amazing powers of reasoning that Holmes possessed.
   ☐ c. never offered assistance to Holmes.

3. Evidence in the story suggests that the ventilator was added to the room to
   ☐ a. let fresh air flow into the chamber.
   ☐ b. permit the swamp adder to enter.
   ☐ c. make the old house look more modern.

4. We may conclude that the "Speckled Band" referred to in the title was a
   ☐ a. band of vagabonds.
   ☐ b. group of wandering musicians.
   ☐ c. snake.

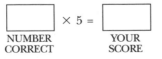

× 5 =

NUMBER CORRECT   YOUR SCORE

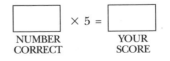

× 5 =

NUMBER CORRECT   YOUR SCORE

STUDY THE **W**RITER'S **C**RAFT. The following questions check your knowledge of skills related to the craft of writing. Put an *x* in the box next to each correct answer. You may refer to pages 4 and 5.

1. Helen told about a night in which she heard a clanging, a crash, and a creaking. This sentence contains
   ☐ a. a metaphor.
   ☐ b. dialogue.
   ☐ c. examples of onomatopoeia.

2. "The trees and flowers were just throwing out their first green shoots, and the air was full of the pleasant smell of the moist earth." This sentence illustrates the author's ability to
   ☐ a. advance the plot rapidly.
   ☐ b. use imagery.
   ☐ c. create interesting characters.

3. Holmes said of Dr. Roylott, "He seems a very charming and amiable person." The quotation
   ☐ a. is ironic and illustrates irony.
   ☐ b. accurately describes Dr. Roylott.
   ☐ c. shows that Holmes badly misjudged Dr. Roylott.

4. Which statement describes how the story is constructed?
   ☐ a. It takes place over the course of an hour or two.
   ☐ b. No conflict is presented.
   ☐ c. It presents unusual objects that are clues to solving the mystery.

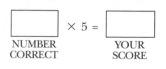

NUMBER
CORRECT

× 5 =

YOUR
SCORE

Questions for Writing and Discussion

- How did Sherlock Holmes know that Helen Stoner had traveled by train and dog-cart? What does this reveal about Holmes?
- Explain in detail why it did not seem possible that someone could have murdered Julia Stoner.
- Why was Dr. Roylott planning to murder Helen Stoner? When did Holmes first become aware that Dr. Roylott might attempt to murder Helen?
- What was the purpose of the bell rope in the room, and why was the bed nailed to the floor?

  See additional questions for extended writing on pages 118 and 119.

Use the boxes below to total your scores for the exercises. Then record your scores on pages 198 and 199.

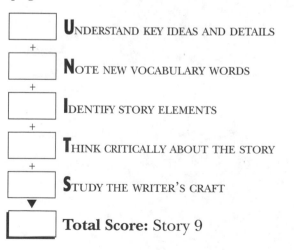

UNDERSTAND KEY IDEAS AND DETAILS

+

NOTE NEW VOCABULARY WORDS

+

IDENTIFY STORY ELEMENTS

+

THINK CRITICALLY ABOUT THE STORY

+

STUDY THE WRITER'S CRAFT

▼

Total Score: Story 9

A Touch of Mystery

Questions for Discussion and Extended Writing

The following questions provide you with opportunities to express your thoughts and feelings about the selections in this unit. Your teacher may assign selected questions. When you write your responses, remember to state your point of view clearly and to support your position by presenting specific details—examples, illustrations, and references drawn from the story and, in some cases, from your life. Organize your writing carefully and check your work for correct spelling, capitalization, punctuation, and grammar.

1. The theme of this unit is "A Touch of Mystery." Briefly explain how each story in the unit is related to this theme.

2. It may be said that clues are the "bricks and mortar" of which mysteries are made. Select two stories in the unit and show how one or more clues in each story prove essential in solving the mystery.

3. Suppose that you are involved in a mystery and that you need a detective. Which detective, from the stories in the unit, would you choose to handle your case? Explain your choice.

4. In "Kim's Game," Nora reflects that "adults are a lot more childish than children in a lot of ways." Do you agree or disagree with that statement? Present reasons to support your opinion.

5. In which story do you think conflict played the most important role? Identify the conflict or conflicts in the story you selected.

6. Select two of the characters in the unit and demonstrate how the characters you chose were successful in overcoming obstacles. Identify the obstacles that the characters faced, as well as the manner in which the characters handled the obstacles. Give titles and authors.

7. Draw upon material found in "The Adventure of the Speckled Band" and "Kim's Game" to write a descriptive essay about the setting or the characters. Give your essay a title.

8. Compare and contrast two of the detectives in the unit. In what ways were they similar? How were they different?

9. "The President Regrets" is the least frightening, or menacing, mystery in the unit. Support this statement in a carefully organized essay that refers to the three stories in the unit. Your essay should have an introduction, a body, and a conclusion.

10. Sherlock Holmes repeatedly gave Helen Stoner excellent advice. Think of a time when someone gave you good advice or a time when you gave good advice to someone. Then write an essay entitled "Good Advice." Describe the person involved, the circumstances related to the advice, and the advice that was given.

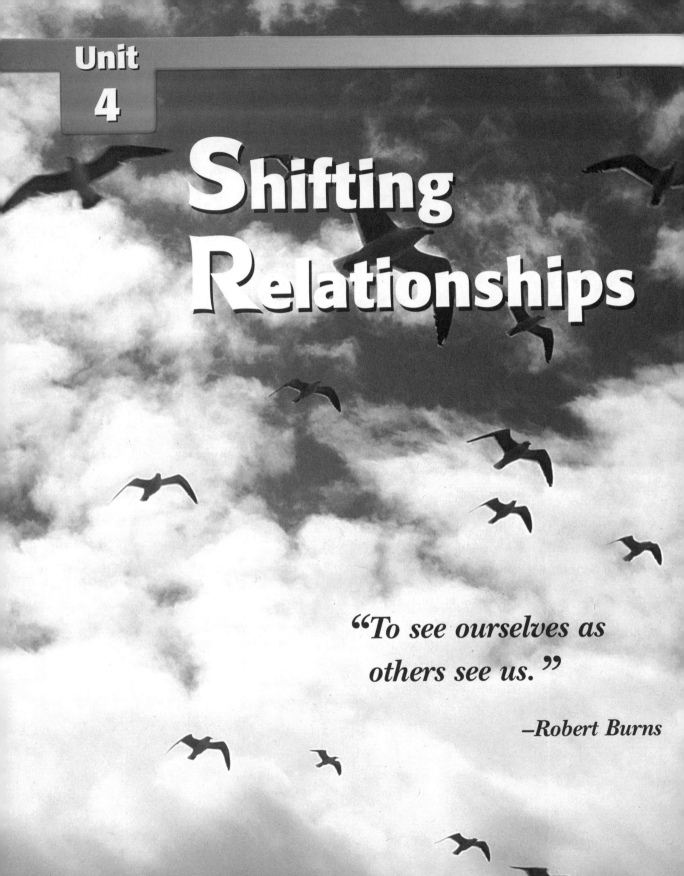

Unit 4

Shifting Relationships

"To see ourselves as others see us."

–Robert Burns

Previewing the Unit

More than two hundred years ago, the Scottish poet Robert Burns lamented in a famous poem the fact that we do not have the power "To see ourselves as others see us." How we see others and how they see us—and the shifting relationships involved—are what this unit is about.

THE TREASURE OF LEMON BROWN In Walter Dean Myers's "The Treasure of Lemon Brown," we meet Greg, a sensitive fourteen-year-old boy whose mood at the beginning of the story is mirrored in the "angry, swirling clouds" that fill the sky. Two days before, Greg had an upsetting incident with his father. During the course of the story, a chance encounter with Lemon Brown, an elderly homeless man, gives Greg the "food for thought" that provides the basis for what may lead to a shift in the relationship between Greg and his father. Like the best of stories, "The Treasure of Lemon Brown" preaches nothing but says a lot.

MOTHER AND DAUGHTER Gary Soto's "Mother and Daughter" tells of the sometimes uneasy, bittersweet relationship between Mrs. Moreno and her daughter, Yollie. Like most of Soto's work, the story combines touches of sadness with humor, in a way that is at once recognizable and real. You will probably enjoy "Mother and Daughter," and you will almost certainly find that the characters are completely believable.

SOMEBODY'S SON The summer that he was eighteen years old, Richard Pindell left home to travel across the country "to find my place in the world." From that journey of personal discovery emerged "Somebody's Son," one of today's finest short stories. "Somebody's Son" is highly autobiographical. According to the author, "I understand that 'Somebody's Son' is going to appear in a unit called 'Shifting Relationships.' I think that that's absolutely appropriate."

SUNDAY IN THE PARK Bel Kaufman has written many hilarious works. But there is nothing funny about "Sunday in the Park." What begins as a pleasant outing in a park ends with an emotional outburst so fierce that the words shock even the character who utters them. Sometimes all kinds of feelings lie hidden beneath the surface, and an upsetting incident can suddenly send them surging up from the deep.

Notice how experiences influence the characters, and how changing outlooks shape their "Shifting Relationships."

They were dangerous and coming closer and closer, and they had just
one thing on their minds—to steal . . .

The Treasure of Lemon Brown

by Walter Dean Myers

The dark sky, filled with angry, swirling clouds, reflected Greg Ridley's mood as he sat on the stoop of his building. His father's voice came to him again, first reading the letter the principal had sent to the house, then lecturing endlessly about his poor efforts in math.

"I had to leave school when I was thirteen," his father had said, "that's a year younger than you are now. If I'd had half the chances that you have, I'd . . ."

Greg had sat in the small, pale green kitchen listening, knowing the lecture would end with his father saying he couldn't play ball with the Scorpions. He had asked his father the week before, and his father had said it depended on his next report card. It wasn't often the Scorpions took on new players, especially fourteen-year-olds, and this was a chance of a lifetime for Greg. He hadn't been allowed to play high-school ball, which he had really wanted to do, but playing for the Community Center team was

the next best thing. Report cards were due in a week, and Greg had been hoping for the best. But the principal had ended the suspense early when she sent that letter saying Greg would probably fail math if he didn't spend more time studying.

"And you want to play *basketball*?" His father's brows knitted over deep brown eyes. "That must be some kind of a joke. Now you just get into your room and hit those books."

That had been two nights before. His father's words, like the distant thunder that now echoed through the streets of Harlem, still rumbled softly in his ears.

It was beginning to cool. Gusts of wind made bits of paper dance between the parked cars. There was a flash of nearby lightning, and soon large drops of rain splashed onto his jeans. He stood to go upstairs, thought of the lecture that probably awaited him if he did anything except shut himself in his room with his math book, and started walking down the street instead.

The Treasure of Lemon Brown

Down the block there was an old tenement that had been abandoned for some months. Some of the guys had held an impromptu checker tournament there the week before, and Greg had noticed that the door, once boarded over, had been slightly ajar.

Pulling his collar up as high as he could, he checked for traffic and made a dash across the street. He reached the house just as another flash of lightning changed the night to day for an instant, then returned the graffiti-scarred building to the grim shadows. He vaulted over the outer stairs and pushed tentatively on the door. It was open, and he let himself in.

The inside of the building was dark except for the dim light that filtered through the dirty windows from the streetlamps. There was a room a few feet from the door, and from where he stood at the entrance, Greg could see a squarish patch of light on the floor. He entered the room, frowning at the musty smell. It was a large room that might have been someone's parlor at one time. Squinting, Greg could see an old table on its side against one wall, what looked like a pile of rags or a torn mattress in the corner, and a couch, with one side broken, in front of the window.

He went to the couch. The side that wasn't broken was comfortable enough, though a little creaky. From this spot he could see the blinking neon sign over the bodega[1] on the corner. He sat a while, watching the sign blink first green then red, allowing his mind to drift to the Scorpions, then to his father. His father had been a postal worker for all Greg's life, and was proud of it, often telling Greg how hard he

had worked to pass the test. Greg had heard the story too many times to be interested now.

For a moment Greg thought he heard something that sounded like a scraping against the wall. He listened carefully, but it was gone.

Outside the wind had picked up, sending the rain against the window with a force that shook the glass in its frame. A car passed, its tires hissing over the wet street and its red tail lights glowing in the darkness.

Greg thought he heard the noise again. His stomach tightened as he held himself still and listened intently. There weren't any more scraping noises, but he was sure he had heard something in the darkness—something breathing!

He tried to figure out just where the breathing was coming from; he knew it was in the room with him. Slowly he stood, tensing. As he turned, a flash of lightning lit up the room, frightening him with its sudden brilliance. He saw nothing, just the overturned table, the pile of rags and an old newspaper on the floor. Could he have been imagining the sounds? He continued listening, but heard nothing and thought that it might have just been rats. Still, he thought, as soon as the rain let up he would leave. He went to the window and was about to look out when he heard a voice behind him.

"Don't try nothin' 'cause I got a razor here sharp enough to cut a week into nine days!"

Greg, except for an involuntary tremor in his knees, stood stock still. The voice was high and brittle, like dry twigs being broken, surely not one he had ever heard before. There was a shuffling sound as the person

---

1. **bodega:** a neighborhood grocery store

who had been speaking moved a step closer. Greg turned, holding his breath, his eyes straining to see in the dark room.

The upper part of the figure before him was still in darkness. The lower half was in the dim rectangle of light that fell unevenly from the window. There were two feet, in cracked, dirty shoes from which rose legs that were wrapped in rags.

"Who are you?" Greg hardly recognized his own voice.

"I'm Lemon Brown," came the answer. "Who're you?"

"Greg Ridley."

"What you doing here?" The figure shuffled forward again, and Greg took a small step backward.

"It's raining," Greg said.

"I can see that," the figure said.

The person who called himself Lemon Brown peered forward, and Greg could see him clearly. He was an old man. His black, heavily wrinkled face was surrounded by a halo of crinkly white hair and whiskers that seemed to separate his head from the layers of dirty coats piled on his smallish frame. His pants were bagged to the knee, where they were met with rags that went down to the old shoes. The rags were held on with strings, and there was a rope around his middle. Greg relaxed. He had seen the man before, picking through the trash on the corner and pulling clothes out of a Salvation Army box. There was no sign of the razor that could "cut a week into nine days."

"What are you doing here?" Greg asked.

"This is where I'm staying," Lemon Brown said. "What you here for?"

"Told you it was raining out," Greg said, leaning against the back of the couch until he felt it give slightly.

"Ain't you got no home?"

"I got a home," Greg answered.

"You ain't one of them bad boys looking for my treasure, is you?" Lemon Brown cocked his head to one side and squinted one eye. "Because I told you I got me a razor."

"I'm not looking for your treasure," Greg answered, smiling. "*If* you have one."

"What you mean, *if* I have one," Lemon Brown said. "Every man got a treasure. You don't know that, you must be a fool!"

"Sure," Greg said as he sat on the sofa and put one leg over the back. "What do you have, gold coins?"

"Don't worry none about what I got," Lemon Brown said. "You know who I am?"

"You told me your name was orange or lemon or something like that."

"Lemon Brown," the old man said, pulling back his shoulders as he did so, "they used to call me Sweet Lemon Brown."

"Sweet Lemon?" Greg asked.

"Yessir. Sweet Lemon Brown. They used to say I sung the blues so sweet that if I sang at a funeral, the dead would commence to rocking with the beat. Used to travel all over Mississippi and as far as Monroe, Louisiana, and east on over to Macon, Georgia. You mean you ain't never heard of Sweet Lemon Brown?"

"Afraid not," Greg said. "What . . . what happened to you?"

"Hard times, boy. Hard times always after a poor man. One day I got tired, sat down to rest a spell and felt a tap on my shoulder. Hard times caught up with me."

"Sorry about that."

"What you doing here? How come you didn't go on home when the rain come. Rain don't bother you young folks none."

"Just didn't," Greg looked away.

"I used to have a knotty-headed boy just like you." Lemon Brown had half walked, half shuffled back to the corner and sat down against the wall. "Had them big eyes like you got. I used to call them moon eyes. Look into them moon eyes and see anything you want."

"How come you gave up singing the blues?" Greg asked.

"Didn't give it up," Lemon Brown said. "You don't give up the blues; they give you up. After a while you do good for yourself, and it ain't nothing but foolishness singing about how hard you got it. Ain't that right?"

"I guess so."

"What's that noise?" Lemon Brown asked, suddenly sitting upright.

Greg listened, and he heard a noise outside. He looked at Lemon Brown and saw the old man was pointing toward the window.

Greg went to the window and saw three men, neighborhood thugs, on the stoop. One was carrying a length of pipe. Greg looked back toward Lemon Brown, who moved quietly across the room to the window. The old man looked out, then beckoned frantically for Greg to follow him. For a moment Greg couldn't move. Then he found himself following Lemon Brown into the hallway and up darkened stairs. Greg followed as closely as he could. They reached the top of the stairs, and Greg felt Lemon Brown's hand first lying on his shoulder, then probing down his arm until he finally took Greg's hand into his own as they crouched in the darkness.

"They's bad men," Lemon Brown whispered. His breath was warm against Greg's skin.

"Hey! Rag man!" A voice called. "We know you in here. What you got up under them rags? You got any money?"

Silence.

"We don't want to have to come in and hurt you, old man, but we don't mind if we have to."

Lemon Brown squeezed Greg's hand in his own hard, gnarled fist.

There was a banging downstairs and a light as the men entered. They banged around noisily, calling for the rag man.

"We heard you talking about your treasure," the voice was slurred. "We just want to see it, that's all."

"You sure he's here?" One voice seemed to come from the room with the sofa.

"Yeah, he stays here every night."

"There's another room over there; I'm going to take a look. You got that flashlight?"

"Yeah, here, take the pipe too."

Greg opened his mouth to quiet the sound of his breath as he sucked it in uneasily. A beam of light hit the wall a few feet opposite him, then went out.

"Ain't nobody in that room," a voice said. "You think he gone or something?"

"I don't know," came the answer. "All I know is that I heard him talking about some kind of treasure. You know they found that shopping bag lady with that money in her bags."

"Yeah. You think he's upstairs?"

"HEY, OLD MAN, ARE YOU UP THERE?"

Silence.

"Watch my back, I'm going up."

There was a footstep on the stairs, and the beam from the flashlight danced crazily along the peeling wallpaper. Greg held his breath. There was another step and a loud crashing noise as the man banged the pipe against the wooden banister. Greg could feel his temples throb as the man slowly neared them. Greg thought about the pipe, wondering what he would do when the man reached them—what he *could* do.

Then Lemon Brown released his hand and moved toward the top of the stairs. Greg looked around and saw stairs going up to the next floor. He tried waving to Lemon Brown, hoping the old man would see him in the dim light and follow him to the next floor. Maybe, Greg thought, the man wouldn't follow them up there. Suddenly, though, Lemon Brown stood at the top of the stairs, both arms raised high above his head.

"There he is!" A voice cried from below.

"Throw down your money, old man, so I won't have to bash your head in!"

Lemon Brown didn't move. Greg felt himself near panic. The steps came closer, and still Lemon Brown didn't move. He was an eerie[2] sight, a bundle of rags standing at the top of the stairs, his shadow on the wall looming over him. Maybe, the thought came to Greg, the scene could be even eerier.

Greg wet his lips, put his hands to his mouth and tried to make a sound. Nothing came out. He swallowed hard, wet his lips once more and howled as evenly as he could.

"What's that?"

As Greg howled, the light moved away from Lemon Brown, but not before Greg saw him hurl his body down the stairs at the men who had come to take his treasure. There was a crashing noise, and then footsteps. A rush of warm air came in as the downstairs door opened, then there was

2. **eerie:** causing fear or dread

only an ominous silence.

Greg stood on the landing. He listened, and after a while there was another sound on the staircase.

"Mr. Brown?" he called.

"Yeah, it's me," came the answer. "I got their flashlight."

Greg exhaled in relief as Lemon Brown made his way slowly back up the stairs.

"You O.K.?"

"Few bumps and bruises," Lemon Brown said.

"I think I'd better be going," Greg said, his breath returning to normal. "You'd better leave, too, before they come back."

"They may hang around outside for a while," Lemon Brown said, "but they ain't getting their nerve up to come in here again. Not with crazy old rag men and howling spooks. Best you stay awhile till the coast is clear. I'm heading out West tomorrow, out to east St. Louis."

"They were talking about treasures," Greg said. "You *really* have a treasure?"

"What I tell you? Didn't I tell you every man got a treasure?" Lemon Brown said. "You want to see mine?"

"If you want to show it to me," Greg shrugged.

"Let's look out the window first, see what them scoundrels be doing," Lemon Brown said.

They followed the oval beam of the flashlight into one of the rooms and looked out the window. They saw the men who had tried to take the treasure sitting on the curb near the corner. One of them had his pants leg up, looking at his knee.

"You sure you're not hurt?" Greg asked Lemon Brown.

"Nothing that ain't been hurt before,"

127

Lemon Brown said. "When you get as old as me all you say when something hurts is, 'Howdy, Mr. Pain, sees you back again.' Then when Mr. Pain see he can't worry you none, he go on mess with somebody else."

Greg smiled.

"Here, you hold this." Lemon Brown gave Greg the flashlight.

He sat on the floor near Greg and carefully untied the strings that held the rags on his right leg. When he took the rags away, Greg saw a piece of plastic. The old man carefully took off the plastic and unfolded it. He revealed some yellowed newspaper clippings and a battered harmonica.

"There it be," he said, nodding his head. "There it be."

Greg looked at the old man, saw the distant look in his eye, then turned to the clippings. They told of Sweet Lemon Brown, a blues singer and harmonica player who was appearing at different theaters in the South. One of the clippings said he had been the hit of the show, although not the headliner. All of the clippings were reviews of shows Lemon Brown had been in more than 50 years ago. Greg looked at the harmonica. It was dented badly on one side, with the reed holes on one end nearly closed.

"I used to travel around and make money for to feed my wife and Jesse—that's my boy's name. Used to feed them good, too. Then his mama died, and he stayed with his mama's sister. He growed up to be a man, and when the war come he saw fit to go off and fight in it. I didn't have nothing to give him except these things that told him who I was, and what he come from. If you know your pappy did something, you know you can do something too.

"Anyway, he went off to war, and I went

off still playing and singing. 'Course by then I wasn't as much as I used to be, not without somebody to make it worth the while. You know what I mean?"

"Yeah," Greg nodded, not quite really knowing.

"I traveled around, and one time I come home, and there was this letter saying Jesse got killed in the war. Broke my heart, it truly did.

"They sent back what he had with him over there, and what it was is this old mouth fiddle and these clippings. Him carrying it around with him like that told me it meant something to him. That was my treasure, and when I give it to him he treated it just like that, a treasure. Ain't that something?"

"Yeah, I guess so," Greg said.

"You *guess* so?" Lemon Brown's voice rose an octave as he started to put his treasure back into the plastic. "Well, you got to guess 'cause you sure don't know nothing. Don't know enough to get home when it's raining."

"I guess . . . I mean, you're right."

"You O.K. for a youngster," the old man said as he tied the strings around his leg, "better than those scalawags what come here looking for my treasure. That's for sure."

"You really think that treasure of yours was worth fighting for?" Greg asked. "Against a pipe?"

"What else a man got 'cepting what he can pass on to his son, or his daughter, if she be his oldest?" Lemon Brown said. "For a big-headed boy you sure do ask the foolishest questions."

Lemon Brown got up after patting his rags in place and looked out the window again.

"Looks like they're gone. You get on out of here and get yourself home. I'll be watching from the window so you'll be all right."

Lemon Brown went down the stairs behind Greg. When they reached the front door the old man looked out first, saw the street was clear and told Greg to scoot on home.

"You sure you'll be O.K.?" Greg asked.

"Now didn't I tell you I was going to east St. Louis in the morning?" Lemon Brown asked. "Don't that sound O.K. to you?"

"Sure it does," Greg said. "Sure it does. And you take care of that treasure of yours."

"That I'll do," Lemon said, the wrinkles about his eyes suggesting a smile. "That I'll do."

The night had warmed and the rain had stopped, leaving puddles at the curbs. Greg didn't even want to think how late it was. He thought ahead of what his father would say and wondered if he should tell him about Lemon Brown. He thought about it until he reached his stoop, and decided against it. Lemon Brown would be O.K., Greg thought, with his memories and his treasure.

Greg pushed the button over the bell marked Ridley, thought of the lecture he knew his father would give him, and smiled.

About the Author

Walter Dean Myers (1937–) was born in Martinsburg, West Virginia. He was one of eight children. After his mother died when he was three years old, Myers was raised by friends of the family in Harlem, New York. Myers loved Harlem, and it became the setting for most of his short stories. Myers began to write fiction on a regular basis, beginning at about the age of ten. He won literary contests, and some of his short stories were published. He had to work at a variety of jobs until he was able to establish himself as a full-time writer. Since 1975, Myers has written more than 25 books, most of them for young adults. He has won two Newbery Awards and four Coretta Scott King Awards. He has also written numerous short stories, many of which appear in collections such as *We Must See: Young Black Storytellers*.

UNDERSTAND KEY IDEAS AND DETAILS. The following questions help you check your reading comprehension. Put an *x* in the box next to the correct answer.

1. Which of the following best describes what the story is mainly about?
   ☐ a. neighborhood thugs
   ☐ b. the plight of homeless people
   ☐ c. the relationship between fathers and sons

2. Greg thought his father would not let him play basketball for the Scorpions because his father
   ☐ a. didn't think that Greg was good enough to make the team.
   ☐ b. wanted Greg to spend more time studying math.
   ☐ c. was afraid that Greg might injure himself.

3. What happened to Lemon Brown's son?
   ☐ a. He was killed in the war.
   ☐ b. He gained fame by singing and playing the blues.
   ☐ c. He got into an argument with his father, and they drifted apart.

4. What were the treasures that Lemon Brown showed Ridley?
   ☐ a. bags of gold
   ☐ b. newspaper clippings and a battered harmonica
   ☐ c. coins and bills that were hidden under the old man's rags

NOTE NEW VOCABULARY WORDS. The following questions check your vocabulary skills. Put an *x* in the box next to the correct answer. Each vocabulary word appears in the story.

1. There were no plans for the contest; it took place on an impromptu basis. The word *impromptu* means
   ☐ a. after much thought and planning.
   ☐ b. with the help of dozens of very talented people.
   ☐ c. without previous thought or preparation.

2. The walls of the old building were scarred with graffiti. Which of the following best defines the word *graffiti?*
   ☐ a. writing or drawings that are scribbled or scratched on a surface
   ☐ b. beautiful pictures painted long ago
   ☐ c. charts and diagrams that are difficult to read

3. Greg had never been in the house, so he pushed on the door tentatively. What does *tentatively* mean?
   ☐ a. happily
   ☐ b. hesitantly
   ☐ c. angrily

4. He was scared; his knees gave "an involuntary tremor," or shaking. The word *involuntary* means
   ☐ a. very painful.
   ☐ b. done on purpose.
   ☐ c. not done willingly.

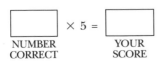

NUMBER CORRECT × 5 = YOUR SCORE

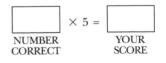

NUMBER CORRECT × 5 = YOUR SCORE

IDENTIFY STORY ELEMENTS. The following questions check your knowledge of story elements. Put an *x* in the box next to each correct answer.

1. What is the *setting* of "The Treasure of Lemon Brown"?
   ☐ a. Mr. Ridley's office
   ☐ b. the kitchen of Greg Ridley's apartment
   ☐ c. an old tenement

2. Which sentence best *characterizes* Mr. Ridley?
   ☐ a. He was a harsh, cruel man who did not care about his son.
   ☐ b. He was determined that his son do well in school.
   ☐ c. He was a wealthy person who lived a life of leisure.

3. Of these events, which happened last in the *plot* of the story?
   ☐ a. Lemon Brown removed rags from his leg and unfolded plastic.
   ☐ b. Greg found shelter from the storm in a building.
   ☐ c. Lemon Brown hurled his body at the men who were coming after him.

4. Which statement best expresses the *theme* of the story?
   ☐ a. Each person's life is a treasure.
   ☐ b. Some people do not really have a place to call home.
   ☐ c. Obtaining a good education is extremely important.

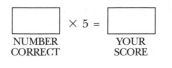

NUMBER CORRECT   × 5 =   YOUR SCORE

THINK CRITICALLY ABOUT THE STORY. The following questions check your critical thinking skills. Put an *x* in the box next to each correct answer.

1. It is likely that Lemon Brown did not
   ☐ a. enjoy the time he spent with Greg Ridley.
   ☐ b. have a very sharp razor that he used as a weapon.
   ☐ c. know how to play the harmonica.

2. Lemon Brown suggested that the most important thing a man has is
   ☐ a. the ability to buy expensive items.
   ☐ b. the knowledge that he has never cheated others.
   ☐ c. something he can pass on to his son or daughter.

3. Lemon Brown's treasure was actually
   ☐ a. his fond memories.
   ☐ b. the many friends who helped him.
   ☐ c. the money he was paid during the years he was a performer.

4. At the conclusion of the story, Greg knew that he would receive a lecture because
   ☐ a. he had not spent time studying that evening.
   ☐ b. he received a lecture every night.
   ☐ c. his father had said earlier that he would speak to Greg that night.

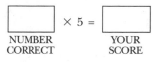

NUMBER CORRECT   × 5 =   YOUR SCORE

STUDY THE WRITER'S CRAFT. The following questions check your knowledge of skills related to the craft of writing. Put an *x* in the box next to each correct answer. You may refer to pages 4 and 5.

1. The author writes of "angry" clouds and of hard times that gave Lemon Brown "a tap" on his shoulder. These are examples of
   ☐ a. dialect.
   ☐ b. onomatopoeia.
   ☐ c. personification.

2. "The voice was high and brittle, like dry twigs being broken." What is true of this sentence?
   ☐ a. It illustrates conflict.
   ☐ b. It contains a simile.
   ☐ c. It provides an example of foreshadowing.

3. The expressions "the distant thunder . . . rumbled" and "tires hissing over the wet street" are
   ☐ a. metaphors.
   ☐ b. similes.
   ☐ c. examples of onomatopoeia.

4. Lemon Brown's "treasure" is a symbol that stands for, or represents,
   ☐ a. riches or great wealth.
   ☐ b. whatever is most meaningful to a person.
   ☐ c. information or knowledge.

Questions for Writing and Discussion

- Why didn't Mr. Ridley permit Greg to play basketball for the team? Do you agree with Mr. Ridley's decision? Explain your answer.
- Lemon Brown said, "If you know your pappy did something, you know you can do something too." Why was that significant to Greg?
- Lemon Brown and his son shared the same treasure. What lesson could this shared treasure provide for Greg?
- At the end of the story, Greg "thought of the lecture he knew his father would give him, and smiled." Why did Greg smile? What has caused this change in him?

See additional questions for extended writing on pages 156 and 157.

Use the boxes below to total your scores for the exercises. Then record your scores on pages 198 and 199.

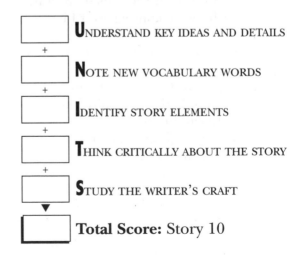

☐ **U**NDERSTAND KEY IDEAS AND DETAILS
+
☐ **N**OTE NEW VOCABULARY WORDS
+
☐ **I**DENTIFY STORY ELEMENTS
+
☐ **T**HINK CRITICALLY ABOUT THE STORY
+
☐ **S**TUDY THE WRITER'S CRAFT
▼
☐ **Total Score:** Story 10

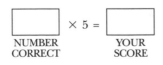

☐ × 5 = ☐

NUMBER   YOUR
CORRECT   SCORE

Life takes unusual twists and turns in the relationship between a . . .

Mother and Daughter

by Gary Soto

Yollie's mother, Mrs. Moreno, was a large woman who wore a muu-muu[1] and butterfly-shaped glasses. She liked to water her lawn in the evening and wave at low-riders, who would stare at her behind their smoky sunglasses and laugh. Now and then a low-rider from Belmont Avenue would make his car jump and shout *"Mamacita!"* But most of the time they just stared and wondered how she got so large.

Mrs. Moreno had a strange sense of humor. Once, Yollie and her mother were watching a late-night movie called *They Came to Look.* It was about creatures from the underworld who had climbed through molten lava to walk the earth. But Yollie, who had played soccer all day with the kids next door, was too tired to be scared. Her eyes closed but sprang open when her mother screamed, "Look, Yollie! Oh, you missed a scary part. The guy's face was all ugly!"

But Yollie couldn't keep her eyes open. They fell shut again and stayed shut, even when her mother screamed and slammed a heavy palm on the arm of her chair.

---

1. **muu-muu:** a long, loose-fitting dress

"Mom, wake me up when the movie's over so I can go to bed," mumbled Yollie.

"OK, Yollie, I wake you," said her mother through a mouthful of popcorn.

But after the movie ended, instead of waking her daughter, Mrs. Moreno laughed under her breath, turned the TV and lights off, and tiptoed to bed. Yollie woke up in the middle of the night and didn't know where she was. For a moment she thought she was dead. Maybe something from the underworld had lifted her from her house and carried her into the earth's belly. She blinked her sleepy eyes, looked around at the darkness, and called, "Mom? Mom, where are you?" But there was no answer, just the throbbing hum of the refrigerator.

Finally, Yollie's grogginess cleared, and she realized her mother had gone to bed, leaving her on the couch. Another of her little jokes.

But Yollie wasn't laughing. She tiptoed into her mother's bedroom with a glass of water and set it on the night stand next to the alarm clock. The next morning, Yollie woke to screams. When her mother reached to turn off the alarm, she had overturned the glass of water.

Yollie burned her mother's morning toast and gloated. "Ha! Ha! I got you back. Why did you leave me on the couch when I told you to wake me up?"

Despite their jokes, mother and daughter usually got along. They watched bargain matinees together and played croquet[2] in the summer and checkers in the winter. Mrs. Moreno encouraged Yollie to study hard because she wanted her daughter to

be a doctor. She bought Yollie a desk, a typewriter, and a lamp that cut glare so her eyes would not grow tired from hours of studying.

Yollie was slender as a tulip, pretty, and one of the smartest kids at Saint Theresa's. She was captain of the crossing guards, an altar girl, and a whiz in the school's monthly spelling bees.

"Tienes que estudiar mucho," Mrs. Moreno said every time she propped her work-weary feet on the hassock. "You have to study a lot, then you can get a good job and take care of me."

"Yes, Mama," Yollie would respond, her face buried in a book. If she gave her mother any sympathy, she would begin her stories about how she had come with her family from Mexico with nothing on her back but a sack with three skirts, all of which were too large by the time she crossed the border because she had lost weight from not having enough to eat.

Everyone thought Yollie's mother was a riot. Even the nuns laughed at her antics. Her brother Raul, a nightclub owner, thought she was funny enough to go into show business.

But there was nothing funny about Yollie needing a new outfit for the eighth-grade fall dance. They couldn't afford one. It was late October, with Christmas around the corner, and their dented Chevy Nova had gobbled up almost one hundred dollars in repairs.

"We don't have the money," said her mother, genuinely sad because they couldn't buy the outfit, even though there was a little money stashed away for college. Mrs. Moreno remembered her teenage years and her hard-working parents, who

---

2. **croquet:** an outdoor game in which players hit wooden balls through a series of wire hoops

picked grapes and oranges and chopped beets and cotton for meager pay around Kerman. Those were the days when "new clothes" meant limp and out-of-style dresses from Saint Vincent de Paul.[3]

The best Mrs. Moreno could do was buy Yollie a pair of black shoes with velvet bows and fabric dye to color her white summer dress black.

"We can color your dress so it will look brand-new," her mother said brightly, shaking the bottle of dye as she ran hot water into a plastic dish tub. She poured the black liquid into the tub and stirred it with a pencil. Then, slowly and carefully, she lowered the dress into the tub.

Yollie couldn't stand to watch. She knew it wouldn't work. It would be like the time her mother stirred up a batch of molasses for candy apples on Yollie's birthday. She'd dipped the apples into the goo and swirled them and seemed to taunt Yollie by singing *Las Mañanitas* to her. When she was through, she set the apples on wax paper. They were hard as rocks and hurt the kids' teeth. Finally, they had a contest to see who could break the apples open by throwing them against the side of the house. The apples shattered like grenades, sending the kids scurrying for cover, and in an odd way the birthday party turned out to be a success. At least everyone went home happy.

To Yollie's surprise, the dress came out shiny black. It looked brand-new and sophisticated, like what people in New York wear. She beamed at her mother, who hugged Yollie and said, "See, what did I tell you?"

The dance was important to Yollie because she was in love with Ernie Castillo, the third-best speller in the class. She bathed, dressed, did her hair and nails, and primped until her mother yelled, "All right already." Yollie sprayed her neck and wrists with Mrs. Moreno's Avon perfume and bounced into the car.

Mrs. Moreno let Yollie out in front of the school. She waved and told her to have a good time but behave herself, then roared off, blue smoke trailing from the tail pipe of the old Nova.

Yollie ran into her best friend, Janice. They didn't say it, but each thought the other was the most beautiful girl at the dance; the boys would fall over themselves asking them to dance.

The evening was warm but thick with clouds. Gusts of wind picked up the paper lanterns hanging in the trees and swung them, blurring the night with reds and yellows. The lanterns made the evening seem romantic, like a scene from a movie. Everyone danced, sipped punch, and stood in knots of threes and fours, talking. Sister Kelly got up and jitterbugged[4] with some kid's father. When the record ended, students broke into applause.

Janice had her eye on Frankie Ledesma, and Yollie, who kept smoothing her dress down when the wind picked up, had her eye on Ernie. It turned out that Ernie had his mind on Yollie, too. He ate a handful of cookies nervously, then asked her for a dance.

"Sure," she said, nearly throwing herself into his arms.

3. **Saint Vincent de Paul:** a charity that sells used items

4. **jitterbugged:** danced in a fast, lively style that first became popular in the 1940s

Mother and Daughter

They danced two fast ones before they got a slow one. As they circled under the lanterns, rain began falling, lightly at first. Yollie loved the sound of the raindrops ticking against the leaves. She leaned her head on Ernie's shoulder, though his sweater was scratchy. He felt warm and tender. Yollie could tell that he was in love, and with her, of course. The dance continued successfully, romantically, until it began to pour.

"Everyone, let's go inside—and, boys, carry in the table and the record player," Sister Kelly commanded.

The girls and boys raced into the cafeteria. Inside, the girls, drenched to the bone, hurried to the restrooms to brush their hair and dry themselves. One girl cried because her velvet dress was ruined. Yollie felt sorry for her and helped her dry the dress off with paper towels, but it was no use. The dress was ruined.

Yollie went to a mirror. She looked a little gray now that her mother's makeup had washed away but not as bad as some of the other girls. She combed her damp hair, careful not to pull too hard. She couldn't wait to get back to Ernie.

Yollie bent over to pick up a bobby pin, and shame spread across her face. A black puddle was forming at her feet. Drip, black drip. Drip, black drip. The dye was falling from her dress like black tears. Yollie stood up. Her dress was now the color of ash. She looked around the room. The other girls, unaware of Yollie's problem, were busy grooming themselves. What could she do? Everyone would laugh. They would know she dyed an old dress because she couldn't afford a new one. She hurried from the restroom with her head down, across the cafeteria floor and out the door. She raced through the storm, crying as the rain mixed with her tears and ran into twig-choked gutters.

When she arrived home, her mother was on the couch eating cookies and watching TV.

"How was the dance, *m'ija?* Come watch the show with me. It's really good."

Yollie stomped, head down, to her bedroom. She undressed and threw the dress on the floor.

Her mother came into the room. "What's going on? What's all this racket, baby?"

"The dress. It's cheap! It's no good!" Yollie kicked the dress at her mother and watched it land in her hands. Mrs. Moreno studied it closely but couldn't see what was wrong. "What's the matter? It's just a little bit wet."

"The dye came out, that's what."

Mrs. Moreno looked at her hands and saw the grayish dye puddling in the shallow lines of her palms. Poor baby, she thought, her brow darkening as she made a sad face. She wanted to tell her daughter how sorry she was, but she knew it wouldn't help. She walked back to the living room and cried.

The next morning, mother and daughter stayed away from each other. Yollie sat in her room turning the pages of an old *Seventeen*, while her mother watered her plants with a Pepsi bottle.

"Drink, my children," she said loud enough for Yollie to hear. She let the water slurp into pots of coleus and cacti. "Water is all you need. My daughter needs clothes, but I don't have no money."

Yollie tossed her *Seventeen* on her bed. She was embarrassed at last night's tirade. It wasn't her mother's fault that they were poor.

When they sat down together for lunch, they felt awkward about the night before. But

Mrs. Moreno had made a fresh stack of tortillas and cooked up a pan of *chile verde*, and that broke the ice. She licked her thumb and smacked her lips.

"You know, honey, we gotta figure a way to make money," Yollie's mother said. "You and me. We don't have to be poor. Remember the Garcias. They make this stupid little tool that fixes cars. They moved away because they're rich. That's why we don't see them no more."

"What can we make?" asked Yollie. She took another tortilla and tore it in half.

"Maybe a screwdriver that works on both ends? Something like that." The mother looked around the room for ideas but then shrugged. "Let's forget it. It's better to get an education. If you get a good job and have spare time, then maybe you can invent something." She rolled her tongue over her lips and cleared her throat. "The county fair hires people. We can get a job there. It will be here next week."

Yollie hated the idea. What would Ernie say if he saw her pitching hay at the cows? How could she go to school smelling like an armful of chickens? "No, they wouldn't hire us," she said.

The phone rang. Yollie lurched from her chair to answer it, thinking it would be Janice wanting to know why she had left. But it was Ernie wondering the same thing. When he found out she wasn't mad at him, he asked if she would like to go to a movie.

"I'll ask," Yollie said, smiling. She covered the phone with her hand and counted to ten. She uncovered the receiver and said, "My mom says it's OK. What are we going to see?"

After Yollie hung up, her mother climbed, grunting, onto a chair to reach the top shelf in the hall closet. She wondered why she hadn't done it earlier. She reached behind a stack of towels and pushed her chubby hand into the cigar box where she kept her secret stash of money.

"I've been saving a little every month," said Mrs. Moreno. "For you, *m'ija.*" Her mother held up five twenties, a blossom of green that smelled sweeter than flowers on that Saturday. They drove to Macy's and bought a blouse, shoes, and a skirt that would not bleed in rain or any other kind of weather.

About the Author

Gary Soto (1952–) has written many stories that deal with the lives and experiences of Mexican Americans. The setting is often Fresno, California, where Soto was born. Soto graduated with honors from California State University, continued his schooling, and currently teaches English and Chicano studies at the University of California. Soto's first book of poems, *The Elements of San Joaquin,* won the United States Award of the International Poetry Forum in 1976. Since then, Soto has written many more volumes of poetry, as well as stories, novels, essays, picture books, and several plays. He is best known, however, for short stories written for and about young adults. Among his most popular collections are *Local News* and *Baseball in April and Other Stories.*

UNDERSTAND KEY IDEAS AND DETAILS. The following questions help you check your reading comprehension. Put an *x* in the box next to the correct answer.

1. This story is mainly about how a mother and daughter
   ☐ a. figure out ways to make money.
   ☐ b. take turns preparing meals for each other.
   ☐ c. deal with a variety of situations.

2. Yollie's dress was ruined when
   ☐ a. someone spilled soda on it.
   ☐ b. rain caused the dye in it to run.
   ☐ c. her mother's makeup washed away and caused stains.

3. Ernie telephoned, and he expressed surprise that she
   ☐ a. had left the dance.
   ☐ b. was willing to go to a movie with him.
   ☐ c. needed her mother's permission to go on a date.

4. At the end of the story, what did Mrs. Moreno buy for Yollie?
   ☐ a. a desk, a typewriter, and a lamp
   ☐ b. a pair of black shoes with velvet bows
   ☐ c. a blouse, shoes, and a skirt

NOTE NEW VOCABULARY WORDS. The following questions check your vocabulary skills. Put an *x* in the box next to the correct answer. Each vocabulary word appears in the story.

1. Mrs. Moreno had a strange sense of humor, but everyone laughed at her antics. Which of the following best defines the word *antics?*
   ☐ a. people who are friends
   ☐ b. a way of dressing
   ☐ c. behavior best described as wildly funny or "clowning around"

2. She stashed away some money for Yollie's college education. The word *stashed* means
   ☐ a. put away.
   ☐ b. borrowed.
   ☐ c. earned.

3. The dress was shiny and black and looked "brand-new and sophisticated." As used here, the word *sophisticated* means
   ☐ a. ugly or unattractive.
   ☐ b. very stylish or fashionable.
   ☐ c. previously worn.

4. After screaming at her mother, Yollie was embarrassed by her tirade. What is the meaning of the word *tirade?*
   ☐ a. entertaining or amusing remarks
   ☐ b. words that express approval
   ☐ c. an angry, scolding speech

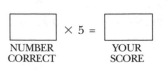

NUMBER CORRECT × 5 = YOUR SCORE

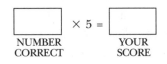

NUMBER CORRECT × 5 = YOUR SCORE

IDENTIFY STORY ELEMENTS. The following questions check your knowledge of story elements. Put an *x* in the box next to each correct answer.

1. Who is the *narrator* of "Mother and Daughter"?
   ☐ a. Yollie
   ☐ b. Mrs. Moreno
   ☐ c. the writer of the story

2. Which statement best *characterizes* Mrs. Moreno?
   ☐ a. She loved Yollie and wanted her to be successful.
   ☐ b. She fought with Yollie all the time and never had fun with her.
   ☐ c. Like her daughter, she was slender and pretty.

3. Of these events, which happened first in the *plot* of the story?
   ☐ a. Mrs. Moreno took five twenty-dollar bills from a cigar box.
   ☐ b. Yollie put a glass of water next to her mother's alarm clock.
   ☐ c. Mrs. Moreno dyed Yollie's dress black.

4. What was the author's *purpose* in writing the story?
   ☐ a. to convince or persuade
   ☐ b. to shock or surprise
   ☐ c. to entertain

THINK CRITICALLY ABOUT THE STORY. The following questions check your critical thinking skills. Put an *x* in the box next to each correct answer.

1. Evidence in the story indicates that Mrs. Moreno thought that the best way for her daughter to get ahead in life was by
   ☐ a. leaving school and getting a job.
   ☐ b. obtaining a good education.
   ☐ c. marrying a wealthy man.

2. Probably, Yollie waited ten seconds before accepting a date with Ernie because she
   ☐ a. had to ask her mother for permission to go out with him.
   ☐ b. was so surprised that she had to stop to catch her breath.
   ☐ c. didn't want Ernie to know that she was eager to accept.

3. Which one of the following statements is *not* true?
   ☐ a. Yollie thought getting a job at the county fair was a good idea.
   ☐ b. Yollie was one of the smartest students at her school.
   ☐ c. Yollie and her mother usually got along.

4. The ending suggests that Mrs. Moreno
   ☐ a. no longer cared about Yollie's future.
   ☐ b. wanted to give her daughter something sooner rather than later.
   ☐ c. was convinced that she and Yollie would eventually become rich.

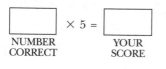

NUMBER CORRECT × 5 = YOUR SCORE

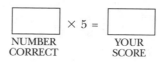

NUMBER CORRECT × 5 = YOUR SCORE

139

STUDY THE WRITER'S CRAFT. The following questions check your knowledge of skills related to the craft of writing. Put an *x* in the box next to each correct answer. You may refer to pages 4 and 5.

1. "The dye was falling from her dress like black tears." This sentence
   ☐ a. is an example of onomatopoeia.
   ☐ b. illustrates characterization.
   ☐ c. contains a simile.

2. "Gusts of wind picked up the paper lanterns hanging in the trees and swung them, blurring the night with reds and yellows." Since this sentence appeals to our senses, it
   ☐ a. is an example of imagery.
   ☐ b. foreshadows how the story will end.
   ☐ c. establishes the mood of the story.

3. The five twenty-dollar bills were "a blossom of green." This statement contains
   ☐ a. a metaphor.
   ☐ b. a simile.
   ☐ c. alliteration.

4. Which sentence does not contain a simile?
   ☐ a. "Yollie was slender as a tulip."
   ☐ b. "For a moment she thought she was dead."
   ☐ c. "The apples shattered like grenades."

Questions for Writing and Discussion

- Describe the jokes that the mother and daughter played on each other.
- Mrs. Moreno and Yollie did a number of things together. Name as many as you can.
- Explain why Yollie rushed home from the dance. Do you think she did the right thing by leaving, or should she have stayed? Give reasons to support your answer.
- Why do you think Mrs. Moreno decided to buy Yollie some new clothes at the end of the story?

See additional questions for extended writing on pages 156 and 157.

Use the boxes below to total your scores for the exercises. Then record your scores on pages 198 and 199.

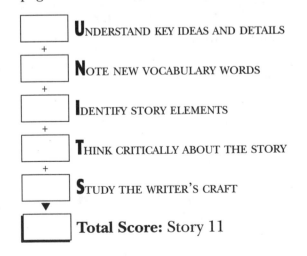

☐ UNDERSTAND KEY IDEAS AND DETAILS
+
☐ NOTE NEW VOCABULARY WORDS
+
☐ IDENTIFY STORY ELEMENTS
+
☐ THINK CRITICALLY ABOUT THE STORY
+
☐ STUDY THE WRITER'S CRAFT
▼
☐ **Total Score:** Story 11

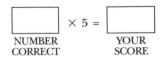

☐ × 5 = ☐
NUMBER CORRECT   YOUR SCORE

He realized just how important it was for him to be . . .

Somebody's Son

by Richard Pindell

He sat, washed up on the side of the highway, a slim, sun-beaten driftwood of a youth. He was hunched on his strapped-together suitcase, chin on hands, elbows on knees, staring down the road. Not a car was in sight. But for him, the dead, still Dakota plains were empty.

Now he was eager to write that letter he had kept putting off. Somehow, writing it would be almost like having company.

He unstrapped his suitcase and fished out of the pocket on the underside of the lid a small, unopened package of stationery. Sitting down in the gravel of the roadside, he closed the suitcase and used it as a desk.

141

Dear Mom,

If Dad will permit it, I would like to come home. I know there's little chance he will. I'm not going to kid myself. I remember he said once, if I ever ran off, I might as well keep on going.

All I can say is that I felt leaving home was something I had to do. Before even considering college, I wanted to find out more about life and about me and the best way for us (life and me) to live with each other. Please tell Dad—and I guess this'll make him sore all over again—I'm still not certain that college is the answer for me. I think I'd like to work for a time and think it over.

You won't be able to reach me by mail, because I'm not sure where I'll be next. But in a few days I hope to be passing by our place. If there's any chance Dad will have me back, please ask him to tie a white cloth to the apple tree in the south pasture—you know the one, the Grimes Golden beside the tracks. I'll be going by on the train. If there's no cloth on the tree I'll just quietly, and without any hard feelings toward Dad—I mean that—keep on going.

    Love, David

The sunset that evening was a violent one. Jagged clouds, trapped in cross-currents, rammed each other like primitive men-of-war and burst into flames, burning one by one into deep purple ash.

It made the boy sad to see the sun go down. He had learned that always at the moment when darkness prevails, loneliness draws closer.

A series of headlights made a domino of the highway. High beams flickered over him curiously. He put out his thumb almost hesitantly, wishing he didn't have to emerge so suddenly, so menacingly. One by one, the cars passed him, their back draft slapping him softly, insultingly, on the cheek.

Much later, turning woodenly to gaze after a car, he saw the glow of taillights intensify. Brakes squealed. The car careened wildly to a stop, and he was running down the road to capture it, his breath rushing against his upturned collar and the taillights glowing nearer as in a dream.

A door was flung open like a friendly arm reaching out to a tired swimmer. "Hop in, boy."

It was a gruff, outdoors voice. "I pretty near missed you. You ain't easy to see out there."

"Thanks, mister."

"Forget it. I used to hitchhike a lot myself when I was a kid."

"How far are you going?" asked David.

The man named a small place in Iowa, about two hundred miles away. David settled back in anticipation of a good ride.

"Where you headin'?" the man asked him.

David glanced at him. His nose was big and jutting; his mouth, wide and gentle. His was a face formed without beauty—and without hesitation. He had a tough-friendly way of accepting David as a man, something which David was still young enough to appreciate as a fine luxury.

The boy looked out on the highway with affection. It would be a good ride with a good companion. "Home," he said with a grin. "I'm heading home."

The man heard the smile in the boy's voice and chuckled. "That's a good feelin', ain't it? Where 'bouts?"

"Maryland. We have a farm about thirty miles outside of Baltimore."

"Where you been?"

"West Coast, Canada, a little of Mexico."

"And now you're hightailin' for home, huh?" There was a note in the man's voice as if this were a pattern he understood intimately.

"Yes, sir."

David smiled wryly to himself, remembering another day. It was in the San Joaquin Valley. He was picking grapes. As usual, the sun ruled mercilessly. Grape leaves drooped. Pickers were hunched over in varying attitudes of defense, some with bandannas covering the backs of their necks. Even the dirt had sagged beneath the blazing heat, crumbling into limp, heavy powder.

David looked down at his feet plowing through the grayish stuff. For four hours now it seemed he had not raised his eyes from his feet. He stopped abruptly and looked back down the row, measuring his progress. He had gone maybe fifty yards.

The faint clink of scissors landing in his half-filled basket came to him and then the foreman was bawling at him, "Hey! Where do you think you're going? It ain't lunchtime yet!" David stared at his feet and the dust; and his feet were stretching out as far as they could reach, his fist was tight around the handle of his suitcase, and the dust swirling madly behind him. He didn't even stop to pick up his money.

When he reached the highway and the cars kept passing him, it was all he could do to keep from jumping out in front of them to make them stop.

"Yeah," the driver was saying now, "I know how it is." The corners of his eyes crinkled as if he were going to smile, but he didn't. "I was out on that same old road when I was a kid. Bummin' around. Lettin' no grass grow under me. Sometimes wishin' it would."

"And then, afterward," David asked, "did you go back home?"

"Nope. I didn't have no home to go back to, like you do. The road was my only home. Lost my ma and pa when I was a little kid. Killed in a car wreck."

"That's rough," David said with such feeling the man glanced at him sharply.

The boy was staring into the night. The man shifted his grip on the wheel, deftly straddling a dead jack rabbit. He spoke softly to the boy as if he were aware he was interrupting important thoughts. "Bet you could do with some sleep."

"You sure you won't be needing me later to help keep you awake?" David asked.

"Don't worry 'bout me none. I like drivin' at night. You just lean back there and help yourself."

"Well, okay," David said. "Thanks."

Sometime later, he was awakened by a sharp decrease in speed. They were entering a town. He sat up and jerked the letter out of his jacket pocket. He had almost forgotten.

"Excuse me, sir, but would you mind stopping at a mailbox so I can mail this? I want to make sure that it gets home before I do."

"Course not," the man said. "Here's one comin' up now." He pulled over to the curb and stopped.

When the boy got back in, the man smiled kindly. "Bet your folks'll be tickled to hear from you."

"I hope so, sir." David tilted his head back and closed his eyes.

The next day, rides were slow. They were what David called "farmer rides," a few miles here, a couple of miles there, with long waits in between.

Toward nightfall, he forsook the unfriendly asphalt and swung onto a panting, slow-moving freight aimed stolidly east. As the train rumbled laboriously over the Mississippi, a few drops of rain slapped the metal floor of his gondola car, and then, suddenly, he was surrounded by water, the river beneath him, and everywhere else, walls of rain. He crawled into a corner and huddled under some scraps of heavy paper that had been used to wrap freight.

For thirty miles, the rain pounded him, slashing his paper hut to tatters and turning his clothes into puddles of mush.

As, cold and wet, he swayed with the motion of the car, his last seven months haunted him. A spinning constellation of faces, flaring up and dying away, careened toward him. Faces of truck drivers, waitresses, salesmen, cops, employment agents, winos, tramps, cowboys, bartenders. Faces of people who had been kind to him; faces of people who had used him. They went on and on.

Well, he would never see them again. He had experienced them quickly, dazedly, as they had experienced him. He had no idea where they were now, and they did not know where he was.

Finally the rain stopped. He lunged erect, inviting the warm, night air to dry him. He looked out over the top of his racketing steel box. He faced east—toward home. They didn't have any idea where he was, either.

The train was hammering along beside a highway. He stared at the houses on the other side. How would it be at home? Would his house be like that one, the one with the porch light burning? Or would it be like that one, where the porch was dark and where over each of the lighted windows a yellow shade was pulled down firmly to the sill?

A couple of days later, in the middle of Maryland, maddeningly close to home, the flow of rides narrowed to a trickle and then ceased altogether. When cars weren't in sight, he walked. After a while, he didn't even bother to stop and hold out his thumb. Furiously, he walked.

Later, seated on the passenger train—the only freights around here ran at night—he wished with slow, frightened heartbeats that he were back on the road, headed the other way.

Three inches from his nose was the dust-stained window through which in a few minutes he would look out across his father's fields. Two different pictures tortured him—the tree with the white cloth and the tree without it. His throat closed and he could hardly breathe.

He tried to fortify himself with the idea that whether or not he still was welcome, at least he would see the place again.

The field was sliding closer, one familiar landmark at a time. He couldn't stop the train. The frenzied wheels were stamping out the end of the crescendo that had begun with the clink of the scissors in his half-filled basket of grapes. Nothing could postpone the denouement[1] now. The tree was around the next bend.

He couldn't look. He was too afraid the cloth would not be there—too afraid he would find, staring back at him, just another

---

1. **denouement:** the ending or final outcome

tree, just another field, just another somebody else's strange place, the way it always is on the long, long road, the nameless staring back at the nameless. He jerked away from the window.

Desperately, he nudged the passenger beside him. "Mister, will you do me a favor? Around this bend on the right, you'll see an apple tree. I wonder if you'll tell me if you see a white cloth tied to one of its branches?"

As they passed the field, the boy stared straight ahead. "Is it there?" he asked with an uncontrollable quaver.

"Son," the man said in a voice slow with wonder, "I see a white cloth tied on almost every twig."

About the Author

Richard Pindell was born in Baltimore, Maryland, and studied at Yale University, where he received a Ph.D. in English. He currently teaches at Binghampton University, where his specialty is the novel and creative writing. He is also a Civil War expert. Pindell has written articles, short stories, and two novels. "Somebody's Son" is based on "a true-life experience, hitchhiking and hopping freights from the Canadian Rockies to Pierre, South Dakota, one summer." The rebellious Pindell had just graduated from high school and wanted "to be on my own without any help from anyone else." Like David, the young man in the story heading back toward Baltimore, Pindell actually wrote a letter home, and so vividly remembers the events that he "can still see the headlights on the highway at Pierre, today." "Somebody's Son" has appeared in many anthologies and is, according to the writer, "far and away my most popular story."

UNDERSTAND KEY IDEAS AND DETAILS. The following questions help you check your reading comprehension. Put an *x* in the box next to the correct answer.

1. What is "Somebody's Son" mainly about?
   - ☐ a. the difficulties one encounters in hitchhiking
   - ☐ b. a young man who heads home in hope of being accepted
   - ☐ c. life on a farm outside Baltimore

2. The purpose of David's letter was
   - ☐ a. to announce that he was coming home, regardless of how his parents felt about that.
   - ☐ b. to say he would never return home.
   - ☐ c. to find out whether his father would allow him to come home.

3. What did David appreciate about the first driver who gave him a lift?
   - ☐ a. The driver accepted David as a man.
   - ☐ b. Although the driver came from a humble background, he was now worth a fortune.
   - ☐ c. The driver didn't want to talk, so David could sit back and relax.

4. At the end of the story, what did the passenger see on the apple tree?
   - ☐ a. twigs and branches, but no piece of white cloth
   - ☐ b. a single piece of white cloth on a branch
   - ☐ c. a white cloth tied on almost every twig

NOTE NEW VOCABULARY WORDS. The following questions check your vocabulary skills. Put an *x* in the box next to the correct answer. Each vocabulary word appears in the story.

1. "Brakes squealed. The car careened wildly to a stop." The word *careened* means
   - ☐ a. crashed.
   - ☐ b. failed or was unable.
   - ☐ c. swerved.

2. "David smiled wryly to himself," thinking about the unpleasant incident. As used in this sentence, the word *wryly* means
   - ☐ a. unable to remember.
   - ☐ b. in a kind of mocking, humorous manner.
   - ☐ c. filled with great joy.

3. The driver deftly swung the wheel to avoid hitting something on the road. What is the meaning of the word *deftly*?
   - ☐ a. quickly and skillfully
   - ☐ b. stupidly or foolishly
   - ☐ c. carelessly or thoughtlessly

4. The train's wheels started with a low sound and ended in a crescendo of noise. The word *crescendo* means
   - ☐ a. the screeching of a whistle.
   - ☐ b. a gradual increase in loudness.
   - ☐ c. a platform or station.

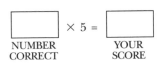

NUMBER CORRECT × 5 = YOUR SCORE

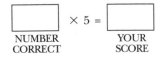

NUMBER CORRECT × 5 = YOUR SCORE

IDENTIFY STORY ELEMENTS. The following questions check your knowledge of story elements. Put an *x* in the box next to each correct answer.

1. The *setting* of "Somebody's Son" is
   ☐ a. a farm near Baltimore.
   ☐ b. Canada and the West Coast.
   ☐ c. highways and rails between the Dakotas and Maryland.

2. It is clear from David's letter that there was *conflict* between
   ☐ a. David and his father.
   ☐ b. David and his mother.
   ☐ c. David and his teachers.

3. Of these events, which happened last in the *plot* of the story?
   ☐ a. The driver stopped to let David mail a letter.
   ☐ b. David asked the man sitting next to him to look at the apple tree.
   ☐ c. David thought about a blazing hot day in the San Joaquin Valley.

4. The *mood* of the story is best described as
   ☐ a. mysterious.
   ☐ b. humorous.
   ☐ c. serious.

THINK CRITICALLY ABOUT THE STORY. The following questions check your critical thinking skills. Put an *x* in the box next to each correct answer.

1. It is reasonable to infer that David
   ☐ a. started college and then dropped out.
   ☐ b. graduated from high school before the story began.
   ☐ c. will never go to college.

2. The fact that David wrote the letter to his mother suggests that
   ☐ a. his mother was able to read much better than his father.
   ☐ b. he had a more comfortable relationship with his mother than with his father.
   ☐ c. his father seldom opened the mail.

3. We may conclude that David asked the passenger to look at the tree because
   ☐ a. David could not see very well.
   ☐ b. David didn't care very much about what was on the tree.
   ☐ c. the situation was such an emotional one for him.

4. We may infer that the tree was covered with white cloths because David's parents
   ☐ a. wanted to make sure that he knew how much they wanted him back.
   ☐ b. were not sure about their feelings toward David.
   ☐ c. thought that the tree looked attractive decorated that way.

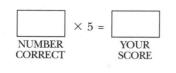

NUMBER CORRECT   × 5 =   YOUR SCORE

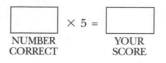

NUMBER CORRECT   × 5 =   YOUR SCORE

STUDY THE WRITER'S CRAFT. The following questions check your knowledge of skills related to the craft of writing. Put an *x* in the box next to each correct answer. You may refer to pages 4 and 5.

1. Since "Somebody's Son" is based on events that took place in the writer's life, the story
   ☐ a. is autobiographical.
   ☐ b. is a biography.
   ☐ c. does not contain a main character.

2. The statement "The highway was a domino of headlights" is
   ☐ a. a simile.
   ☐ b. a metaphor.
   ☐ c. an example of onomatopoeia.

3. "As usual, the sun ruled mercilessly." This sentence provides an example of
   ☐ a. alliteration.
   ☐ b. conflict.
   ☐ c. personification.

4. During the story, the writer presents an event—David's experience picking grapes—that occurred at an earlier time. This is known as
   ☐ a. foreshadowing.
   ☐ b. imagery.
   ☐ c. a flashback.

Questions for Writing and Discussion

- About how old do you think David was? Explain how you arrived at your answer.
- David and his father obviously disagreed about college. What do you believe each person thought? Who do you think was right? Explain why.
- Why do you think David decided to go home?
- How do we know that David's family was eager to have David come back? Why do you think David's father changed his mind about his son?

See additional questions for extended writing on pages 156 and 157.

Use the boxes below to total your scores for the exercises. Then record your scores on pages 198 and 199.

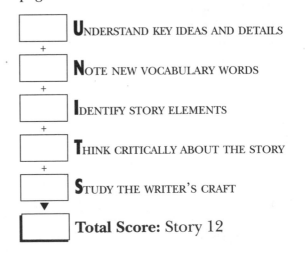

	UNDERSTAND KEY IDEAS AND DETAILS
+	NOTE NEW VOCABULARY WORDS
+	IDENTIFY STORY ELEMENTS
+	THINK CRITICALLY ABOUT THE STORY
+	STUDY THE WRITER'S CRAFT
▼	**Total Score:** Story 12

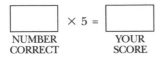

	× 5 =	
NUMBER CORRECT		YOUR SCORE

Tension suddenly erupts in what starts out as a pleasant . . .

Sunday
IN THE
Park

by Bel Kaufman

It was still warm in the late-afternoon sun, and the city noises came muffled through the trees in the park. She put her book down on the bench, removed her sunglasses, and sighed contentedly. Morton was reading the *Times Magazine* section, one arm flung around her shoulder; their three-year-old son, Larry, was playing in the sandbox: a faint breeze fanned her hair softly against her cheek. It was five-thirty of a Sunday afternoon, and the small playground, tucked away in a corner of the park, was all but deserted. The swings and seesaws stood

149

motionless and abandoned, the slides were empty, and only in the sandbox two little boys squatted diligently side by side. *How good this is,* she thought, and almost smiled at her sense of well-being. They must go out in the sun more often; Morton was so city-pale, cooped up all week inside the gray factorylike university. She squeezed his arm affectionately and glanced at Larry, delighting in the pointed little face frowning in concentration over the tunnel he was digging. The other boy suddenly stood up and with a quick, deliberate swing of his chubby arm threw a spadeful of sand at Larry. It just missed his head. Larry continued digging; the boy remained standing, shovel raised, stolid[1] and impassive.

"No, no, little boy." She shook her finger at him, her eyes searching for the child's mother or nurse. "We mustn't throw sand. It may get in someone's eyes and hurt. We must play nicely in the nice sandbox." The boy looked at her in unblinking expectancy. He was about Larry's age but perhaps ten pounds heavier, a husky little boy with none of Larry's quickness and sensitivity in his face. Where was his mother? The only other people left in the playground were two women and a little girl on roller skates leaving now through the gate, and a man on a bench a few feet away. He was a big man, and he seemed to be taking up the whole bench as he held the Sunday comics close to his face. She supposed he was the child's father. He did not look up from his comics, but spat once deftly out of the corner of his mouth. She turned her eyes away.

At that moment, as swiftly as before, the fat little boy threw another spadeful of sand

at Larry. This time some of it landed on his hair and forehead. Larry looked up at his mother, his mouth tentative; her expression would tell him whether to cry or not.

Her first instinct was to rush to her son, brush the sand out of his hair, and punish the other child, but she controlled it. She always said that she wanted Larry to learn to fight his own battles.

"Don't *do* that, little boy," she said sharply, leaning forward on the bench. "You mustn't throw sand!"

The man on the bench moved his mouth as if to spit again, but instead he spoke. He did not look at her, but at the boy only.

"You go right ahead, Joe," he said loudly. "Throw all you want. This here is a *public* sandbox."

She felt a sudden weakness in her knees as she glanced at Morton. He had become aware of what was happening. He put his *Times* down carefully on his lap and turned his fine, lean face toward the man, smiling the shy, apologetic smile he might have offered a student in pointing out an error in his thinking. When he spoke to the man, it was with his usual reasonableness.

"You're quite right," he said pleasantly, "but just because this is a public place. . . ."

The man lowered his funnies and looked at Morton. He looked at him from head to foot, slowly and deliberately. "Yeah?" His insolent voice was edged with menace. "My kid's got just as good right here as yours, and if he feels like throwing sand, he'll throw it, and if you don't like it, you can take your kid the hell out of here."

The children were listening, their eyes and mouths wide open, their spades forgotten in small fists. She noticed the muscle in Morton's jaw tighten. He was

---

1. **stolid:** without emotion

rarely angry; he seldom lost his temper. She was suffused[2] with a tenderness for her husband and an impotent rage against the man for involving him in a situation so alien and so distasteful to him.

"Now, just a minute," Morton said courteously, "you must realize. . . ."

"Aw, shut up," said the man.

Her heart began to pound. Morton half rose; the *Times* slid to the ground. Slowly the other man stood up. He took a couple of steps toward Morton, then stopped. He flexed his great arms, waiting. She pressed her trembling knees together. Would there be violence, fighting? How dreadful, how incredible. . . . She must do something, stop them, call for help. She wanted to put her hand on her husband's sleeve, to pull him down, but for some reason she didn't.

Morton adjusted his glasses. He was very pale. "This is ridiculous," he said unevenly. "I must ask you. . . ."

"Oh, yeah?" said the man. He stood with his legs spread apart, rocking a little, looking at Morton with utter scorn. "You and who else?"

For a moment the two men looked at each other nakedly. Then Morton turned his back on the man and said quietly, "Come on, let's get out of here." He walked awkwardly, almost limping with self-consciousness, to the sandbox. He stooped and lifted Larry and his shovel out.

At once Larry came to life; his face lost its rapt expression and he began to kick and cry. "I don't *want* to go home, I want to play better, I don't *want* any supper, I don't *like* supper. . . ." It became a chant as they walked, pulling their child between them, his

2. **suffused:** filled with

feet dragging on the ground. In order to get to the exit gate they had to pass the bench where the man sat sprawling again. She was careful not to look at him. With all the dignity she could summon, she pulled Larry's sandy, perspiring little hand, while Morton pulled the other. Slowly and with head high she walked with her husband and child out of the playground.

Her first feeling was one of relief that a fight had been avoided, that no one was hurt. Yet beneath it there was a layer of something else, something heavy and inescapable. She sensed that it was more than just an unpleasant incident, more than defeat of reason by force. She felt dimly it had something to do with her and Morton, something acutely personal, familiar, and important.

Suddenly Morton spoke. "It wouldn't have proved anything."

"What?" she asked.

"A fight. It wouldn't have proved anything beyond the fact that he's bigger than I am."

"Of course," she said.

"The only possible outcome," he continued reasonably, "would have been— what? My glasses broken, perhaps a tooth or two replaced, a couple of days' work missed—and for what? For justice? For truth?"

"Of course," she repeated. She quickened her step. She wanted only to get home and to busy herself with her familiar tasks; perhaps then the feeling, glued like heavy plaster on her heart, would be gone. *Of all the stupid, despicable bullies,* she thought, pulling harder on Larry's hand. The child was still crying. Always before she had felt a tender pity for his defenseless little body, the frail arms, the narrow shoulders with sharp, winglike shoulder blades, the thin and unsure legs, but now her mouth tightened in resentment.

"Stop crying," she said sharply. "I'm ashamed of you!" She felt as if all three of them were tracking mud along the street. The child cried louder.

If there had been an issue involved, she thought, *if there had been something to fight for. . . . But what else could he possibly have done? Allow himself to be beaten? Attempt to educate the man? Call a policeman? "Officer, there's a man in the park who won't stop his child from throwing sand on mine. . . ."* The whole thing was as silly as that, and not worth thinking about.

"Can't you keep him quiet, for Pete's sake?" Morton asked irritably.

"What do you suppose I've been trying to do?" she said.

Larry pulled back, dragging his feet.

"If you can't discipline this child, I will," Morton snapped, making a move toward the boy.

But her voice stopped him. She was shocked to hear it, thin and cold and penetrating with contempt. "Indeed?" she heard herself say. "You and who else?"

About the Author

Bel Kaufman's experiences during a 20-year career as a teacher in New York City high schools led her to write *Up the Down Staircase,* a best-selling novel that was made into a popular movie. Kaufman was born in Berlin, Germany, and raised in Russia. She came to the United States at the age of 12. She received a B.A. at Hunter College and an M.A. at Columbia University. Kaufman's works include a novel, *Love, Etc.,* articles, lyrics for musicals, and a number of short stories, of which "Sunday in the Park" is the best known. The author is a popular public speaker who lectures about humor, education, and her grandfather, Sholem Aleichem, a famous writer whose amusing tales of the Yiddish-speaking Jews of Eastern Europe were adapted into a popular Broadway musical, *Fiddler on the Roof.*

UNDERSTAND **K**EY **I**DEAS AND **D**ETAILS. The following questions help you check your reading comprehension. Put an *x* in the box next to the correct answer.

1. "Sunday in the Park" is mainly about
   - ☐ a. how an incident in a park brings a wife's emotions to the surface.
   - ☐ b. the need for people to learn how to live in peace.
   - ☐ c. why young people need the protection of adults.

2. When Morton lifted his son out of the sandbox, Larry
   - ☐ a. readily agreed to go home.
   - ☐ b. asked his mother what to do.
   - ☐ c. complained loudly about leaving.

3. Joe's father said that Joe might throw sand if he wanted to because
   - ☐ a. Joe loved to throw sand.
   - ☐ b. Joe was bigger than the other boy.
   - ☐ c. the sandbox was a public place.

4. At the end of the story, the wife
   - ☐ a. helped her husband discipline their child.
   - ☐ b. challenged her husband.
   - ☐ c. looked for a police officer.

NOTE **N**EW **V**OCABULARY **W**ORDS. The following questions check your vocabulary skills. Put an *x* in the box next to the correct answer. Each vocabulary word appears in the story.

1. The boys in the sandbox were diligently digging "side by side." The word *diligently* means
   - ☐ a. industriously and steadily.
   - ☐ b. foolishly or in a silly manner.
   - ☐ c. sadly or sorrowfully.

2. Joe stood without moving or showing any emotion; he was impassive. Which of the following best defines the word *impassive?*
   - ☐ a. too young to talk
   - ☐ b. not interested in anything
   - ☐ c. not expressing any feelings

3. "At once Larry came to life; his face lost its rapt expression." What is the meaning of the word *rapt?*
   - ☐ a. lively
   - ☐ b. very deep in thought
   - ☐ c. shocked or surprised

4. She believed that the man was a despicable bully. When you think someone is *despicable,* you
   - ☐ a. admire the person.
   - ☐ b. despise or scorn the person.
   - ☐ c. care about the person.

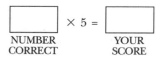

NUMBER CORRECT   × 5 =   YOUR SCORE

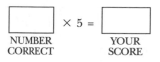

NUMBER CORRECT   × 5 =   YOUR SCORE

IDENTIFY STORY ELEMENTS. The following questions check your knowledge of story elements. Put an *x* in the box next to each correct answer.

1. Which of the following best illustrates *character development* that reveals change?
   - ☐ a. At the beginning of the story, the wife had a sense of well-being; at the end of the story, she expressed anger and contempt.
   - ☐ b. Although he didn't like the way Joe's father was acting, Morton thought that he could do little about it.
   - ☐ c. The man took a couple of steps toward Morton, ready to fight.

2. Of these events, which happened first in the *plot* of the story?
   - ☐ a. Morton took Larry from the sand-box.
   - ☐ b. Larry's mother told Joe not to throw sand.
   - ☐ c. Joe's father walked toward Morton.

3. Which sentence illustrates *inner conflict*?
   - ☐ a. Joe's father told Morton to shut up.
   - ☐ b. Morton's wife wanted to help her husband but seemed unable to.
   - ☐ c. The boy began to cry, "I don't want to go home."

4. Which of the following is the most important line of *dialogue* in the story?
   - ☐ a. "This is ridiculous."
   - ☐ b. "I don't *want* any supper."
   - ☐ c. "You and who else?"

THINK CRITICALLY ABOUT THE STORY. The following questions check your critical thinking skills. Put an *x* in the box next to each correct answer.

1. Evidence in the story indicates that Morton
   - ☐ a. was stronger and far more powerful than his appearance suggested.
   - ☐ b. often became annoyed and lost his temper.
   - ☐ c. worked at a university.

2. We may infer that Joe's father was
   - ☐ a. ready, willing, and eager to fight Morton.
   - ☐ b. the kind of person who is always willing to listen to reason.
   - ☐ c. loud-mouthed and annoying but not dangerous.

3. Clues in the story suggest that
   - ☐ a. Morton's wife wished that her husband were stronger.
   - ☐ b. Morton might have beaten Joe's father in a fight.
   - ☐ c. Larry and Joe would eventually become friends.

4. Although Morton's wife thought "the whole thing was silly . . . and not worth thinking about," the incident
   - ☐ a. helped to bring Morton and her closer together.
   - ☐ b. affected her greatly.
   - ☐ c. made Joe's father realize that he had acted like a bully.

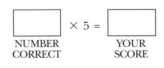

NUMBER CORRECT   × 5 =   YOUR SCORE

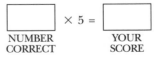

NUMBER CORRECT   × 5 =   YOUR SCORE

STUDY THE **W**RITER'S **C**RAFT. The following questions check your knowledge of skills related to the craft of writing. Put an *x* in the box next to each correct answer. You may refer to pages 4 and 5.

1. Morton is reading the *Times Magazine* section, while Joe's father is reading the Sunday comics, or cartoons. This is the author's way of showing
   - ☐ a. that most people like to read when they are in a park.
   - ☐ b. that newspapers have various sections.
   - ☐ c. differences between the characters.

2. The boy "with a quick, deliberate swing of his chubby arm threw a spadeful of sand at Larry." As used here, what is the connotation of the word *chubby?*
   - ☐ a. cute
   - ☐ b. strong
   - ☐ c. weak

3. She had a feeling that was "glued like heavy plaster on her heart." What figure of speech is used in this sentence?
   - ☐ a. a simile
   - ☐ b. alliteration
   - ☐ c. personification

4. Morton's wife felt that "beneath it there was a layer of something else, something heavy." The "layer" refers to
   - ☐ a. emotions.
   - ☐ b. beauty.
   - ☐ c. education.

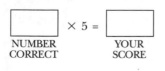

NUMBER CORRECT × 5 = YOUR SCORE

Questions for Writing and Discussion

- Do you approve of the way Joe's father acted? Explain your answer.
- Most people would agree that Morton was in a difficult situation. Do you think that he did the right thing by avoiding a fight? Tell why.
- There is a conflict between the two fathers in the story. But the greater conflict is the one between Morton and his wife. Do you agree with this statement? Discuss.
- Explain the significance of the wife's last four words in the story—"You and who else?"

See additional questions for extended writing on pages 156 and 157.

Use the boxes below to total your scores for the exercises. Then record your scores on pages 198 and 199.

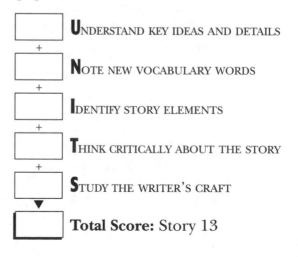

UNDERSTAND KEY IDEAS AND DETAILS

+

NOTE NEW VOCABULARY WORDS

+

IDENTIFY STORY ELEMENTS

+

THINK CRITICALLY ABOUT THE STORY

+

STUDY THE WRITER'S CRAFT

▼

Total Score: Story 13

Shifting Relationships

Questions for Discussion and Extended Writing

The following questions provide you with opportunities to express your thoughts and feelings about the selections in this unit. Your teacher may assign selected questions. When you write your responses, remember to state your point of view clearly and to support your position by presenting specific details—examples, illustrations, and references drawn from the story and, in some cases, from your life. Organize your writing carefully and check your work for correct spelling, capitalization, punctuation, and grammar.

1. The theme of this unit is "Shifting Relationships." Select three stories from the unit and briefly explain how each is related to that theme.

2. Someone once said, "Success in a relationship is not so much about finding the right person as about *being* the right person." This statement suggests that for relationships to succeed, some degree of change may be necessary. Pick two stories from the unit and show how a character in each story changes or seems willing to change to improve a relationship. Give titles and authors.

3. In which story in the unit do characters seem to have the closest relationship? Support your answer by providing examples and illustrations from the story.

4. Compare and contrast Mr. Ridley in "The Treasure of Lemon Brown" and David's father in "Somebody's Son." In what ways are they similar? How are they different?

5. "Sunday in the Park" shows a dramatic shift in a relationship. Support that statement by referring to specific details in the story.

6. According to Lemon Brown, everyone has "a treasure." Write an essay in which you tell what the characters in "Mother and Daughter" treasured. Give your essay a title.

7. In "Sunday in the Park" and "The Treasure of Lemon Brown," it is not clear what the characters will do as the story ends. Pick a character from each story and explain how you think that character will act following the conclusion of the story.

8. Which character in the unit did you most admire or care about? Explain why.

9. In many ways, "Sunday in the Park" is very different from the other stories in the unit. Support this statement in a carefully organized essay that has an introduction, a body, and a conclusion.

10. The Greek philosopher Aristotle wrote, "Friendship is a slow-ripening fruit." This suggests that friendship develops over time as the result of a *relationship.* What qualities do you look for in a friend? Do you think that you are a good friend? What are some tests of friendship? Think about these questions. Then write an essay entitled "A True Friend."

The Way Things End

"All's well that ends well."

–William Shakespeare

Previewing the Unit

Since this is the final unit in *Choices*, it is perhaps only fitting that it be titled "The Way Things End." According to William Shakespeare, "All's well that ends well." While we cannot guarantee that each story will "end well"—have a happy ending—we feel confident that you will enjoy each one.

SOMETHING GREEN In "Something Green" you will meet McGarry, a strange and fascinating character created by science fiction writer Frederic Brown. McGarry has been stranded for years on a planet named Kruger III. We realize in due time that, alone and isolated (or so it would seem) on a planet far different from Earth, McGarry has undergone a startling transformation, or change. But let's not get ahead of ourselves. See what happens in this unusual tale—but be warned of the way things end!

THE INN OF LOST TIME Lensey Namioka's "The Inn of Lost Time" is based on a Japanese folktale. The characters are interesting and varied, and the setting plays a significant role. But the plot will probably prove the most fascinating element. Steer your course through the twists and turns of the plot, and just when you think that you've come to the end of the road and know all, you'll find still another surprise awaits you. As the title suggests, the story is about time—time now, time in the past, and maybe even time in the future. It's lots of fun. But how will it all end?

AUNTY MISERY *and* THOSE THREE WISHES This brings us to the final two selections in our volume. The first story, "Aunty Misery," is a folktale that has been retold by Judith Ortiz Cofer. The second story, "Those Three Wishes," is by Judith Gorog, an author best known for her tales of horror. Both selections are quite short, and both deal with the same subject—wishes. The stories will remind you of an old saying that warns "Be careful what you wish for. It may come true." You'll see how that proverb applies. Interestingly, one story concludes with the suggestion that something *never* will end, while the other story ends—rather *abruptly*, let us say.

As you read, anticipate what will happen. All will become clear when you finish and discover . . . "The Way Things End."

He had only one thing on his mind—to get back to Earth and see . . .

Something Green

by Frederic Brown

The big sun was crimson in a violet sky. At the edge of the brown plain, dotted with brown bushes, lay the red jungle.

McGarry strode toward it. It was tough work and dangerous work, searching in those red jungles, but it had to be done. And he'd searched a thousand of them; this was just one more.

He said, "Here we go, Dorothy. All set?"

The little five-limbed creature that rested on his shoulder didn't answer, but then it never did. It couldn't talk, but it was something to talk to. It was company. In size and weight it felt amazingly like a hand resting on his shoulder.

He'd had Dorothy for—how long? At a guess, four years. He'd been here about five, as nearly as he could reckon it, and it had been about a year before he'd found her. Anyway, he assumed that Dorothy was a "she," if for no better reason than the gentle way she rested on his shoulder, like a woman's hand.

"Dorothy," he said, "reckon we'd better get ready for trouble. Might be lions or tigers in there."

He unbuckled his sol-gun holster and let his hand rest on the butt of the weapon, ready to draw it quickly. For the thousandth time, at least, he thanked his lucky stars that the weapon he'd managed to salvage from the wreckage of his spacer had been a sol-gun, the one and only weapon that worked practically forever without refills or ammunition. A sol-gun soaked up energy. And, when you pulled the trigger, it dished it out. With any weapon but a sol-gun he'd never have lasted even one year on Kruger III.

Yes, even before he quite reached the edge of the red jungle, he saw a lion. Nothing like any lion ever seen on Earth, of course. This one was bright magenta,[1] just enough different in color from the purplish bushes it crouched behind so he could see it. It had eight legs, all jointless and as supple and strong as an elephant's trunk, and a scaly head with a beak like a toucan's.

McGarry called it a lion. He had as much right to call it that as anything else, because it had never been named. Or if it had, the namer had never returned to Earth to report on the flora and fauna[2] of Kruger III. Only one spacer had ever landed here before McGarry's, as far as the records showed, and it had never taken off again. He was looking for it now; he'd been looking for it systematically for the five years he'd been here.

If he found it, it might—just barely might—contain intact some of the electronic transistors which had been destroyed in the

crash-landing of his own spacer. And if it contained enough of them, he could get back to Earth.

He stopped ten paces short of the edge of the red jungle and aimed the sol-gun at the bushes behind which the lion crouched. He pulled the trigger and there was a bright green flash, brief but beautiful—oh, so beautiful—and the bushes weren't there any more, and neither was the lion.

McGarry chuckled softly. "Did you see that, Dorothy? That was *green,* the one color you don't have on this bloody red planet of yours. The most beautiful color in the universe, Dorothy. *Green!* And I know where there's a world that's mostly green, and we're going to get there, you and I. Sure we are. It's the world I came from, and it's the most beautiful place there is, Dorothy. You'll love it."

He turned and looked back over the brown plain with brown bushes, the violet sky above, the crimson sun. The eternally crimson sun Kruger, which never set on the day side of this planet, one side of which always faced it as one side of Earth's moon always faces Earth.

No day and night—unless one passed the shadow line into the night side, which was too freezingly cold to sustain life. No seasons. A uniform, never-changing temperature, no wind, no storms.

He thought for the thousandth, or the millionth, time that it wouldn't be a bad planet to live on, if only it were green like Earth, if only there was something green upon it besides the occasional flash of his sol-gun. It had breathable atmosphere, moderate temperature ranging from about forty Fahrenheit near the shadow line to about ninety at the point directly under the

---

1. **magenta:** purplish red

2. **flora and fauna:** plants and animals

red sun, where its rays were straight down instead of slanting. Plenty of food, and he'd learned long ago which plants and animals were, for him, edible and which made him ill. Nothing he'd ever tried was outright poisonous.

Yes, a wonderful world. He'd even got used, by now, to being the only intelligent creature on it. Dorothy was helpful, there. Something to talk to, even if she didn't talk back.

Except—oh!—he wanted to see a *green* world again.

Earth, the only planet in the known universe where green was the predominant color, where plant life was based on chlorophyll.

Other planets, even in the solar system, Earth's neighbors, had no more to offer than greenish streaks in rare rocks, an occasional tiny life-form of a shade that might be called brownish green if you wanted to call it that. Why, you could live years on any planet but Earth, anywhere in the cosmos, and never see green.

McGarry sighed. He'd been thinking to himself, but now he thought out loud, to Dorothy, continuing his thoughts without a break. It didn't matter to Dorothy. "Yes, Dorothy," he said, "it's the only planet worth living on—Earth! Green fields, grassy lawns, green trees. Dorothy, I'll never leave it again, once I get back there. I'll build me a shack out in the woods, in the middle of trees, but not trees so thick that the grass doesn't grow under them. *Green* grass. And I'll paint the shack green, Dorothy. We've even got green pigments[3] back on Earth."

He sighed and looked at the red jungle ahead of him.

"What's that you asked, Dorothy?" She hadn't asked anything, but it was a game to pretend that she talked back, a game to keep him sane. "Will I get married when I get back? Is that what you asked?"

He gave it consideration. "Well, it's like this, Dorothy. Maybe and maybe not. You were named after a woman back on Earth, you know. A woman I was going to marry. But five years is a long time, Dorothy. I've been reported missing and presumably dead. I doubt if she's waited this long. If she has, well, I'll marry her, Dorothy.

"Did you ask, what if she hasn't? Well, I don't know. Let's not worry about that till I get back, huh? Of course, if I could find a woman who was *green,* or even one with green hair, I'd love her. But on Earth almost everything is green *except* the women."

He chuckled at that and, sol-gun ready, went on into the jungle, the red jungle that had nothing green except the occasional flash of his sol-gun.

Funny about that. Back on Earth, a sol-gun flashed violet. Here under a red sun, it flashed green when he fired it. But the explanation was simple enough. A sol-gun drew energy from a nearby star and the flash it made when fired was the complementary color of its source of energy. Drawing energy from Sol, a yellow sun, it flashed violet. From Kruger, a red sun, green.

Maybe that, he thought, had been the one thing that, aside from Dorothy's company, had kept him sane. A flash of green several times a day. Something green to remind him what the color *was.* To keep his eyes attuned to it, if he ever saw it again.

---

3. **pigments:** powders used to make various colors

It turned out to be a small patch of jungle, as patches of jungle went on Kruger III. One of what seemed countless millions of such patches. And maybe it really was millions; Kruger III was larger than Jupiter. But less dense, so the gravity was easily bearable. Actually it might take him more than a lifetime to cover it all. He knew that, but did not let himself think about it. No more than he let himself think that the ship might have crashed on the dark side, the cold side. Or than he let himself doubt that, once he found the ship, he would find the transistors he needed to make his own spacer operative again.

The patch of jungle was less than a mile square, but he had to sleep once and eat several times before he had finished it. He killed two more lions and one tiger. And when he finished it, he walked around the circumference of it, blazing each of the larger trees along the outer rim so he wouldn't repeat by searching this particular jungle again. The trees were soft; his pocketknife took off the red bark down to the pink core as easily as it would have taken the skin off a potato.

Then out across the dull brown plain again, this time holding his sol-gun in the open to recharge it.

"Not that one, Dorothy. Maybe the next. The one over there near the horizon. Maybe it's there."

Violet sky, red sun, brown plain.

"The green hills of Earth, Dorothy. Oh, how you'll love them."

The brown never-ending plain.

The never-changing violet sky.

Was there a sound up there? There couldn't be. There never had been. But he looked up. And saw it.

A tiny black speck high in the violet, moving. *A spacer. It had to be a spacer. There were no birds on Kruger III. And birds don't trail jets of fire behind them—*

He knew what to do; he'd thought of it a million times, how he could signal a spacer if one ever came in sight. He raised his sol-gun, aimed it straight into the violet air and pulled the trigger. It didn't make a big flash, from the distance of the spacer, but it made a *green* flash. The pilot couldn't miss a green flash on a world with no other green.

He pulled the trigger again.

And the pilot of the spacer *saw*. He cut and fired his jets three times—the standard answer to a signal of distress—and began to circle.

McGarry stood there trembling. So long a wait, and so sudden an end to it. He touched his left shoulder and touched the five-legged pet that felt to his fingers as well as to his naked shoulder so like a woman's hand.

"Dorothy," he said, "it's—" He ran out of words.

The spacer was closing in for a landing now. McGarry looked down at himself, suddenly aware and ashamed of himself, as he would look to a rescuer. He was dirty and probably smelled, although he could not smell himself. And under the dirt his body looked thin and wasted, almost old, but that was due of course to diet deficiencies; a few months of proper food, Earth food, would take care of that.

Earth! The green hills of Earth!

He ran now, stumbling sometimes in his eagerness, toward the point where the spacer was landing. He could see now that it was a one-man job, like his own had been. But that was all right; it could carry two in

163

an emergency, at least as far as the nearest planet where he could get other transportation back to Earth. To the green hills, the green fields, the green valleys.

As he ran, there were tears running down his cheeks.

He was there, waiting, as the door opened and a tall slender young man in the uniform of the Space Patrol stepped out.

"You'll take me back?" he shouted.

"Of course," said the young man calmly. "Been here long?"

"Five years!" McGarry knew that he was crying, but he couldn't stop.

"I'm Lieutenant Archer. Of course I'll take you back, man, as soon as my jets cool enough for a takeoff. I'll take you as far as Carthage, on Aldebaran II, anyway; you can get a ship out of there for anywhere. Need anything right away? Food? Water?"

McGarry shook his head dumbly. Food, water—What did such things matter now?

The green hills of Earth! He was going back to them. *That* was what mattered, and all that mattered. So long a wait, then so sudden an ending. He saw the violet sky swimming and then it suddenly went black as his knees buckled under him.

He was lying flat and the young man was holding a flask to his lips and he took a long drink and sat up and felt better. He looked to make sure the spacer was still there; it was, and he felt wonderful.

The young man said, "Buck up, old-timer; we'll be off in half an hour. You'll be in Carthage in six hours. Want to talk, till you get your bearings again? Want to tell me all about it, everything that's happened?"

They sat in the shadow of a brown bush, and McGarry told him about it, everything about it. The five-year search for the other

ship he'd read had crashed on the planet and which might have intact the parts he needed to repair his own ship. The long search. About Dorothy, perched on his shoulder, and how she'd been something to talk to.

But somehow, the face of Lieutenant Archer was changing as McGarry talked. It grew even more solemn, even more compassionate.[4]

"Old-timer," Archer asked gently, "what year was it when you came here?"

McGarry saw it coming. How can you keep track of time on a planet whose sun and seasons are unchanging? A planet of eternal day, eternal summer—

He said flatly, "I came here in twenty-two forty-two. How much have I misjudged, Lieutenant? How old am I—instead of thirty, as I've thought?"

"It's twenty-two seventy-two, McGarry. You came here thirty years ago. You're fifty-five. But don't let that worry you too much. Medical science has advanced. You still have a long time to live."

McGarry said it softly. "Fifty-five. *Thirty years.*"

The lieutenant looked at him pityingly. He said, "Old-timer, do you want it all in a lump, all the rest of the bad news? There are several items of it. I'm no psychologist but I think maybe it's best for you to take it now, all at once, while you can still throw into the scale against it the fact that you're going back. Can you take it, McGarry?"

There couldn't be anything worse than he'd learned already. The fact that thirty years of his life had already been wasted here. Sure, he could take the rest of

---

4. **compassionate:** feeling sympathy or pity

whatever it was, as long as he was getting back to Earth, green Earth.

He stared at the violet sky, the red sun, the brown plain. He said, very quietly, "I can take it. Dish it out."

"You've done wonderfully for thirty years, McGarry. You can be thankful for the fact that you believed Marley's spacer crashed on Kruger III; it was Kruger IV. You'd have never found it here, but the search, as you say, kept you—reasonably sane." He paused a moment. His voice was gentle when he spoke again. "There isn't anything on your shoulder, McGarry. This Dorothy is a figment[5] of your imagination. But don't worry about it; that particular delusion[6] has probably kept you from cracking up completely."

McGarry put up his hand. It touched his shoulder. Nothing else.

Archer said, "It's marvelous that you're *otherwise* okay. Thirty years alone; it's almost a miracle. And if your one delusion persists, now that I've told you it *is* a delusion, a psychiatrist back at Carthage or on Mars can fix you up in a jiffy."

McGarry said dully, "It doesn't persist. It isn't there now. I—I'm not even sure, Lieutenant, that I ever did really believe in Dorothy. I think I made her up on purpose, to talk to, so I'd remain sane except for that. She was—she was like a woman's hand, Lieutenant. Or did I tell you that?"

"You told me. Want the rest of it now, McGarry?"

McGarry stared at him. "The rest of it? What rest can there be? I'm fifty-five instead

of thirty. I've spent thirty years, since I was twenty-five, hunting for a spacer I'd never have found, since it's on another planet. I've been crazy—in one way, but only one— most of that time. But none of that matters now that I can go back to Earth."

Lieutenant Archer was shaking his head slowly. "Not back to Earth, old-timer. To Mars if you wish, the beautiful brown and yellow hills of Mars. Or, if you don't mind heat, to purple Venus. But not to Earth, McGarry. Nobody lives there any more."

"Earth is—gone? I don't—"

"Not gone, McGarry. It's there. But it's black and barren, a charred ball. The war with the Arcturians, twenty years ago. They struck first, and got Earth. We got *them*, we won, we exterminated them, but Earth was gone before we started. I'm sorry, but you'll have to settle for somewhere else."

McGarry said, "No Earth." There was no expression in his voice. No expression at all.

Archer said, "That's the works, old-timer. But Mars isn't so bad. You'll get used to it. It's the center of the solar system now, and there are three billion humans on it. You'll miss the green of Earth, sure, but it's not so bad."

McGarry said, "No Earth." There was no expression in his voice. No expression at all.

Archer nodded. "Glad you can take it that way, old-timer. It must be rather a jolt. Well, I guess we can get going. The tubes ought to have cooled enough by now. I'll check and make sure."

He stood up and started toward the little spacer.

McGarry's sol-gun came out of its holster. McGarry shot him, and Lieutenant Archer wasn't there any more. McGarry stood up and walked to the little spacer. He aimed

---

5. figment: something made up

6. delusion: a false belief

the sol-gun at it and pulled the trigger. Part of the spacer was gone. Half a dozen shots and it was completely gone. Little atoms that had been the spacer and little atoms that had been Lieutenant Archer of the Space Patrol may have danced in the air, but they were invisible.

McGarry put the gun back into its holster and started walking toward the red splotch of jungle near the horizon.

He put his hand up to his shoulder and touched Dorothy and she was there, as she'd been there now for four of the five years he'd been on Kruger III. She felt, to his fingers and to his bare shoulder, like a woman's hand.

He said, "Don't worry, Dorothy. We'll find it. Maybe this next jungle is the right one. And when we find it—"

He was near the edge of the jungle now, the red jungle, and a tiger came running out to meet him and eat him. A tiger with six legs and a head like a barrel. McGarry aimed his sol-gun and pulled the trigger, and there was a bright green flash, brief but beautiful— oh, so beautiful—and the tiger wasn't there any more.

McGarry chuckled softly. "Did you see that, Dorothy? That was *green*, the color there isn't much of on any planet but the one we're going to. The only green planet in the system, and it's the one I came from. You'll love it."

She said, "I know I will, Mac." Her low throaty voice was completely familiar to him, as familiar as his own; she'd always answered him. He reached up his hand and touched her as she rested on his naked shoulder. She felt like a woman's hand.

He turned and looked back over the brown plain dotted with brown bushes, the violet sky above, the crimson sun. He laughed at it. Not a mad laugh, a gentle one. It didn't matter because soon now he'd find the spacer so he could go back to Earth.

To the green hills, the green fields, the green valleys. Once more he patted the hand upon his shoulder and spoke to it, listened to its answer.

Then, gun at ready, he entered the red jungle.

About the Author

Frederic Brown (1906–1972) burst onto the literary scene when his novel *The Fabulous Clipjoint* won the Edgar Allan Poe Award in 1948 for the best first mystery novel. From that point on, Brown produced a vast amount of writing, including numerous science fiction stories and novels, as well as all kinds of tales of crime and suspense. Brown, who was born in Cincinnati, Ohio, and went to school at the University of Cincinnati and Hanover College, had a rich imagination. He explored unusual and interesting themes. He created many original characters and placed them in odd and extraordinary situations that challenged the reader. "Something Green" is a good example of Brown's style of writing.

UNDERSTAND KEY IDEAS AND DETAILS. The following questions help you check your reading comprehension. Put an *x* in the box next to the correct answer.

1. "Something Green" is mainly about
   ☐ a. a space traveler who is unable to accept the truth.
   ☐ b. the beauty of Earth, which most people take for granted.
   ☐ c. why one should never give up hope, no matter how desperate a situation seems to be.

2. How long had McGarry been on Kruger III?
   ☐ a. five years
   ☐ b. thirty years
   ☐ c. fifty-five years

3. When he met Lieutenant Archer, McGarry became excited about
   ☐ a. the delicious food he would be eating soon.
   ☐ b. receiving fresh, cool water.
   ☐ c. seeing Earth again.

4. At the end of the story, McGarry
   ☐ a. entered the jungle.
   ☐ b. examined Archer's spaceship.
   ☐ c. fired his sol-gun into the air.

NOTE NEW VOCABULARY WORDS. The following questions check your vocabulary skills. Put an *x* in the box next to the correct answer. Each vocabulary word appears in the story.

1. It was "as supple and strong as an elephant's trunk." Something that is *supple* is
   ☐ a. flexible and bends easily.
   ☐ b. not very intelligent.
   ☐ c. weak.

2. McGarry knew "which plants and animals . . . were edible and which made him ill." The word *edible* means
   ☐ a. large and dangerous.
   ☐ b. difficult to find.
   ☐ c. fit to eat.

3. McGarry stated that Earth was the only planet "where green was the predominant color." Define the word *predominant*.
   ☐ a. only
   ☐ b. main
   ☐ c. brightest

4. McGarry was "reported missing and presumably dead." What is the meaning of the word *presumably*?
   ☐ a. almost
   ☐ b. thought to be
   ☐ c. injured or hurt

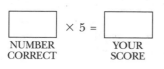

NUMBER CORRECT × 5 = YOUR SCORE

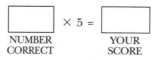

NUMBER CORRECT × 5 = YOUR SCORE

IDENTIFY STORY ELEMENTS. The following questions check your knowledge of story elements. Put an *x* in the box next to each correct answer.

1. Which statement best *characterizes* McGarry?
   ☐ a. He was eager to start a new life on another planet.
   ☐ b. He went insane after living alone for many years.
   ☐ c. He planned to marry a woman who he hoped still waited for him.

2. What is the *setting* of "Something Green"?
   ☐ a. a spaceship somewhere in the universe
   ☐ b. a planet named Kruger III, many years in the future
   ☐ c. Earth, more than two hundred years in the future

3. The *climax* of the story occurs when
   ☐ a. McGarry's spaceship lands on Kruger III.
   ☐ b. McGarry fires his sol-gun to alert the Space Patrol pilot of his existence.
   ☐ c. McGarry is told that there is no longer any life on Earth.

4. Which best expresses the story's *theme*?
   ☐ a. False hope can inspire, but it can also lead to disaster.
   ☐ b. No one can really tell what the future will bring.
   ☐ c. A man who had been lost for many years is finally found.

THINK CRITICALLY ABOUT THE STORY. The following questions check your critical thinking skills. Put an *x* in the box next to each correct answer.

1. Evidence in the story indicates that McGarry created Dorothy
   ☐ a. because he thought she would give him excellent advice.
   ☐ b. because she looked exactly like a woman on Earth named Dorothy.
   ☐ c. to keep him company and help him stay sane.

2. One reason it was difficult for McGarry to know how long he had been on Kruger III was that
   ☐ a. there were no seasons on that planet.
   ☐ b. there was nothing green on the planet.
   ☐ c. the planet was very large, even larger than Jupiter.

3. McGarry probably shot Lieutenant Archer because
   ☐ a. Archer was about to attack him.
   ☐ b. McGarry was unable to believe what Archer had said about Earth.
   ☐ c. Dorothy suggested he do so.

4. Which statement is most likely true?
   ☐ a. McGarry will succeed in finding Earth one day.
   ☐ b. McGarry will discover the remains of Marley's crashed spaceship.
   ☐ c. McGarry will never get back to Earth.

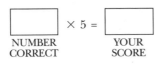

NUMBER CORRECT × 5 = YOUR SCORE

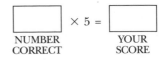

NUMBER CORRECT × 5 = YOUR SCORE

STUDY THE **W**RITER'S **C**RAFT. The following questions check your knowledge of skills related to the craft of writing. Put an *x* in the box next to each correct answer. You may refer to pages 4 and 5.

1. The narrator tells of "the brown plain with brown bushes, the violet sky above, the crimson sun." What is true of this sentence?
   ☐ a. It indicates to the reader where the story takes place.
   ☐ b. It illustrates the narrator's concern with colors.
   ☐ c. It shows inner conflict.

2. A striking thing about "Something Green" is the author's ability to
   ☐ a. demonstrate how a character can escape from a planet that has no other human being living on it.
   ☐ b. make a character who acts very strangely seem believable and real.
   ☐ c. create a story that does not contain dialogue.

3. What is true—and interesting—about the way the story is constructed?
   ☐ a. At the beginning and at the conclusion, a man enters a red jungle.
   ☐ b. It contains many flashbacks.
   ☐ c. There is no main character.

4. "Something Green" is an example of a
   ☐ a. detective story.
   ☐ b. folktale.
   ☐ c. science fiction story.

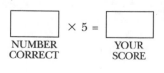

NUMBER CORRECT   × 5 =   YOUR SCORE

Questions for Writing and Discussion

- How did McGarry end up on the planet Kruger III? Why did he consider himself lucky?
- What was McGarry seeking as he made his way through the jungles? Do you think he will ever find the object of his search? Explain why.
- Why do you think McGarry created Dorothy? Why did he tell Archer that she did not exist—and then create her again at the end of the story?
- Read the next-to-last line of the story again. What does it prove, or confirm? What other incident in the story supports your answer?

See additional questions for extended writing on page 196 and 197.

Use the boxes below to total your scores for the exercises. Then record your scores on pages 198 and 199.

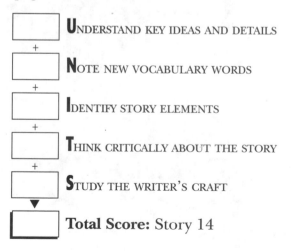

UNDERSTAND KEY IDEAS AND DETAILS

+

NOTE NEW VOCABULARY WORDS

+

IDENTIFY STORY ELEMENTS

+

THINK CRITICALLY ABOUT THE STORY

+

STUDY THE WRITER'S CRAFT

▼

Total Score: Story 14

They had never stayed at a stranger place than . . .

The Inn of Lost Time

by Lensey Namioka

"**W**ill you promise to sleep if I tell you a story?" said the father. He pretended to put on a stern expression.

"Yes! Yes!" the three little boys chanted in unison. It sounded like a nightly routine.

The two guests smiled as they listened to the exchange. They were wandering ronin, or unemployed samurai,[1] and they enjoyed watching this cozy family scene.

---

1. **samurai:** trained professional warriors in Japan long ago

170

The father gave the guests a helpless look. "What can I do? I have to tell them a story, or these little rascals will give us no peace." Clearing his throat, he turned to the boys. "All right. The story tonight is about Urashima Taro."

Instantly the three boys became still. Sitting with their legs tucked under them, the three little boys, aged five, four, and three, looked like a descending row of stone statuettes. Matsuzo, the younger of the two ronin, was reminded of the wayside half-body statues of Jizo, the God of Travelers and Protector of Children.

Behind the boys the farmer's wife took up a pair of iron chopsticks and stirred the ashes of the fire in the charcoal brazier.[2] A momentary glow brightened the room. The lean faces of the two ronin, lit by the fire, suddenly looked fierce and hungry.

The farmer knew that the two ronin were supposed to use their arms in defense of the weak. But in these troubled times, with the country torn apart by civil wars, the samurai didn't always live up to their honorable code.

Then the fire died down again and the subdued red light softened the features of the two ronin. The farmer relaxed and began his story.

The tale of Urashima Taro is familiar to every Japanese. No doubt the three little boys had heard their father tell it before— and more than once. But they listened with rapt attention.

---

2. **brazier:** a large metal pan that holds charcoal or coal

Urashima Taro, a fisherman, rescued a turtle from some boys who were battering it with stones. The grateful turtle rewarded Taro by carrying him on his back to the bottom of the sea, where he lived happily with the Princess of the Undersea. But Taro soon became homesick for his native village and asked to go back on land. The princess gave him a box to take with him but warned him not to peek inside.

When Taro went back to his village, he found the place quite changed. In his home he found his parents gone, and living there was another old couple. He was stunned to learn that the aged husband was his own son, whom he had last seen as a baby! Taro thought he had spent only a pleasant week or two undersea with the princess. On land, seventy-two years had passed! His parents and most of his old friends had long since died.

Desolate, Taro decided to open the box given him by the princess. As soon as he looked inside, he changed in an instant from a young man to a decrepit old man of more than ninety.

At the end of the story the boys were close to tears. Even Matsuzo found himself deeply touched. He wondered why the farmer had told his sons such a poignant[3] bedtime story. Wouldn't they worry all evening instead of going to sleep?

3. **poignant:** very intense

But the boys recovered quickly. They were soon laughing and jostling each other, and they made no objections when their mother shooed them toward bed. Standing in order of age, they bowed politely to the guests, and then lay down on the mattresses spread out for them on the floor. Within minutes the sound of their regular breathing told the guests that they were asleep.

Zenta, the older of the two ronin, sighed as he glanced at the peaceful young faces. "I wish I could fall asleep so quickly. The story of Urashima Taro is one of the saddest that I know among our folk tales."

The farmer looked proudly at his sleeping sons. "They're stout lads. Nothing bothers them much."

The farmer's wife poured tea for the guests and apologized. "I'm sorry this is only poor tea made from coarse leaves."

Zenta hastened to reassure her. "It's warm and heartening on a chilly autumn evening."

"You know what I think is the saddest part of the Urashima Taro story?" said Matsuzo, picking up his cup and sipping the tea. "It's that Taro lost not only his family and friends, but a big piece of his life as well. He had lost the most precious thing of all: time."

The farmer nodded agreement. "I wouldn't sell even one year of my life for money. As for losing seventy-two years, no amount of gold will make up for that!"

Zenta put his cup down on the floor and looked curiously at the farmer. "It's interesting that you should say that. I had an opportunity once to observe exactly how much gold a person was willing to pay for some lost years of his life." He smiled grimly. "In this case the man went as far as one gold piece for each year he lost."

"That's bizarre!" said Matsuzo. "You never told me about it."

"It happened long before I met you," said Zenta. He drank some tea and smiled ruefully. "Besides, I'm not particularly proud of the part I played in that strange affair."

"Let's hear the story!" urged Matsuzo. "You've made us all curious."

The farmer waited expectantly. His wife sat down quietly behind her husband and folded her hands. Her eyes looked intently at Zenta.

"Very well, then," said Zenta. "Actually, my story bears some resemblance to that of Urashima Taro. . . . "

It happened about seven years ago, when I was a green, inexperienced youngster not quite eighteen years old. But I had had a good training in arms, and I was able to get a job as a bodyguard for a wealthy merchant from Sakai.

As you know, wealthy merchants are relatively new in our country. Traditionally the rich have been noblemen, landowners, and warlords with thousands of followers. Merchants, considered as parasites in our society, are a despised class. But our civil wars have made people unusually mobile and stimulated trade between various parts of the country. The merchants have taken advantage of this to conduct businesses on a scale our fathers could not imagine. Some of them have become more wealthy than a warlord with thousands of samurai under his command.

The man I was escorting, Tokubei, was one of this new breed of wealthy merchants. He was trading not only with outlying provinces but even with the Portuguese from across the sea. On this particular journey he was not carrying much gold with him. If he had, I'm sure he would have hired an older and more experienced bodyguard. But if the need should arise, he could always write a message to his clerks at home and have money forwarded to him. It's important to remember this.

The second day of our journey was a particularly grueling one, with several steep hills to climb. As the day was drawing to its close, we began to consider where we should spend the night. I knew that within an hour's walking was a hot-spring resort known to have several attractive inns.

But Tokubei, my employer, said he was already very tired and wanted to stop. He had heard of the resort, and knew the inns there were expensive. Wealthy as he was, he did not want to spend more money than he had to.

While we stood talking, a smell reached our noses, a wonderful smell of freshly cooked rice. Suddenly I felt ravenous. From the way Tokubei swallowed, I knew he was feeling just as hungry.

We looked around eagerly, but the area was forested and we could not see very far in any direction. The tantalizing smell seemed to grow and I could feel the saliva filling my mouth.

"There's an inn around here, somewhere," muttered Tokubei. "I'm sure of it."

We followed our noses. We had to leave the well-traveled highway and take a narrow, winding footpath. But the mouth-watering smell of the rice and the vision of fluffy, freshly aired cotton quilts drew us on.

The sun was just beginning to set. We passed a bamboo grove, and in the low evening light the thin leaves turned into little golden knives. I saw a gilded clump of bamboo shoots. The sight made me think of the delicious dish they would make when boiled in soy sauce.

We hurried forward. To our delight we soon came to a clearing with a thatched house standing in the middle. The fragrant smell of rice was now so strong that we were certain a meal was being prepared inside.

Standing in front of the house was a pretty girl beaming at us with a welcoming smile. "Please honor us with your presence," she said, beckoning.

There was something a little unusual about one of her hands, but, being hungry and eager to enter the house, I did not stop to observe closely.

You will say, of course, that it was my duty as a bodyguard to be suspicious and to look out for danger. Youth and inexperience should not have prevented me from wondering why an inn should be found hidden away from the highway. As it was, my stomach growled, and I didn't even

hesitate but followed Tokubei to the house.

Before stepping up to enter, we were given basins of water to wash our feet. As the girl handed us towels for drying, I saw what was unusual about her left hand: she had six fingers.

Tokubei had noticed it as well. When the girl turned away to empty the basins, he nudged me. "Did you see her left hand? She had—" He broke off in confusion as the girl turned around, but she didn't seem to have heard.

The inn was peaceful and quiet, and we soon discovered the reason why. We were the only guests. Again, I should have been suspicious. I told you that I'm not proud of the part I played.

Tokubei turned to me and grinned. "It seems that there are no other guests. We should be able to get extra service for the same amount of money."

The girl led us to a spacious room which was like the principal chamber of a private residence. Cushions were set out for us on the floor and we began to shed our traveling gear to make ourselves comfortable.

The door opened and a grizzled-haired man entered. Despite his vigorous-looking face his back was a little bent and I guessed his age to be about fifty. After bowing and greeting us he apologized in advance for the service. "We have not always been innkeepers here," he said, "and you may find the accommodations lacking. Our good intentions must make up for our inexperience. However, to compensate for our inadequacies, we will charge a lower fee than that of an inn with an established reputation."

Tokubei nodded graciously, highly pleased by the words of our host, and the evening began well. It continued well when the girl came back with some flasks of wine, cups, and dishes of salty snacks.

While the girl served the wine, the host looked with interest at my swords. From the few remarks he made, I gathered that he was a former samurai, forced by circumstances to turn his house into an inn.

Having become a bodyguard to a tight-fisted merchant, I was in no position to feel superior to a ronin turned innkeeper. Socially, therefore, we were more or less equal.

We exchanged polite remarks with our host while we drank and tasted the salty snacks. I looked around at the pleasant room. It showed excellent taste, and I especially admired a vase standing in the alcove.

My host caught my eyes on it. "We still have a few good things that we didn't have to sell," he said. His voice held a trace of bitterness. "Please look at the panels of these doors. They were painted by a fine artist."

Tokubei and I looked at the pair of sliding doors. Each panel contained a landscape painting, the right panel depicting a winter scene and the left one the same scene in late summer. Our host's words were no idle boast. The pictures were indeed beautiful.

Tokubei rose and approached the screens for a closer look. When he sat down again, his eyes were calculating. No doubt he was trying to estimate what price the paintings would fetch.

After my third drink I began to feel very tired. Perhaps it was the result of drinking on an empty stomach. I was glad when the girl brought in two dinner trays and a lacquered container of rice. Uncovering the rice container, she began filling our bowls.

Again I noticed her strange left hand with its six fingers. Any other girl would have tried to keep that hand hidden, but this girl made no effort to do so. If anything, she seemed to use that hand more than her other one when she served us. The extra little finger always stuck out from the hand, as if inviting comment.

The hand fascinated me so much that I kept my eyes on it, and soon forgot to eat. After a while the hand looked blurry. And then everything else began to look blurry. The last thing I remembered was the sight of Tokubei shaking his head, as if trying to clear it.

When I opened my eyes again, I knew that time had passed, but not how much time. My next thought was that it was cold. It was not only extremely cold but damp.

I rolled over and sat up. I reached immediately for my swords and found them safe on the ground beside me. *On the ground?* What was I doing on the ground? My last memory was of staying at an inn with a merchant called Tokubei.

The thought of Tokubei put me into a panic. I was his bodyguard, and instead of watching over him, I had fallen asleep and had awakened in a strange place.

I looked around frantically and saw that he was lying on the ground not far from where I was. Had he been killed?

I got up shakily, and when I stood up my head was swimming. But my sense of urgency gave some strength to my legs. I stumbled over to my employer and to my great relief found him breathing—breathing heavily, in fact.

When I shook his shoulder, he grunted and finally opened his eyes. "Where am I?" he asked thickly.

It was a reasonable question. I looked around and saw that we had been lying in a bamboo grove. By the light I guessed that it was early morning, and the reason I felt cold and damp was because my clothes were wet with dew.

"It's cold!" said Tokubei, shivering and climbing unsteadily to his feet. He looked around slowly, and his eyes became wide with disbelief. "What happened? I thought we were staying at an inn!"

His words came as a relief. One of the possibilities I had considered was that I had gone mad and that the whole episode with the inn was something I had imagined. Now I knew that Tokubei had the same memory of the inn. I had not imagined it.

But why were we out here on the cold ground, instead of on comfortable mattresses in the inn?

"They must have drugged us and robbed us," said Tokubei. He turned and looked at me furiously. "A fine bodyguard you are!"

There was nothing I could say to that. But at least we were both alive and unharmed. "Did they take all your money?" I asked.

Tokubei had already taken his wallet out of his sash and was peering inside. "That's funny! My money is still here!"

This was certainly unexpected. What did the innkeeper and his strange daughter intend to do by drugging us and moving us outside?

At least things were not as bad as we had feared. We had not lost anything except a comfortable night's sleep, although from the heaviness in my head I had certainly slept deeply enough—and long enough too. Exactly how much time had elapsed since we drank wine with our host?

All we had to do now was find the highway again and continue our journey. Tokubei suddenly chuckled. "I didn't even have to pay for our night's lodging!"

As we walked from the bamboo grove, I saw the familiar clump of bamboo shoots, and we found ourselves standing in the same clearing again. Before our eyes was the thatched house. Only it was somehow different. Perhaps things looked different in the daylight than at dusk.

But the difference was more than a change of light. As we approached the house slowly, like sleepwalkers, we saw that the thatching was much darker. On the previous evening the thatching had looked fresh and new. Now it was dark with age. Daylight should make things appear brighter, not darker. The plastering of the walls also looked more dingy.

Tokubei and I stopped to look at each other before we went closer. He was pale, and I knew that I looked no less frightened. Something was terribly wrong. I loosened my sword in its scabbard.[4]

We finally gathered the courage to go up to the house. Since Tokubei seemed unable to find his voice, I spoke out. "Is anyone there?"

After a moment we heard shuffling footsteps and the front door slid open. The face of an old woman appeared. "Yes?" she inquired. Her voice was creaky with age.

What set my heart pounding with panic, however, was not her voice. It was the sight of her left hand holding on to the frame of the door. The hand was wrinkled and crooked with the arthritis of old age—and it had six fingers.

I heard a gasp beside me and knew that Tokubei had noticed the hand as well.

The door opened wider and a man appeared beside the old woman. At first I thought it was our host of the previous night. But this man was much younger, although the resemblance was strong. He carried himself straighter and his hair was black, while the innkeeper had been grizzled and slightly bent with age.

"Please excuse my mother," said the man. "Her hearing is not good. Can we help you in some way?"

Tokubei finally found his voice. "Isn't this the inn where we stayed last night?"

The man stared. "Inn? We are not innkeepers here!"

"Yes, you are!" insisted Tokubei. "Your daughter invited us in and served us with wine. You must have put something in the wine!"

The man frowned. "You are serious? Are you sure you didn't drink too much at your inn and wander off?"

"No, I didn't drink too much!" said Tokubei, almost shouting. "I hardly drank at all! Your daughter, the one with six fingers in her hand, started to pour me a second cup of wine . . ." His voice trailed off, and he stared again at the left hand of the old woman.

"I don't have a daughter," said the man slowly. "My mother here is the one who has six fingers in her left hand, although I hardly think it polite of you to mention it."

"I'm getting dizzy," muttered Tokubei and began to totter.

"I think you'd better come in and rest a bit," the man said to him gruffly. He glanced at me. "Perhaps you wish to join your friend. You don't share his delusion about the inn, I hope?"

---

4. **scabbard:** a case or holder for a sword

"I wouldn't presume to contradict my elders," I said carefully. Since both Tokubei and the owner of the house were my elders, I wasn't committing myself. In truth I didn't know what to believe, but I did want a look at the inside of the house.

The inside was almost the same as it was before but the differences were there when I looked closely. We entered the same room with the alcove and the pair of painted doors. The vase I had admired was no longer there, but the doors showed the same landscapes painted by a master. I peered closely at the pictures and saw that the colors looked faded. What was more, the left panel, the one depicting a winter scene, had a long tear in one corner. It had been painstakingly mended, but the damage was impossible to hide completely.

Tokubei saw what I was staring at and he became even paler. At this stage we had both considered the possibility that a hoax[5] of some sort had been played on us. The torn screen convinced Tokubei that our host had not played a joke: the owner of a valuable painting would never vandalize it for a trivial reason.

As for me, I was far more disturbed by the sight of the sixth finger on the old woman's hand. Could the young girl have disguised herself as an old crone?[6] She could put rice powder in her hair to whiten it, but she could not transform her pretty straight fingers into old fingers twisted with arthritis. The woman here with us now was genuinely old, at least fifty years older than the girl.

It was this same old woman who finally gave us our greatest shock. "It's interesting that you should mention an inn, gentlemen," she croaked. "My father used to operate an inn. After he died, my husband and I turned this back into a private residence. We didn't need the income, you see."

"Your . . . your . . . f-father?" stammered Tokubei.

"Yes," replied the old woman. "He was a ronin, forced to go into inn-keeping when he lost his position. But he never liked the work. Besides, our inn had begun to acquire an unfortunate reputation. Some of our guests disappeared, you see."

Even before she finished speaking, a horrible suspicion had begun to dawn on me. Her *father* had been an innkeeper, she said, her father who used to be a ronin. The man who had been our host was a ronin turned innkeeper. Could this mean that this old woman was actually the same person as the young girl we had seen?

I sat stunned while I tried to absorb the implications. What had happened to us? Was it possible that Tokubei and I had slept while this young girl grew into a mature woman, got married, and bore a son, a son who is now an adult? If that was the case, then we had slept for fifty years!

The old woman's next words confirmed my fears. "I recognize you

---

5. **hoax:** a trick

6. **crone:** an old woman

now! You are two of the lost guests from our inn! The other lost ones I don't remember so well, but I remember you because your disappearance made me so sad. Such a handsome youth, I thought, what a pity that he should have gone the way of the others!"

A high wail came from Tokubei, who began to keen[7] and rock himself back and forth. "I've lost fifty years! Fifty years of my life went by while I slept at this accursed inn!"

The inn was indeed accursed. Was the fate of the other guests similar to ours? "Did anyone else return as we did, fifty years later?" I asked.

The old woman looked uncertain and turned to her son. He frowned thoughtfully. "From time to time wild-looking people have come to us with stories similar to yours. Some of them went mad with the shock."

Tokubei wailed again. "I've lost my business! I've lost my wife, my young and beautiful wife! We had been married only a couple of months!"

A gruesome chuckle came from the old woman. "You may not have lost your wife. It's just that she's become an old hag like me!"

That did not console Tokubei, whose keening became louder. Although my relationship with my employer had not been characterized by much respect on either side, I did begin to feel very sorry for him. He was right: he had lost his world.

---

7. **keen:** to cry out in a sad and mournful way

As for me, the loss was less traumatic. I had left home under extremely painful circumstances, and had spent the next three years wandering. I had no friends and no one I could call a relation. The only thing I had was my duty to my employer. Somehow, some way, I had to help him.

"Did no one find an explanation for these disappearances?" I asked. "Perhaps if we knew the reason why, we might find some way to reverse the process."

The old woman began to nod eagerly. "The priestess! Tell them about the shrine priestess!"

"Well," said the man, "I'm not sure if it would work in your case. . . . "

"What? What would work?" demanded Tokubei. His eyes were feverish.

"There was a case of one returning guest who consulted the priestess at our local shrine," said the man. "She went into a trance and revealed that there was an evil spirit dwelling in the bamboo grove here. This spirit would put unwary travelers into a long, unnatural sleep. They would wake up twenty, thirty, or even fifty years later."

"Yes, but you said something worked in his case," said Tokubei.

The man seemed reluctant to go on. "I don't like to see you cheated, so I'm not sure I should be telling you this."

"Tell me! Tell me!" demanded Tokubei. The host's reluctance only made him more impatient.

"The priestess promised to make a

spell that would undo the work of the evil spirit," said the man. "But she demanded a large sum of money, for she said that she had to burn some very rare and costly incense[8] before she could begin the spell."

At the mention of money Tokubei sat back. The hectic flush died down on his face and his eyes narrowed. "How much money?" he asked.

The host shook his head. "In my opinion the priestess is a fraud and makes outrageous claims about her powers. We try to have as little to do with her as possible."

"Yes, but did her spell work?" asked Tokubei. "If it worked, she's no fraud!"

"At least the stranger disappeared again," cackled the old woman. "Maybe he went back to his own time. Maybe he walked into a river."

Tokubei's eyes narrowed further. "How much money did the priestess demand?" he asked again.

"I think it was one gold piece for every year lost," said the host. He hurriedly added, "Mind you, I still wouldn't trust the priestess."

"Then it would cost me fifty gold pieces to get back to my own time," muttered Tokubei. He looked up. "I don't carry that much money with me."

"No, you don't," agreed the host.

Something alerted me about the way he said that. It was as if the host knew already that Tokubei did not carry much money on him.

Meanwhile Tokubei sighed. He had come to a decision. "I do have the means to obtain more money, however. I can send a message to my chief clerk and he will remit the money when he sees my seal."

"Your chief clerk may be dead by now," I reminded him.

"You're right!" moaned Tokubei. "My business will be under a new management and nobody will even remember my name!"

"And your wife will have re-married," said the old woman, with one of her chuckles. I found it hard to believe that the gentle young girl who had served us wine could turn into this dreadful harridan.[9]

"Sending the message may be a waste of time," agreed the host.

"What waste of time!" cried Tokubei. "Why shouldn't I waste time? I've wasted fifty years already! Anyway, I've made up my mind. I'm sending that message."

"I still think you shouldn't trust the priestess," said the host.

That only made Tokubei all the more determined to send for the money. However, he was not quite resigned to the amount. "Fifty gold pieces is a large sum. Surely the priestess can buy incense for less than that amount?"

"Why don't you try giving her thirty gold pieces?" cackled the old woman. "Then the priestess will send you back thirty years, and your wife will only be middle-aged."

---

8. **incense:** gives a sweet smell when burned

9. **harridan:** a bad-tempered, scolding woman

While Tokubei was still arguing with himself about the exact sum to send for, I decided to have a look at the bamboo grove. "I'm going for a walk," I announced, rising and picking up my sword from the floor beside me.

The host turned sharply to look at me. For an instant a faint, rueful smile appeared on his lips. Then he looked away.

Outside, I went straight to the clump of shoots in the bamboo grove. On the previous night—or what I perceived as the previous night—I had noticed that clump of bamboo shoots particularly, because I had been so hungry that I pictured them being cut up and boiled.

The clump of bamboo shoots was still in the same place. That in itself proved nothing, since bamboo could spring up anywhere, including the place where a clump had existed fifty years earlier. But what settled the matter in my mind was that the clump looked almost exactly the way it did when I had seen it before, except that every shoot was about an inch taller. That was a reasonable amount for bamboo shoots to grow overnight.

Overnight. Tokubei and I had slept on the ground here overnight. We had not slept here for a period of fifty years.

Once I knew that, I was able to see another inconsistency: the door panels with the painted landscapes. The painting with the winter scene had been on the *right* last night and it was on the *left* this morning. It wasn't simply a case of the panels changing places, because the depressions in the panel for the handholds had been reversed. In other words, what I saw just now was not a pair of paintings faded and torn by age. They were an entirely different pair of paintings.

But how did the pretty young girl change into an old woman? The answer was that if the screens could be different ones, so could the women. I had seen one woman, a young girl, last night. This morning I saw a different woman, an old hag.

The darkening of the thatched roof? Simply blow ashes over the roof. The grizzled-haired host of last night could be the same man who claimed to be his grandson today. It would be a simple matter for a young man to put gray in his hair and assume a stoop.

And the purpose of the hoax? To make Tokubei send for fifty pieces of gold, of course. It was clever of the man to accuse the shrine priestess of fraud and pretend reluctance to let Tokubei send his message.

I couldn't even feel angry toward the man and his daughter—or mother, sister, wife, whatever. He could have killed me and taken my swords, which he clearly admired. Perhaps he was really a ronin and felt sympathetic toward another one.

When I returned to the house, Tokubei was looking resigned. "I've decided to send for the whole fifty gold pieces." He sighed.

"Don't bother," I said. "In fact we

should be leaving as soon as possible. We shouldn't even stop here for a drink, especially not of wine."

Tokubei stared. "What do you mean? If I go back home, I'll find everything changed!"

"Nothing will be changed," I told him. "Your wife will be as young and beautiful as ever."

"I don't understand," he said. "Fifty years. . . . "

"It's a joke," I said. "The people here have a peculiar sense of humor, and they've played a joke on us."

Tokubei's mouth hung open. Finally he closed it with a snap. He stared at the host, and his face became first red and then purple. "You—you were trying to swindle me!" He turned furiously to me. "And you let them do this!"

"I'm not letting them," I pointed out. "That's why we're leaving right now."

"Are you going to let them get away with this?" demanded Tokubei. "They might try to swindle someone else!"

"They only went to this much trouble when they heard of the arrival of a fine fat fish like you," I said. I looked deliberately at the host. "I'm sure they won't be tempted to try the same trick again."

"And that's the end of your story?" asked Matsuzo. "You and Tokubei just went away? How did you know the so-called innkeeper wouldn't try the trick on some other luckless traveler?"

Zenta shook his head. "I didn't know. I merely guessed that once the trick was exposed, they wouldn't take the chance of trying it again. Of course I thought about revisiting the place to check if the people there were leading an honest life."

"Why didn't you?" asked Matsuzo. "Maybe we could go together. You've made me curious about that family now."

"Then you can satisfy your curiosity," said Zenta, smiling. He held his cup out for more tea, and the farmer's wife came forward to pour.

Only now she used both hands to hold the pot, and for the first time Matsuzo saw her left hand. He gasped. The hand had six fingers.

"Who was the old woman?" Zenta asked the farmer's wife.

"She was my grandmother," she replied. "Having six fingers is something that runs in my family."

At last Matsuzo found his voice. "You mean this is the very house you visited? This is the inn where time was lost?"

"Where we *thought* we lost fifty years," said Zenta. "Perhaps I should have warned you first. But I was almost certain that we'd be safe this time. And I see that I was right."

He turned to the woman again. "You and your husband are farmers now, aren't you? What happened to the man who was the host?"

"He's dead," she said quietly. "He was my brother, and he was telling you the truth when he said that he was a ronin. Two years ago he found work with another warlord, but he was killed in battle only a month later."

Matsuzo was peering at the pair of sliding doors, which he hadn't noticed before. "I see that you've put up the faded set of paintings. The winter scene is on the left side."

The woman nodded. "We sold the newer pair of doors. My husband said that we're farmers now and that people in our position don't need valuable paintings. We used the money to buy some new farm implements."

She took up the teapot again. "Would you like another cup of tea?" she asked Matsuzo.

Staring at her left hand, Matsuzo had a sudden qualm. "I—I don't think I want any more."

Everybody laughed.

About the Author

Lensey Namioka (1929–) was born in Beijing, China, and as a young adult, came with her parents to the United States. As readers of "The Inn of Lost Time" might suspect, Namioka loves to write about the Japan of long ago. Married to a Japanese mathematician, Namioka draws heavily on background information provided by her husband. The author has stated, "My involvement with Japan started before my marriage, since my mother spent many years in Japan." Namioka has written many award-winning novels, including *Valley of the Broken Trees, White Serpent Castle, Phantom of Tiger Mountain,* and *Who's Hu?* Zenta and Matsuzo, the two samurai you met in "The Inn of Lost Time," appear in a number of Namioka's exciting adventure novels that take place in 16th-century Japan.

UNDERSTAND KEY IDEAS AND DETAILS. The following questions help you check your reading comprehension. Put an *x* in the box next to the correct answer.

1. "The Inn of Lost Time" is mainly about
    ☐ a. a bedtime story that a father tells his children.
    ☐ b. an innkeeper who serves his guests wine and salty snacks.
    ☐ c. how a wealthy merchant is almost tricked out of fifty pieces of gold.

2. The most striking thing about the girl at the inn was the fact that she
    ☐ a. said almost nothing to the merchant and his bodyguard.
    ☐ b. had six fingers on her left hand.
    ☐ c. gave the guests basins of water and towels to wash and dry their feet.

3. When Zenta and Tokubei woke up, they found themselves
    ☐ a. in a spacious room.
    ☐ b. lying outside on the ground.
    ☐ c. on cushions that had been placed on the floor.

4. Zenta realized that he had *not* slept for fifty years by closely observing
    ☐ a. a clump of bamboo shoots and the painted door panels.
    ☐ b. the expressions on the faces of the family at the inn.
    ☐ c. the roof of the house, which seemed darker than before.

NOTE NEW VOCABULARY WORDS. The following questions check your vocabulary skills. Put an *x* in the box next to the correct answer. Each vocabulary word appears in the story.

1. The man changed "from a young man to a decrepit old man of more than ninety." The word *decrepit* means
    ☐ a. lively and vigorous.
    ☐ b. considerate or kind.
    ☐ c. weakened by old age.

2. No inn seemed to be near, but the wonderful tantalizing smell of freshly cooked rice reached their noses. Which of the following best defines the word *tantalizing?*
    ☐ a. wretched or awful
    ☐ b. desirable but out of reach
    ☐ c. expensive but well worth the price

3. One panel contained a painting "depicting a winter scene." The word *depicting* means
    ☐ a. describing or portraying.
    ☐ b. ruining or spoiling.
    ☐ c. missing or omitting.

4. The merchant believed that his wife and his business were gone; the loss was traumatic. What is the meaning of the word *traumatic?*
    ☐ a. expected
    ☐ b. somewhat surprising
    ☐ c. emotionally shocking

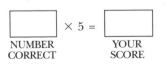

NUMBER CORRECT   × 5 =   YOUR SCORE

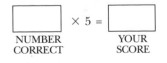

NUMBER CORRECT   × 5 =   YOUR SCORE

IDENTIFY STORY ELEMENTS. The following questions check your knowledge of story elements. Put an *x* in the box next to each correct answer.

1. "The Inn of Lost Time" is *set* in Japan
   ☐ a. at the present time.
   ☐ b. hundreds of years ago.
   ☐ c. at some time in the future.

2. Which of the following is an example of *inner conflict?*
   ☐ a. Tokubei kept "arguing with himself" about how much money to pay the priestess.
   ☐ b. Zenta realized that the innkeeper could easily have killed him.
   ☐ c. The old woman seemed amused at the awkward situation Zenta and Tokubei were in.

3. Which sentence from the story is an example of *foreshadowing?*
   ☐ a. "The farmer looked proudly at his sleeping sons."
   ☐ b. As we began our journey, Tokubei knew that "he could always write a message to his clerks at home and have money forwarded to him."
   ☐ c. "We finally gathered the courage to go up to the house."

4. The *theme* of the story deals mostly with
   ☐ a. warriors and bodyguards.
   ☐ b. food and drink.
   ☐ c. what should be most valued in life—time.

THINK CRITICALLY ABOUT THE STORY. The following questions check your critical thinking skills. Put an *x* in the box next to each correct answer.

1. It is fair to say that the innkeeper and his family
   ☐ a. were actually honest people who were misunderstood.
   ☐ b. did not think of a clever plan.
   ☐ c. almost succeeded in stealing money from the merchant.

2. We can tell from Zenta's actions that he was
   ☐ a. not concerned at all about the fate of Tokubei.
   ☐ b. more alert to details and more thoughtful than his employer.
   ☐ c. the kind of man who longed for revenge.

3. Undoubtedly the wine that Tokubei and Zenta drank was
   ☐ a. drugged.
   ☐ b. not too strong.
   ☐ c. very old and very costly.

4. Which one of the following facts is most important to the story?
   ☐ a. The events that Zenta tells about took place when he was not quite eighteen years old.
   ☐ b. The farmer's wife apologized for serving her guests poor tea.
   ☐ c. Having six fingers was a trait that ran in the wife's family.

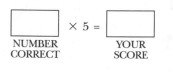

NUMBER CORRECT   × 5 =   YOUR SCORE

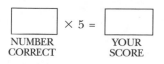

NUMBER CORRECT   × 5 =   YOUR SCORE

185

STUDY THE WRITER'S CRAFT. The following questions check your knowledge of skills related to the craft of writing. Put an *x* in the box next to each correct answer. You may refer to pages 4 and 5.

1. Zenta told his tale of the inn to three characters in the story. This is known as
   ☐ a. telling two stories at the same time.
   ☐ b. offering words of advice.
   ☐ c. telling a story within a story.

2. In the evening light, the thin leaves in the bamboo grove "turned into little golden knives." This sentence contains
   ☐ a. a simile.
   ☐ b. a metaphor.
   ☐ c. personification.

3. "The Inn of Lost Time" is constructed so that it most closely resembles
   ☐ a. a detective story.
   ☐ b. a science fiction story.
   ☐ c. an autobiography.

4. What is true of the conclusion of "The Inn of Lost Time"?
   ☐ a. It is intended to frighten the reader.
   ☐ b. It makes the reader feel sad.
   ☐ c. It contains still another surprise.

Questions for Writing and Discussion

- In what important ways is the tale of Urashima Taro similar to the story that Zenta told?
- Zenta thought that he should have been suspicious of any inn "hidden away from the highway." What did Zenta mean? Why was the merchant, Tokubei, selected to be a victim?
- What was the most convincing element of the hoax, or trick, to steal Tokubei's money? Explain how the family arranged that part of the plan.
- Matsuzo said that time is "the most precious thing of all." What do you think Matsuzo meant by that? Do you agree? Explain your answer.

See additional questions for extended writing on pages 196 and 197.

Use the boxes below to total your scores for the exercises. Then record your scores on pages 198 and 199.

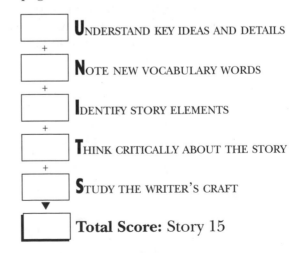

☐ **U**NDERSTAND KEY IDEAS AND DETAILS
+
☐ **N**OTE NEW VOCABULARY WORDS
+
☐ **I**DENTIFY STORY ELEMENTS
+
☐ **T**HINK CRITICALLY ABOUT THE STORY
+
☐ **S**TUDY THE WRITER'S CRAFT
▼
☐ **Total Score:** Story 15

☐ × 5 = ☐

NUMBER   YOUR
CORRECT   SCORE

An old saying warns, "Be careful what you wish for. It may come true." See if this is so in "Aunty Misery" and "Those Three Wishes."

Aunty Misery

retold by Judith Ortiz Cofer

This is a story about an old, very old woman who lived alone in her little hut with no other company than a beautiful pear tree that grew at her door. She spent all her time taking care of her pear tree. But the neighborhood children drove the old woman crazy by stealing her fruit. They would climb her tree, shake its delicate limbs, and run away with armloads of golden pears, yelling insults at "Aunty Misery," as they called her.

One day, a pilgrim[1] stopped at the old woman's hut and asked her permission to spend the night under her roof. Aunty Misery saw that he had an honest face and bade the traveler come in. She fed him and made a bed for him in front of her hearth. In the morning while he was getting ready to leave, the stranger told her that he would show his gratitude for her hospitality by granting her one wish.

"There is only one thing that I desire," said Aunty Misery.

---

1. **pilgrim:** a traveler

187

Aunty Misery *and* Those Three Wishes

"Ask, and it shall be yours," replied the stranger, who was a sorcerer[2] in disguise.

"I wish that anyone who climbs up my pear tree should not be able to come back down until I permit it."

"Your wish is granted," said the stranger, touching the pear tree as he left Aunty Misery's house.

And so it happened that when the children came back to taunt the old woman and to steal her fruit, she stood at her window watching them. Several of them shimmied up the trunk of the pear tree and immediately got stuck to it as if with glue. She let them cry and beg her for a long time before she gave the tree permission to let them go, on the condition that they never again steal her fruit or bother her.

Time passed, and both Aunty Misery and her tree grew bent and gnarled with age. One day another traveler stopped at her door. This one looked suffocated and exhausted, so the old woman asked him what he wanted in her village. He answered her in a voice that was dry and hoarse, as if he had swallowed a desert: "I am Death, and I have come to take you with me."

Thinking fast, Aunty Misery said, "All right, but before I go I would like to pluck some pears from my beloved pear tree to remember how much pleasure it brought

me in this life. But I am a very old woman and cannot climb to the tallest branches where the best fruit is; will you be so kind as to do it for me?"

With a heavy sigh like wind through a catacomb,[3] Death climbed the pear tree. Immediately he became stuck to it as if with glue. And no matter how much he cursed and threatened, Aunty Misery would not give the tree permission to release Death.

Many years passed, and there were no deaths in the world. The people who make their living from death began to protest loudly. The doctors claimed no one bothered to come in for examinations or treatments anymore, because they did not fear dying; the pharmacists' business suffered too, because medicines are, like magic potions, bought to prevent or postpone the inevitable; undertakers were unhappy with the situation also, for obvious reasons. There were also many old folks tired of life who wanted to pass on to the next world to rest from the miseries of this one.

Aunty Misery realized all this, and not wishing to be unfair, she made a deal with her prisoner, Death: if he promised not ever to come for her again, she would give him his freedom. He agreed. And that is why so long as the world is the world, Aunty Misery will always live.

---

2. sorcerer: someone who practices magic

3. catacomb: an underground burial chamber

About the Author

Judith Ortiz Cofer (1952–) was born in Hormingueros, Puerto Rico, but she actually spent much of her early life in two different worlds. As a very young child, her family moved to Patterson, New Jersey. When her father joined the U.S. Navy and went to sea, Cofer returned to Puerto Rico, where she lived for long periods of time with her grandmother. As a result of the constant movement back and forth between the United States and Puerto Rico, the question of cultural identity became very meaningful to Cofer. It has been a major theme in much of her writing. Originally trained as a teacher, Cofer attended Oxford University and later lectured and taught at many colleges. She has written poetry, novels, stories, and essays. Her first novel, *The Line of the Sun,* published in 1989, was nominated for a Pulitzer Prize, and she has received awards for nonfiction writing and for her short stories.

No one ever said that Melinda Alice was nice. That wasn't the word used. No, she was clever, even witty. She was called—never to her face, however—Melinda Malice.[1] Melinda Alice was clever and cruel. Her mother, when she thought about it at all, hoped Melinda would grow out of it. To her father, Melinda's very good grades mattered.

It was Melinda Alice, back in the eighth grade, who had labeled the shy, myopic[2] new girl "Contamination" and was the first to pretend that anything or anyone touched by the new girl had to be cleaned, inoculated, or avoided. High school had merely given Melinda Alice greater scope for her talents.

The surprising thing about Melinda Alice was her power. No one trusted her, but no one avoided her either. She was always included, always in the middle. If you had

---

1. **malice:** the desire to see others suffer or be hurt

2. **myopic:** nearsighted; unable to readily see things that are far away

Those Three Wishes

by Judith Gorog

seen her, pretty and witty, in the center of a group of students walking past your house, you'd have thought, "There goes a natural leader."

Melinda Alice had left for school early. She wanted to study alone in a quiet spot because there was going to be a big math test, and Melinda Alice was not prepared. That "A" mattered, so Melinda Alice walked to school alone, planning her studies. She didn't usually notice nature much, so she nearly stepped on a beautiful snail that was making its way across the sidewalk.

"Ugh. Yucky thing," thought Melinda Alice. Not wanting to step on the snail accidentally was one thing, but now she lifted her shoe to crush it.

"Please don't," said the snail.

"Why not?" retorted Melinda Alice.

"I'll give you three wishes," replied the snail evenly.

"Agreed," said Melinda Alice. "My first wish is that my next," she paused a split second, "my next thousand wishes come true." She smiled triumphantly and opened her bag to take out a small notebook and pencil to keep track.

Melinda Alice was sure she heard the snail say, "What a clever girl," as it made it to the safety of an ivy bed beside the sidewalk.

During the rest of the walk to school, Melinda was occupied with wonderful ideas. She would have beautiful clothes. "Wish number two, that I will always be perfectly dressed," and she was just that. True, her new outfit was not a lot different from the one she had worn leaving the house, but that only meant Melinda Alice liked her own taste.

After thinking awhile, she wrote, "Wish number three. I wish for pierced ears and small gold earrings." Her father had not allowed Melinda to have pierced ears, but now she had them anyway. She felt her new earrings and shook her beautiful hair in delight. "I can have anything: stereo, tapes,

TV, videodisk, moped, car, anything! All my life!" She hugged her books to herself in delight.

By the time she reached school, Melinda was almost an altruist.[3] She could wish for peace. Then she wondered, "Is the snail that powerful?" She felt her ears, looked at her perfect blouse, skirt, jacket, shoes. "I could make ugly people beautiful, cure cripples . . ." She stopped. The wave of altruism had washed past. "I could pay people back who deserve it!" Melinda Alice

looked at the school, at all the kids. She had an enormous sense of power. "They all have to do what I want now." She walked down the crowded halls to her locker. Melinda Alice could be sweet. She could be witty. She could—The bell rang for homeroom. Melinda Alice stashed her books, slammed the locker shut, and just made it to her seat.

"Hey, Melinda Alice," whispered Fred. "You know that big math test next period?"

"Oh, no," grimaced Melinda Alice. Her thoughts raced; "That snail made me late, and I forgot to study."

"I'll blow it," she groaned aloud. "I wish I were dead."

---

3. **altruist:** a person who does good for completely unselfish reasons

About the Author

Judith Gorog (1938–) has gained fame as a writer of chilling tales for young adults. Born in Madison, Wisconsin, Gorog began writing stories and plays—and even her own versions of the Greek myths—when she was still a child. Since she loved reading, and she enjoyed writing and telling stories, it is not surprising that Gorog eventually became an author. Most of Gorog's stories are relatively short and feature scary, strange, or fantastic elements. "Those Three Wishes" is a good example of her work. Gorog's short story collections include *Three Dreams and a Nightmare* and *No Swimming in Dark Pond and Other Chilling Tales.* She has also written a novel for young adults, *Winning Scheherazade.*

UNDERSTAND KEY IDEAS AND DETAILS. The following questions help you check your reading comprehension. Put an *x* in the box next to the correct answer.

1. Which of the following best expresses the main difference between the two stories?
   ☐ a. One story is short; the other is long.
   ☐ b. In one story, the main character is an old woman; in the other story, the main character is a girl.
   ☐ c. A wish works out well for one character and poorly for another.

2. In "Aunty Misery," the stranger granted Aunty Misery a wish because he
   ☐ a. was upset that "neighborhood children drove the old woman crazy."
   ☐ b. was grateful for her kindness.
   ☐ c. frequently granted wishes to elderly people.

3. In "Those Three Wishes," the snail granted Melinda Alice three wishes because she
   ☐ a. was so witty.
   ☐ b. was a natural leader at school.
   ☐ c. agreed not to crush it.

4. The key difference between the endings of the stories is that
   ☐ a. Aunty Misery is unable die, while Melinda Alice will die at once.
   ☐ b. Aunty Misery has used her wish, but Melinda Alice still has many left.
   ☐ c. Aunty Misery seems satisfied, but Melinda Alice doesn't.

NOTE NEW VOCABULARY WORDS. The following questions check your vocabulary skills. Put an *x* in the box next to the correct answer. Each vocabulary word appears in the story.

1. The old tree was "bent and gnarled with age." The word *gnarled* means
   ☐ a. twisted.
   ☐ b. tall.
   ☐ c. covered with leaves.

2. Although some people want to live forever, death is inevitable. What is the meaning of the word *inevitable*?
   ☐ a. far off in the future
   ☐ b. sometimes painful
   ☐ c. impossible to avoid

3. Melinda Alice pretended that anyone who touched "the new girl had to be cleaned, inoculated, or avoided." Which of the following best defines the word *inoculated*?
   ☐ a. offered congratulations
   ☐ b. given an injection to prevent the spread of illness
   ☐ c. made the subject of discussion

4. Melinda Alice grimaced, realizing that she had forgotten to study. The word *grimaced* means
   ☐ a. shouted loudly enough for everyone to hear.
   ☐ b. twisted one's face with displeasure.
   ☐ c. asked for assistance.

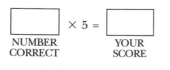

NUMBER
CORRECT   × 5 =   YOUR
SCORE

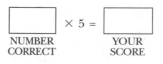

NUMBER
CORRECT   × 5 =   YOUR
SCORE

IDENTIFY STORY ELEMENTS. The following questions check your knowledge of story elements. Put an *x* in the box next to each correct answer.

1. What happened last in the *plot* of "Aunty Misery"?
   ☐ a. Death came to take Aunty Misery.
   ☐ b. A pilgrim granted Aunty Misery a wish.
   ☐ c. Aunty Misery freed Death from the tree.

2. Which sentence best *characterizes* Melinda Alice?
   ☐ a. She was very clever—perhaps too clever for her own good.
   ☐ b. She was pretty and witty, but because she could not be trusted, her classmates avoided her.
   ☐ c. She hoped to do well in school but didn't care much about her grades.

3. The *motive* behind Aunty Misery's wish was her desire to
   ☐ a. live forever.
   ☐ b. prevent children from stealing her fruit.
   ☐ c. bring peace to the world.

4. In both stories, the *narrator* is
   ☐ a. the main character in the story.
   ☐ b. a character in the story who is not the main character.
   ☐ c. the writer of the story.

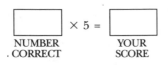

NUMBER CORRECT   × 5 =   YOUR SCORE

THINK CRITICALLY ABOUT THE STORY. The following questions check your critical thinking skills. Put an *x* in the box next to each correct answer.

1. Which of the following statements is true?
   ☐ a. Essentially, Aunty Misery was a kind person and Melinda Alice was not.
   ☐ b. Aunty Misery had a beloved pear tree and many helpful friends.
   ☐ c. Melinda Alice loved and appreciated nature.

2. Aunty Misery asked that Death climb to the top of the pear tree. This demonstrates that she
   ☐ a. could not reach the fruit on the tree.
   ☐ b. desired to enjoy some pears just before she died.
   ☐ c. had cleverly thought of a way to "cheat Death."

3. Evidence in the story suggests that Melinda Alice would have used a wish or wishes to
   ☐ a. bring great happiness to people.
   ☐ b. gain power over others.
   ☐ c. cure all the diseases in the world.

4. Judging from what you have read in the stories, you may infer that
   ☐ a. Melinda Alice was very nice, although most people wouldn't describe her that way.
   ☐ b. if you are helpful to strangers, you will always be rewarded.
   ☐ c. Aunty Misery is still alive.

NUMBER CORRECT   × 5 =   YOUR SCORE

STUDY THE WRITER'S CRAFT. The following questions check your knowledge of skills related to the craft of writing. Put an *x* in the box next to each correct answer. You may refer to pages 4 and 5.

1. In "Aunty Misery" and "Those Three Wishes," Death and a snail are able to speak. This illustrates
   ☐ a. descriptive language.
   ☐ b. personification.
   ☐ c. imagery.

2. "Aunty Misery" is an example of
   ☐ a. an autobiographical story.
   ☐ b. a story of mystery and suspense.
   ☐ c. a folktale.

3. Because a lesson can be drawn from both stories, each story may be said to offer
   ☐ a. dialogue.
   ☐ b. the same mood.
   ☐ c. a moral.

4. Although the stories present characters who are quite different, each story
   ☐ a. depends on the granting of a wish.
   ☐ b. has a similar setting.
   ☐ c. contains a long and complicated plot.

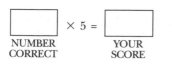

NUMBER CORRECT × 5 = YOUR SCORE

Questions for Writing and Discussion

- In what ways are "Aunty Misery" and "Those Three Wishes" similar? How are the stories different?
- Aunty Misery and Melinda Malice are *nicknames*—descriptive, informal names. Did each character deserve her nickname? Tell why.
- Did you find "Those Three Wishes" to be an amusing story or a sad story? What do you think the writer intended? Explain your answers.
- In each story, do you think that the main character deserved her fate? Why? Which story did you enjoy more? Tell why.

See additional questions for extended writing on pages 196 and 197.

Use the boxes below to total your scores for the exercises. Then record your scores on pages 198 and 199.

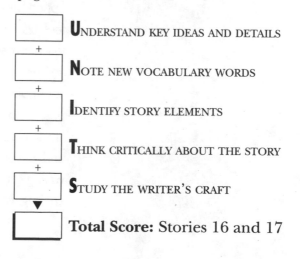

UNDERSTAND KEY IDEAS AND DETAILS
+
NOTE NEW VOCABULARY WORDS
+
IDENTIFY STORY ELEMENTS
+
THINK CRITICALLY ABOUT THE STORY
+
STUDY THE WRITER'S CRAFT
▼
Total Score: Stories 16 and 17

The Way Things End

Questions for Discussion and Extended Writing

The following questions provide you with opportunities to express your thoughts and feelings about the selections in this unit. Your teacher may assign selected questions. When you write your responses, remember to state your point of view clearly and to support your position by presenting specific details—examples, illustrations, references drawn from the story and, in some cases, from your life. Organize your writing carefully and check your work for correct spelling, capitalization, punctuation, and grammar.

1. The theme of this unit is "The Way Things End." Briefly explain how each story in the unit is related to that theme.

2. The poet Thomas Stearns Eliot wrote, "This is the way the world ends. Not with a bang but a whimper." Select two characters in the unit and discuss how their worlds end—with a bang or with a whimper.

3. Although something dramatic occurred in "Something Green," it is a story that ends much the way it begins. Show that this statement is true by referring to the story.

4. "The Inn of Lost Time" is a story that has many endings. Support this statement by providing examples from the story.

5. Compare and contrast Aunty Misery and Melinda Alice. In what ways are they similar? How are they different?

6. In which two selections in the unit does the setting of the story play the most significant role? Give titles and authors, and present reasons for your answer.

7. Select two stories in the unit and demonstrate how one or more characters in each story confronted and overcame danger. Provide titles and authors.

8. In many ways, McGarry is the strangest character in any story in this unit. Support this statement in a carefully organized essay that has an introduction, a body, and a conclusion.

9. Which characters in this unit would you consider the most clever? Refer to the actions of the characters to support your conclusion.

10. Justice Oliver Wendell Holmes Jr. once wrote, "Life is an end in itself." What do you think this statement means? What are some of the plans that you have for your life? How do you intend to make your plans come true? Have you already started working on some of those plans? If so, how? Think about these questions. Then write an essay entitled "Life, an End in Itself."

Progress Chart

1. Write in your score for each exercise.
2. Write in your Total Score.

Story	U	N	I	T	S	Total Score
1						
2						
3						
4						
5						
6						
7						
8						
9						
10						
11						
12						
13						
14						
15						
16 & 17						

Progress Graph

1. Write your Total Score in the box under the number for each story.
2. Put an *x* along the line above each box to show your Total Score for that story.
3. Make a graph of your progress by drawing a line to connect the *x*'s.

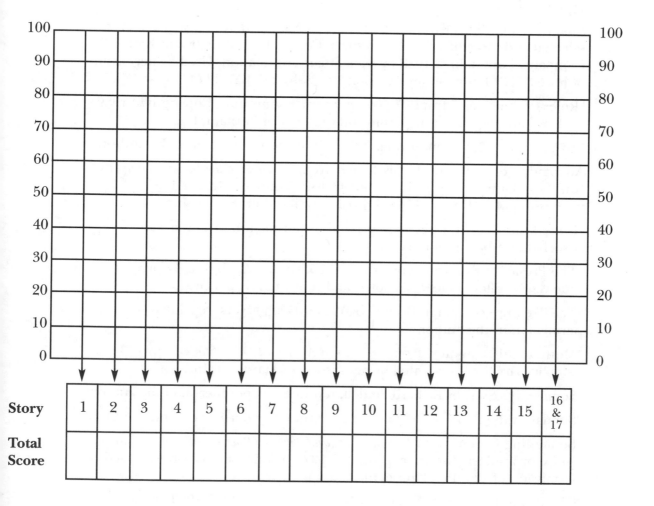

Acknowledgments

Acknowledgment is gratefully made to the following publishers, authors, and agents for permission to reprint these works. Every effort has been made to determine copyright owners. In case of any omissions, the Publisher will be pleased to make suitable acknowledgments in future editions. Adaptations and abridgments are by Burton Goodman. All rights reserved.

"American Sandwich" by Edite Cunhã. Adapted and reprinted by permission of the author.

Adapted from "This Farm for Sale" in *A Jesse Stuart Reader: Stories and Poems,* selected and introduced by Jesse Stuart. Copyright © 1963 by McGraw-Hill Company. Copyright © 1988 by Jesse Stuart Foundation. Used by permission of Jesse Stuart Foundation, P.O. Box 391, Ashland, KY 41114.

"Rules of the Game" from *The Joy Luck Club* by Amy Tan. Copyright © 1989 by Amy Tan. Reprinted by permission of Penguin Putnam, Inc.

"To Serve Man" by Damon Knight. Reprinted by permission of the author.

Adaptation of "Who Am I This Time?" from *Welcome to the Monkey House* by Kurt Vonnegut Jr., copyright © 1961 by Kurt Vonnegut Jr. Used by permission of Dell Publishing, a division of Random House, Inc.

"Kim's Game" by M. D. Lake, reprinted by permission of Lowenstein Associates on behalf of the author.

"The President Regrets" copyright © 1965, Diner's Club, Inc. Copyright renewed by Ellery Queen. Adapted and reprinted by permission.

"The Treasure of Lemon Brown" by Walter Dean Myers, reprinted by permission of the author.

"Mother and Daughter" from *Baseball in April and Other Stories,* copyright © 1990 by Gary Soto, reprinted by permission of Harcourt, Inc.

"Somebody's Son" by Richard Pindell, reprinted by permission of the author.

"Sunday in the Park" by Bel Kaufman, reprinted by permission of the author.

"Something Green" from *Paradox Lost and Twelve Other Great Science Fiction Stories,* by Frederic Brown, copyright © 1973 by Elizabeth C. Brown. Used by permission of Random House, Inc.

"The Inn of Lost Time" by Lensey Namioka. Copyright © 1989 by Lensey Namioka. Reprinted by permission of Lensey Namioka. All rights reserved by the author.

"Aunty Misery" by Judith Ortiz Cofer, reprinted by permission of the author.

Credits

Illustrations

David Cunningham: pp. 19, 66, 101, 170–171
Tom Foty: pp. 82–83, 160, 190–191
Greg Hargreaves: pp. 30–31, 141, 187
Yoshi Miyake: pp. 44, 94, 122–123
Lance Paladino: pp. 8–9, 56, 133, 149

Photographs

Henryk Kaiser/eStock Photography/PictureQuest: front cover
PhotoDisc, Inc.: pp. 6, 40, 80, 118, back cover
Richard Megna/Fundamental Photographs: pp. 42, 78
McDonald Wildlife Photography/Animals Animals: pp. 120, 156
Bruce Burkhardt/Corbis: pp. 158, 196